THE BEST OF

Lennie Lower

THE REST OF

Lennie Lower

THE BEST OF
Lennie Lower

SELECTED BY
CYRIL PEARL

ANGUS
& ROBERTSON
PUBLISHERS

ANGUS & ROBERTSON PUBLISHERS

First published in 1963 by Lansdowne Press
This edition published in 1990 by Angus & Robertson Publishers
Unit 4, Eden Park, 31 Waterloo Road, North Ryde, NSW, Australia 2113;
and 16 Golden Square, London W1R 4BN, United Kingdom

National Library of Australia
Cataloguing-in-Publication data:

Lower, Lennie, 1903-1947.
The best of Lennie Lower.
ISBN 0 207 16461 4.
1. Australian wit and humor. I. Pearl, Cyril, 1906-
II. Title.
A828.209

Printed by Griffin Press

Contents

Introduction

"ONCE UPON A TIME THERE WAS A FUNNY MAN"
By Cyril Pearl

ONE NIGHT IN THE late 1930's, I went to a Journalists' Ball in Sydney. Like every other trade junket, whether of jam-makers, jugglers or gigolos, it was a pretty dull affair — the traditional *mélange* of back-slapping and back-stabbing — save for one very pleasing and for a while quite inexplicable novelty. Soon after I arrived, coyly hidden in the brown robes of a Franciscan monk, I was overlaid by great waves of girls, some encouragingly nubile, and all dedicated to the noble mission of craving my autograph.

As a recent refugee from the austerities of Melbourne C.1 (it was long before the era of such saturnalia as madcap Moomba, with its Heliogabalian orgies of lemonade and chiko rolls in the Fitzroy Gardens) I was a little startled, and not a little flattered, by the continuing attentions of these uninhibited Sydney odalisques. But I was smartly chastened by the observation that their interest in me evaporated as soon as I had delivered my autograph. Some made rude remarks. Others just folded their discontents like Arabs and silently stole away.

I discovered the reason for all this a little later. One of my fellow-guests, Mr. L. W. Lower, had broadcast the intelligence that the man concealed in the Franciscan cowl was none other than Mr. L. W. Lower. He was unmoved when I taxed him with his perfidy, which he explained as a rational act of self-protection. But he vouchsafed me by way of compensation, and as a veteran of innumerable trade balls, some aged-in-the-wood advice: "It's hard to hide a bottle in that monkish get-up," he said. "Why not come as a St. Bernard and carry the stuff round your neck?"

I recall this Curious Episode of the Clamant Autograph-Hunters only to demonstrate the enormous affection in which Lower was held by the citizens of Sydney. With his friend and illustrator, W. E. Pidgeon ("Wep"), as distinguished an artist as Lower was a writer, he had become an integral part of Sydney life. In clubs and pubs, in lolly-shops and lupanars, in the towering clinker-brick *château* of the millionaire pork-packer and the underground tiled *chalet-de-necessité* of the troubled pedestrian, in the streets and on the beaches, he was a man of infinite legend, a man of infinite laughs, a much-loved man. Even the Sydney taxi-driver, hunched ape-like over his frayed cigarette, would emit an approving, almost-human grunt if you asked him to deposit you at the newspaper office where Lower worked.

Si monumentum requiris, Sport, well there it is . . . .

Lower's transcendent popularity is easily explained. He was an individualist in an era of creeping conformity. He was a rebel in a country of suffocating acquiescence. A Darlinghurst Don Quixote, he tilted at windbags, punctured pomposity, slaughtered sacred cows, all with tremendous gusto. He saw that much of life was absurd, and his laughter echoed down its stuffy corridors, lusty, irreverent and irrepressible.

As a humorist, Lower deployed a vast array of talents. He had a superb ear for dialogue, a searching eye for detail, a glorious sense of the ridiculous. He was a master of comedy in its multiform guises: subtle, vulgar, zany, verbal, ratbag, slapstick, nonsensical. His humour can be as realistic as a greasy sink, or as remote as the laugh of a leprechaun. He blends Tyl Eulenspiegel, Puck, Lewis Carroll, Edward Lear, W. S. Gilbert, P. G. Wodehouse, Groucho Marx and Roy ("Mo") Rene with a refreshing flavour of gum-leaves. Some day, some humourless academic will write a profound and unreadable thesis on the protean nature of humour, using Lower's collected work as source material.

Leonard Waldemar Lower was born in Dubbo, a town about half way between Sydney and Bourke, in September 1903. His father died when he was seven, and his stepfather took him to Sydney to attend the Barcom Avenue State School, Darlinghurst. At "Darlo," as the natives call it affectionately, Little Lennie acquired the rudiments of his education, as well as the more polite parts. (For details of this process, the earnest student is referred to Chapter 6, "Putting Curry Into The Curriculum.") Soon after leaving school, he joined the Royal Australian Navy. His career in the Senior Service was brief and obscure, but according to an obituarist in *Smith's Weekly*, Lower "grew impatient with Navy methods and gave the exact range to a gun crew, which resulted in severe damage to a valuable target." I have no reason to doubt this. In one of Lower's rare naval reminiscences, "All At Sea" (page 36) he recalls how his squadron went out on manoeuvres with ten battleships and returned with two.

Lower began writing when he was in the Navy ("the silly stuff that later made my name, and, of course, the usual adolescent poetry"), but he was about 23 when his first piece was published — in *Beckett's Budget*, a sleazy scandal-sheet of the late 1920's. Soon after, he got a job on the *Labor Daily*, then the voice of the Lang

Labour Party. For most of the period between Navy and news-paper, Lower served in Sydney's growing army of unemployed. He did a bit of road-mending, slept in the Domain, carried his swag, and became adept at jumping the rattler. Years later, in the *Labor Daily*, he advised any romantic who regarded train-jumping "as another sort of joy-riding" to try it:

> The temptation to "jump the rattler" is great.
>
> Twenty miles that would take a day to walk can be covered in less than an hour on a goods train. And the man who walks all day must have food. . . .
>
> The gain is worth the risk of imprisonment or sudden death, from one point of view.
>
> But death is always within call, the policeman is never far away. . . .
>
> I saw one poor old man who missed his grip on a flying truck and clung to the buffer for half a mile, clawing like a feeble monkey to retain his hold — and wouldn't let go his swag! The look in his eyes when at last I managed to get his hands on to the edge of the truck, I shall never forget . . .
>
> I have ridden smothered in coal on an enginetender, astride a buffer in the dead of night, in an empty truck which had con-tained lime, and still contained sufficient to blind and choke a man as the motion of the truck stirred it, while the train shunted about a clamorous depot — and I lay on my stomach breathing lime. I have clung to the side of a high wheat truck, afraid to move, and sweated under tarpaulins; but for sheer hell commend me to the under-the-seat method.
>
> The space is so narrow that chest and backbone seem as one, and breathing is both staccato and pianissimo. To those people who suffer from train sickness while sitting on their well-padded seats, I proffer as a curiosity the man who lies with his face to the floor and the seat pressing on his back, while the train jolts and rattles on.

For the *Labor Daily*, Lower wrote a daily column of comment, verse and humour, first under the pen-name of T. I. Red, later under his own name. He also wrote pungent social and political satire. Australia was stumbling into its blackest days since the great economic collapse of the Grey Nineties, and Lower, with far more justification than any self-pitying contemporary exploiter of the label, became a very Angry Young Man, indeed. "Not by wrath but by laughter do we slay," said Nietzsche. But it wasn't always easy to laugh in 1928. And there were plenty of monsters to slay. There was, for instance, the new cult of "social" reporting, the most emetic form of Australian journalism, which consists of chronicling the activities of people who don't matter for the enlightenment of people who don't care.

At least 80,000 families in New South Wales were on the dole, and Sydney's Sunday papers were filling columns with inanities about nonentities. It was too much for Lower, as for any reader of adult cerebration. With a dash of muriatic acid in his inkwell, he turned out a piece that showed he could have risen to great heights as a social writer:

LET'S PEEP INSIDE

Imitation is the sincerest form of flattery, and in borrowing this idea from the *Sunday Sun* and *Sunday Telegraph*, we show our appreciation of the new domestic journalism.

The charming home of Mr. and Mrs. John Bowyang, tucked away in Pelican Street, Surry Hills, is a revelation in piquancy. From the backyard one has a view of every other backyard in the street, and the tall chimneystack of Tooth's Brewery looms majestically in the distance.

An antique casket, known to connoisseurs as a "dirt-tin," stands by the back entrance. It is one of Mrs. Bowyang's great sorrows that the lid has been pinched.

Mrs. Bowyang has an artistic taste and an eye for effect. Two lines have been stretched between long poles at either end of the yard, and when these lines are full of clothes, the sight is bewitching in the extreme.

Empty salmon tins, kindly thrown over the fence by the next-door neighbours, and a worn-out bath and a coil of wire-netting on top of the washhouse roof, complete the picture.

Fascinating though the yard is, it is not until one enters the house itself that one gets a glimpse of the interior.

The motif throughout the whole house is one of antiquity. The wallpaper is mellow with age, and the ceilings have not been kalsomined for forty-seven years.

Hardly any of the doors shut properly, and the windows are held open by bright clean lemonade bottles.

Mrs. Bowyang points with pride to an old meat safe which hangs in the drawing-room, where the lodger sleeps.

There is a history attached to the old safe.

It was rescued from Mark Foy's big fire many years ago, and for a long time the parrot lived in it; but as the family grew the parrot had to be given away and the infant Bowyang sleeps in it now.

The old clock is another interesting relic. It was given to Mrs. Bowyang by her mother, who was one of the Maloneys — the Woolloomooloo Maloneys who were so prominent in society a few years ago when the younger set ran a two-up school down at the wharves.

Though it has been in the family for many years — excepting occasional visits to the pawnshop — the alarm still works.

The bedroom furnishings are symbolic of that affectionate family life which seems to be fading into oblivion in these modern times. There are two double beds and a stretcher in the room, cleverly arranged so that one may walk from one bed to the other without climbing over.

Mr. and Mrs. Bowyang and little Jacky sleep in one double bed, the three youngest girls in the other, and Mr. Bowyang's brother-in-law, who is out of work, sleeps in the stretcher.

Mrs. Bowyang's hobbies are washing and mending, and some of the mending she does is nothing short of marvellous.

Business takes Mr. Bowyang away every morning at 6.30, he being engaged in the sewer-digging profession; but he still finds time for his diversions, namely, washing up and placing tins where the rain comes in. The younger children have a magnificent playground in Pelican Street, where they have a jolly time daubing themselves with mud, eating stray apple-cores, and escaping being run over by passing lorries.

Viewed from the front, Mrs. Bowyang's home is extremely attractive. It seems to attract all the dust in the streets, and although it has never been renovated since it was built, it is remarkably cheap for 25/- a week, and the brass door-knob takes an excellent polish.

The writer was intrigued by the quaint, old-world, worn-out, bashed-in atmosphere of the locality, and it was with great reluctance that he left. He lingered for a while, hoping to see the owner of Mrs. Bowyang's residence, with the idea of strangling him when he saw him, but realizing the futility of the idea he left.

Lower had moved to the *Daily Guardian*, and its parent, *Smith's Weekly* when his comic masterpiece, *Here's Luck*, appeared in 1930. It remains, pre-eminently, Australia's funniest book, as ageless as Pickwick or Tom Sawyer, a work of "weird genius," as one reviewer put it, written by "a Chaplin of words." Yet beneath the coruscating humour there is acute observation, sardonic comment, and, as John Dalley pointed out, "an undertone of tragic disillusionment."

In the chorus of critical acclaim which greeted *Here's Luck* was one dissenting voice. Appropriately, it came from Melbourne, a city which still regards alcohol as a product of Beelzebub & Co., especially when absorbed after 6.15 p.m. "A very distasteful note is struck," wrote the now-forgotten *Argus*, "by making father and son the central figures in orgies of intoxication and more reprehensible behaviour, in which the example of the father is excelled by the son." Lower was not given to orgies of intoxication or anything else, but like many sensitive and creative men, he had a healthy respect for the evocations, persuasions and consolations of grog. One of the most eloquent passages in *Here's Luck* is a paean to fermented liquor which Mr. Sloove, a grandiloquent Sydney politician, delivers to an audience of fellow-drinkers:

"How many paltry figures have ranted against it, shrieked their censure," he cried, "and faded back to the earth from which they come — to fertilize the vines.

"Gaze on your glass of beer.

"See how the lambent, lazy bubbles drift to the top, as men

drift through life; linger a while in the froth, and burst of old age, or are cut off in their prime in Fate's thirsty gulp? This scourge, this shame, this liquid degradation — what is it? . . .

"It links the extremes of mankind in one common friendly girdle. The labourer disturbing the rocks of ages with his pick, and Shakespeare in his favourite inn — and Attila, the Scourge of God, who died of too much mead . . .

"Noah . . . the greatest navigator of all times; cooped in the ark with his relations and a lot of other wild animals, drifting in a landless world. Chosen from countless teetotallers drowned in their favourite drink;

"When the awful responsibility of beginning a new world had eased — what happened? . . .

"The Bible says his son found him lying in the vineyard, his back teeth awash and a happy, boozed smile on his face . . .

"Says the earnest reformer," continued Sloove, "supposing that, instead of drinking whisky, you drank milk. Look at the benefits to your health, your pocket, and the race is general. Against this horrible suggestion there is, thank heaven, a stone-wall fact, a gesture in granite, one great unshakable answer, 'I don't like milk.'

"It is an axiom of economists that supply follows demand like the blood follows a punch on the nose. We want beer. Therefore there is beer. Peer into the murky mystery of your orange phosphate. What do you see? A chemical laboratory. A bit of this being added, a bit of that tipped in. And in the translucent depths of booze? Hop-fields, rippling acres of barley, and whistling boys in the sunshine, picking grapes. You would have me drink this coloured eye-lotion? Consider, then, this awful possibility.

"Two old friends meet.

"'Bill! Why, you old son of a gun.'

"'Where've you been? Haven't seen you for years!'

"A moment of happy grins, of surging happy memories, of hand-shakes truly meant.

"'Well — well — well!'

"Glad. Awkward. Lost for words.

"'Come and have an *orangeade!*'"

He paused, while a wave of horror swept over the company.

"I *ask* you!" he exclaimed passionately.

Lower never wrote another novel, but till the last day of his life, he never ceased writing. His output was prodigious, and the consistency of his work, astonishing. His humour renewed itself miraculously, inexhaustibly. At one period, when he was working for the *Australian Women's Weekly*, the *Sunday Telegraph*, and the *Daily Telegraph*, he was turning out eight funny pieces, two of considerable length, each week — a darg that must be unexampled even in the greediest days of Grub Street. He was sacked by the *Telegraph*, and returned to *Smith's Weekly* at the end of 1940, after an historic meeting with Mr. Noel Coward, then visiting Australia on a morale-building mission. There are many versions of the brief encounter. The commonly accepted one is that when Mr. Coward greeted Lower as the King of Australian humorists, Mr. Lower returned the compliment by invoking another Royal personage . . .

Lower died in Sydney Hospital, still writing his funny pieces for *Smith's Weekly*, on July 10 1947. The Sydney papers, for the most part, took little notice of his death. The death of a Bellevue Hill bookmaker would have received more editorial attention. It was, of course, a foolish day on which to die, even for a man with an exquisite sense of humour, because that day the linotypes were running hot with the news of the engagement of Princess Elizabeth to Lieutenant Philip Mountbatten. The *Daily Telegraph*, which revealed clairvoyantly that the Royal couple would honeymoon in Australia, announced Lower's death in its gossip column. The *Bulletin*, that rusty megaphone of Australian nationalism, gave Australia's greatest humorist nineteen lines. In the same issue, "Ek Dum," the *Bulletin's* omniscient military soothsayer, described at much greater length the uniform worn by Field Marshal Bernard Montgomery, Viscount of Alamein and of Hindhead ("His tunic collar is wide open at the front and on one wing he wears the R.S.L. badge, on the other he wears a burnished metal kangaroo," etc.). The *Sydney Morning Herald*, like the *Daily Telegraph*, disposed of Lower in its gossip column. This paragraph, it is true, was augmented by seven additional lines the following day. But these, in the "Death" notices, were paid for at 1/9 a line. For twenty years, Lower had been Sydney's laureate of laughter. Only one Sydney paper, *Smith's Weekly*, attempted an adequate assessment of his importance. Acclaiming him as "the greatest of all Australian humorists," it followed a brief biographical note with a warm appreciation of his work:

> Great secret of Lower's humour is that he was always himself, he never let anyone or anything get in the way of his natural genius. Editors could tell him what to write about, he would go away and come back with something entirely different. Lennie Lower's humour was the real thing, it grew as naturally as fruit, and right out of life . . .
> As Lennie Lower himself, so his novel, *Here's Luck*, speaks for the people. Written as a mad and highly individualist extravaganza, it was soon seen to be much closer to the life and language of people who back horses and get drunk and enjoy themselves at parties in Sydney and suburbs than many much more seriously conceived works. A book with a scene in it that recalls the glories of Falstaff, a book which showed Sydney people to themselves as they had never seen themselves before.

As editor of the *Sunday Telegraph*, I had the honour of devoting the leader-page to Lower's memory. I reprinted one of his delightful fairy-tales, and invited Wep to write a personal note about his old colleague.

This is what he wrote:

ONCE UPON A TIME THERE WAS A FUNNY MAN . . .

"There was once an aged bootmaker named Franz, who lived in a valley just crawling with mad bears."

In the *Telegraph* ten years ago lots of whimsies began like that.

Now that their like can never appear again, we shall have to tell our own, and the prefix will be "there was once Lennie Lower . . ."

And, as long as his contemporaries' memories last, Lower will become part of the fable and legend he liked so much to build.

Even during his lifetime apocryphal stories about him were legion.

The average accepted image of the man was composed of hearsay evidence and an interpretation of him from his work.

It is a conglomerate picture of errant elf, harassed householder, screwball, and comic, that is likely to survive the reality.

The reality, indeed, was hard to find.

Close personal contact with him was difficult — he was too reserved and fundamentally shy to let anyone in behind the protective barriers of his personality.

There was much of the child in his makeup — he had its simplicity, irresponsibility, and, perhaps, its improvidence — certainly he had its fresh and devastating powers of observation.

He was one of those original spirits whose vision never wearies and who, in the common, unlooked-at aspects of life, finds always a new and amazing something.

How unerringly he cut those cameos of the standard husband-wife relationship—how much of everyone's domesticity was packed in so little.

And those wonderful journeys he took us into the lands of fairies and witches and giants and ogres!

It was his extraordinary keenness of observation and uncanny ability to assimilate the essence of a place or situation that gave salt and earthiness to his humour.

I remember long ago when I was with him on a caravan trip by the Snowy River being continually amazed at the apparently casual and indifferent attitude he adopted.

Yet not once did he fail to spot the local colour or pick the choicest cut of character.

I have never seen him scratch for, or alter, a word. He caught *the type with a dialogue of precision and economy that has scarce been matched since. Henry Lawson, too, did his piece for the man in the street.*

He seemed to have few close friends, those nearest him were older but possessed of the same irresponsible adolescence.

It is hard to realize that he is dead.

For me and a million others he still lives while we can read.

His obituary is written, not in the newspapers, but in the trams, and the bars, and in the hearts of human men.

There was nothing more to say . . .

1 The Secret Lives of Lennie Lower

From pawnbroker to poultice-mixer, from baker to bushranger, Lower changed jobs as often as he changed his socks. He was also a polar explorer, a blacksmith, a lion-tamer and a fire-engine.

Where The Cooler Bars Grow

I'm only a city boy. Until a short time ago I'd never seen a sheep all in one piece or with its fur on. That's why, when people said to me, "Go west, young man, or east, if you like, but go," I went.

Truth to tell, I thought it would be safer. I had a shotgun and a rifle, and a bag of flour, and two sealed kerosene tins of fresh water in the luggage van. I thought of taking some coloured beads for the natives, but decided it was too expensive.

I forget now where it was I went to. Anyhow, it was full of wheat silos and flies, and there was a horse standing on three legs under a tree. There were no other signs of life except a faint curl of smoke coming from the hotel chimney.

When I walked into the bar there was nobody there, so I walked out the back to the kitchen and there was nobody there. I went out to the front veranda again, and saw a little old man picking burrs off his socks.

"Good-day!" I said.

"Day!" he replied.

"Where's everybody?" I asked.

"Never heard of him. Unless you mean old Smith. He's down by the crick. You're a stranger, aren't you?"

"Just got off the train. Where's the publican?"

"Do you want a drink?"

"Yes."

"Orright!"

So we went into the bar and had a drink.

"I want to book a room here," I told him.

"Don't be silly!" he replied. "Sleep out on the veranda with the rest of us if you've got blankets. They're decoratin' the School of Arts with the sheets. You going to the dance?"

"I can't dance!"

"Strike me pink, who wants to! We leave that to the women. There ought to be some good fights at this one. When I was younger there wasn't a man could stand up to me on the dance floor. Here comes somebody now."

"Day."

"Day. Don't you bring that horse into the bar! Hang it all, you've been told about that before."

"He's quiet. I broke him in yesterday. Hear about Snowy? Got his arm caught in the circular saw up at the timber mill."

"That's bad."

"Too right it is! They've got to get a new saw. Whoa there!"

"Take him out into the kitchen. The flies are worryin' him."

"Goodo. Pour me out a beer."

"Pour it out yourself."

"Go to bed, you old mummified ox!"

"I'll give you a belt in the ear, you red-headed son of a convict!"

"Give it to your uncle. Giddap!"

"One of me best friends," said the old man, as the horse was led into the kitchen.

"I suppose," said the red-headed one, returning, "it'll be all right if he eats that cake on the kitchen table? Won't do him any harm, will it?"

"That's for supper at the dance!"

"Well, I'll go and take it off him. There's a good bit of it left."

Outside on the veranda voices were heard.

"I wouldn't sell that dog for a thousand pounds."

"I wouldn't give you two bob for 'im."

"You never had two bob in your life! You ever seen a sheep dog trial? That dog has won me more prizes at the Show than ten other dogs.

"Why," he continued, "you could hang up a fly-veil, point out one particular hole in it and that dog could cut a fly out of a bunch and work him through that hole."

"Good-day!"

"Day!"

"No sign of rain yet."

"No. I heard of a swaggie who had to walk eighty miles to get water to boil his billy, and when he got there he found he'd forgotten his cup and saucer, and by the time he'd walked back for his cup and saucer there was a bushfire started in the water-hole, it was that dry."

"Don't bring your horses into the bar!"

"Don't take any notice of the old crank. Why don't you put this beer out in the sun to get cool? If it was any flatter you'd have to serve it in a plate. Going to the Show this year?"

"Of course I am. Why don't you teach that horse some manners?"

"Good-day, Mrs. Smith."

"Who put that horse in my kitchen?"

"Is he in the kitchen? Well, what do you think of that!"

"Fancy him being in the kitchen!"

"In the kitchen, of all places!"

"Who could have let him in?"

"Never mind about that. Get him out at once, Jack! Wipe up that counter. I told you to cut some wood this morning. And put

3

that dog outside and get the broom and sweep up the bar. Wash those glasses first."

By this time we were all out on the veranda.

"She hasn't found out about the horse eating the cake yet," said somebody.

"Better go for a walk somewhere, eh?"

But that was years ago. They've got radios and refrigerators in the bush now, and that's why you see me mournfully wandering about the cattle stalls at Show time. I'm thinking of the good old days before the squatters took up polo, and started knitting their own berets. When men were men, and women were useful about the farm when the plough horse took sick.

> *Wrap me up in my stockwhip and blanket*
> *And bury me deep down below*
> *Where the farm implement salesmen won't molest me,*
> *In the shades where the cooler bars grow.*

Ah, me!

Circus Tricks In A Pawnshop

I've given up the pawnbroking business. I've always maintained that if you're in a business where nothing turns up the best thing is to turn it down and start off square all round. I'm not sure how you do that last bit, but you know what I mean.

I will say, though, that having a pawnshop has polished my education to such a degree that I can hold my own — and anyone else's, for that matter — with anybody. I can play "Home, Sweet Home" on the mandoline, cornet, saxophone, concertina, flute, and banjo with variations. I'm so good at the variations that people have often mistaken my "Home, Sweet Home" for "Rule, Britannia." Nobody ever pawned a piano with me, so that's an instrument I've never had a chance to have a smack at. I also know how to work theodolites. You put it up on a tripod and you get a man to hold a stick on the ground, and then you point the thing at him and look through it. After you've done that you go away and do it somewhere else.

Quite a lot of interesting things used to come into my shop, but you've got to know the trade.

A man might come into your shop with a watch. He says, "How much will you lend me on this?" You take it and look at it scornfully, open the back, smile pityingly, and hand it back to him.

"No good to me," you say, and turn your back and pretend to be busy examining a pair of gum-boots or something.

The chap says, "Will you buy it?" You turn around with a pained, weary expression, take the watch back, have another look at it, and say, "I'm robbing myself, but I'll give you four and six-pence for it. I wouldn't do it only you remind me of my poor dead brother. I'm a fool to myself, that's what I am."

After a bit of haggling you give him four and nine and keep the watch. Then you rush over the road to the rival pawnbroker and wave it in front of him and say, "How's this for a bargain! Only four and nine. Have you ever seen anything like that before?"

And he looks at it and says, "Yes; I sold it to a fellow ten minutes minutes ago for two bob."

Then you go outside and faint in the gutter, and when you come to you find that someone's pinched the watch off you.

Of course, it wasn't anything like that that put me out of the game, and it wasn't lack of business. The trouble was, I had too much business.

It all started when the proprietor of a circus pawned the big drum with me. I'd always had a yearning to play a drum, and many was the happy hour I spent whanging it behind the counter, although "Home, Sweet Home" sounds a bit monotonous on a drum after about the third verse.

Well, this chap from the circus became quite friendly, and one day he came into the shop dragging a cage with a lion in it. I'd never had a lion before, and after a bit of hesitation I decided to lend him ten shillings on the cage and five shillings on the lion, making a total of 12/6 in all.

I hung it up outside the shop, and used to put fresh sand in his cage every morning, and sandpaper his perch so he wouldn't fall off, and we got quite pally.

He used to like me to play the drum. When I played he used to roar with delight, and what with me playing the drum and the lion roaring I can tell you there was not a dull moment from start to finish.

Anyhow, the circus proprietor kept bringing me odds and ends until I thought I had everything in the circus, except the tent-pole.

I had forgotten about the elephant. He came in, bringing the front of the building with him. I was in the Pledge Department at the time, doing a bit of pledging, and as soon as the elephant saw me he recognized me. (When I was in the Indian jungle rabbit-trapping, this same elephant used to fill the car radiator for me.) He stood up on his hind legs, placed his front paws on my shoulders, and burst out crying.

By the time I'd peeled the shop off him there was not much left except the goodwill, and that was bent so badly as to be of no further use.

The elephant and I are now living happily together, but I have given up pawnbroking for good.

Last Words On First Aid

When I was in the ambulance brigade — you didn't know I was in the ambulance brigade? Oh, my word, yes! Many's the few bob I've made driving people into town when they've missed their trains. As I was saying, when I was in the ambulance brigade I was renowned throughout the length and breadth and thickness of the land for my skill. Anything from confession of the brain down to minor scratches and confusions I could handle with ease and celery. At inserting stitches I was nulli secundus. I could do plain or fancy stitching, rucking and smocking. I can tell you that when I stitched anyone they knew they were stitched.

I was also an expert poultice-mixer. I could turn out a bread poultice with ridiculous ease, also the more tasty ones with jam on them. Nobody in my district was game to try and get drowned when I was about. I would just fling them on the ground and administer artificial perspiration to them till their spirits were broken.

Snake bites!

They were child's play to me. For a snake to bite anybody when I was within cooee of the spot was a sheer waste of time. It was just a matter of tying a ligature round the snake, carving the bitten portion off the patient, and rubbing permarmalade of potash in it. In about eighteen months' time the wound would be healed, and the patient would be able to be wheeled about in a chair. All due to me.

Of course, things were not always so easy, especially in the country districts. I remember a time when word came to me that a man was lying with a fraction of the leg in a paddock. It seems that a riderless horse had returned to the homestead and begun barking furiously to attract attention. After a while the interested spectators began to think that there was something amiss, so they followed the horse through wild and mountainous country until they came upon a man lying helpless in the thick underwear. (*Undergrowth, fool!*) Undergrowth.

6

Word was sent to me. Hastily mounting my ambulance, I rushed to the spot. I could see that the man was in great pain, so I had a stiff brandy, which seemed to relieve him a little. Then, unrolling my tourniquet, I set to work. (I hope I am not confusing you with all these technical terms?). I placed the leg in splints, and bandaged it, dabbed a bit of sticking plaster here and there, and he was set.

It was when we started to shift him that I found that I had treated the wrong leg, but I had made such a nice job of it in the first place that I thought I'd let it go at that.

Getting him through that rugged country was an experience which I shall never forget. We had to tie a rope around his waist and drag him. So rapid was the progress of his complaint that, by the time we got him home he had his other leg broken, twelve ribs fractured, a piece out of his back, and he was all over gravel rash.

Three or four years later, when he was able to sit up, he had the ingratitude and effrontery to sue me for wilfully and maliciously rendering first aid. Needless to say, I got out of it, the magistrate saying that it wasn't first aid within the meaning of the Act.

But it just shows you what a man has to put up with when he's out doing the Florence Nightingale act from dawn till dark.

There is precious little reward for one's work in the ambulance brigade. Occasionally I'd get a few shillings when the victim was unconscious, but I found that very few people have much money on them when they meet with an accident. I had to go eight miles for a chap once, and all I got out of him was a box of matches and a couple of old letters.

The casual observer might think that an ambulance man has a wonderful time riding around in ambulances, and breaking traffic regulations, and exspeeding the seed limit, and getting his photo taken standing next to the spot marked X, and all that, but it's all wrong. It's better to be a patient than an ambulance man. You go and get run over by a bus, and see if I'm not right.

Behind The Bread Lines

Just because we bakers put up the price of bread occasionally, there's no reason for you girls to get so crusty about it. A baker's life is very hard.

My father said to me some years ago, "My boy, the way you

throw the dough about it's easily seen that you are a born baker."
So that's how I came to enter the trade.

My very first attempt was a startling success, and the original loaf may be seen at the Technological Museum. You will find it mentioned in all the text books as the Lower Five-way Loaf.

When removed from the oven it was charcoal on the outside (very good for dyspepsia), a little further toward the centre it was toast, and farther in still there was bread. The next internal layer was a kind of scone material and the kernel was pure dough. The master baker was so astonished that he was almost frightened.

Then there was the wholemeal loaf I made. It was just the same as ordinary bread, only it was four feet long and two feet thick, and anybody who couldn't make a whole meal out of a loaf like that is a hog.

When I got my own bakery, I took Wep into partnership. This was a hideous mistake. I put him on the dough mixing for a start, and he managed to fall into the dough. I saw the dough heaving up and down, and heard queer, guffling noises, and when I went to investigate I was just in time to see him coming up for the third time.

I rescued him, but there was a complaint the next day from a woman who said that she'd bought a loaf of bread with a left boot in it. That didn't do the business a vast amount of good.

I thought that the best thing I could do would be to send him out on the carts. At the end of his first day he came back to the bakery with both eyes bunged up, and the next morning there were four husbands, two with shot-guns and two with axes, waiting outside the bakery for him.

After that I put him in the business office, where he seemed to do better.

He came to me one day and said, "I've some bad news for you." I was lighting the primus under a loaf of bread at the time. "Out with it!" I said tersely, "I'm busy."

"The price of flour has gone up fourpence a ton," he said in a hushed voice. For a moment I reeled and went as pale as death.

"Good Heavens!" I cried, "we're ruined!"

I pulled myself together and wiped the dough from my forehead. "We must do something," I said in a stern voice. "How much are the customers paying for bread now?"

"Tenpence halfpenny over the counter, a bob under the counter, one and a halfpenny delivered, nothing undelivered," he replied smartly.

"Well, we'll have to charge an extra twopence a loaf, that's all," I said. "If we can get away with it for a fortnight we ought to be able to retire from the bakery business and buy a yacht each. In the meantime ring up all the newspapers and tell 'em we're ruined. By the way, you know that a baker's dozen is thirteen?"

"You can't alter that?" replied Wep.

"No," I said, "but in future every shilling we have to collect automatically becomes one and a penny . . . do you get me? And we'll have to put more holes in the bread. Order four more sacks of holes."

Of course there were a lot of letters in the papers about it from "Housewife," "Indignant," "British Justice," and "Mother of Ten," but a fat lot we cared, with the elections eighteen months off.

After a few weeks, when we were properly ruined, we sold the bakery and regretfully announced that, entirely due to our efforts to sell bread at less than the cost of production, we were compelled to sell out.

I bought a steam yacht and went for a cruise of the Mediterranean, and Wep bought a villa on the Riviera.

If ever the price of flour goes up again, I'm going to hop right back into the baking business. There's a fortune in it.

On A Wet And Woisterous Night

When I was born I sat up in bed and said, "I want to be a bee farmer." And my father said, "Fancy him bee-having like that so young!"

I made a half-hitch in my binder (not worn these days, I believe — they have backless nappies) and said, "Being a newcomer to this family, I should not like to cause any disruption in a hitherto happy ménage, therefore I am willing to become a baker, a bootmaker, a butcher, a bridge-builder, a bosun, a blister . . . anything that starts with a B." My father, who was a man of great business acumen, decided that I should become a bushranger.

Now, I don't want all you old ladies of eighty and ninety saying, "Yes, I remember when I was a girl, Fireball Lower called at my father's farm for a new flint for his lighter. Father was away at the time. He was always very gentle with women, and he kissed me as he was riding through the slip-rails."

"No," said the old lady to our reporter, "I don't think that girls are what they used to be, what with their coloured fingernails and cocktails and fal de lals." Still, I suppose other days, other ways. Hey ho! (When are you going to get on with this story?) Damned typewriter roll won't go around. Do all my typewriting with a pen in future.

I was just a poor, hard-working lad when I was unjustly pinched for horse-strangling and sentenced to three months or the rising of the court. I came out of that living hell an embittered man, and immediately became an enthusiastic bushranger. My first hold-up was on a wild, wet, windy, woisterous night when the gale howled and trees were blown down and branches were scattered all over the place.

I got shot that night. As a matter of fact, if I hadn't been shot I wouldn't have had the nerve to go through with the business. I waited in the darkness on the side of the road. It was bitterly cold, and I pulled my ambush more closely around me. I could hear the poach accroaching (*pull yourself together*) and, as it drew level with me, I urged my faithful horse into the road.

"Bail up!" I cried in clear, ringing tones. To this I added: "Stand and deliver!" "Halt!" and "Whoa!" to make sure of the thing.

The coach-driver reined in his panting horses and got down off his seat. "Listen," he said, "this is getting monotonous. What's the big idea bailing me up every night in the same place?"

"Don't you know that I own the refreshment-room on the other side of the road, mug?" I replied. You've got to be pretty stern with these coach-drivers. I went home in a taxi the other night and the driver had the gall to ask me for eight shillings for a five-bob ride. Did I tell him off! I'll say. And did I pay him the eight shillings? Yes.

"All passengers out of the coach," I commanded. "Men on one side of the road and women on the other. Search yourselves and toss the lot into this barrel." I forgot to tell you that I never travel without a barrel.

Well, I was chucking a comely wench under the chin and chucking a dirty big loafer into the ditch when there came the sound of clattering hoofs. "The troopers!" gasped the coach-driver, smiling malignantly. Malignantly. Dashed good. I must use that word more often. It was the troopers. I stood my ground as they came up.

"Ha! Ha!" said the main or head trooper. "Nice goings on, I must say. A fine how d'y do!" He turned to the coachman. "You are pinched," he said, "for loitering in a public place and for parking in a non-parking area.

"And as for you, Fireball," he said, turning to me, "you'll have to give up this bushranging. You're out in all weathers and, goodness knows, you might catch your death of cold. Why don't you take up politics instead?"

"Sir," I said, drawing myself and horse up to our full height, "I may be a bushranger but, damitall, only on a small scale. I resent your suggestion."

He bowed and shook my hand while the tears rolled down his face. "We need more men like you in this country," he said. I malignanted at him and rode off.

But he was right. There ought to be more men like me.

Wasting Time In The Arctic Wastes

Not that you're interested, but I must tell you about my Russian flight to the North Pole. Personally, I'm sick of the place. Nothing to see but a pole. All right for adventurous and blasé people who are sick of other poles. Still I must tell you! I simply must!

Among those present on my last Russian expedition were Captain Skoffski, Koffski, Vitchisvitch, and Movemoff.

I was graphologist. You know what a graphologist is? Good! That let's me out.

We found the Pole. It just looked like a pole to us. So we came home.

BUT. In that terse, not to say laconic, sentence lies a world of meaning. Beneath the surface is a story of heroism and fortitude which you'd hardly believe. And you'd be almost right.

On our last expedition the dogs (or mucklucks, as the Eskimos call them) broke loose and ate all the stores. We were (to use one of the Eskimo words, and I hope you'll pardon me for what may seem a vulgar display of erudition) stonkered. There we were, crowded in our hut trying to make the best of things. Playing on the harpoon and keeping our spirits up by putting water in the stuff. A blizzard sprang up, but though snowed in and in perilous circumstances we sang songs while gathered about the old college radiator, and the bears and walruses — or walri — howled and bawled outside.

> I'm sittin' and knittin' a mitten
> To save me hands gittin'
> Frost-bitten——

I forget the rest.

I shall not go on any more Arctic expeditions. Last time I came home covered with seals, and I was so frostbitten that when I put my feet in the ice-chest to warm them the thing burst into flames.

11

And we are still paying 5/- per week on the ice-chest! Of course, we'd be doing that in any case, but it just shows you.

In some ways, I'm glad to be back. And yet, if you were to ask me I might ponder. Out in the snowy wastelands one comes face to face with one's soul. A horrible sight. You can't argue with your soul in a desolate waste. And, I can't do anything with this typewriter. Curse the thing!

What would you do in a white, flat, cold place where no bird sings and no beast moves and slumberous slabs of snow roll down and just flatten you? Where great slabs of ice crack open and leave you stranded all alone in a still world with not a soul around. And the deep gloom of the arctic night casts a pall. . . . We'd better snap out of this. It's bad for you.

How jolly to romp through the sparkling, crisp fairy snow! To hear the jolly laughter of the little Eskimo children ringing through the cold, clean air. See! Yonder is a hungry bear! How white he seems! Let us all bolt like blazes. *Of course you would spoil it.*

But note: The aureorear whatsisname flashes its message in the sky. With pink and flaming yellow. (If I don't get a purple certificate for this there's something wrong.)

See yon majestic iceberg! With what pompous majesty it serenely sails! Borne on the tide which bears the fate of men. . . . (That's not bad. Or is it?) Anyhow, let's have a go.

> *On ice-floe walrus doth make speech with seal:*
> *And swordfish doth with snout impale*
> *The dolphin which, with melancholy wail,*
> *Turns south to Rio Grande, braving the gale.*

I don't like that last bit much. I can do better than that when properly goaded. I could do even worse, but I've got to go home now. As a matter of fact, I'll have to do much better than that when I get home.

When, as I said before, I get home —— But I don't think I'll go home. And even if I do I'll go out into the garden and eat polar bears.

Confessions Of Village Blacksmith

Having retired now from active blacksmithing, I think it is fairly safe to tell you something about my life as "The Village Blacksmith."

I was rather a brawny chap in my time, with arms like iron bands and a voice like brass bands. As a matter of fact, the villagers used to call me a mighty man. This was because sometimes I might do a job and then again I mightn't.

My poor wife died of psittacosis, otherwise known as parrot's disease. If you were to ask me did she have any last words, I would reply, "Yes; all of 'em"; however, as you haven't asked me, we won't go into the matter.

My three daughters were all named after flowers. There was Geranium, the eldest, who used to sit on the horses' chests while I shod them Then there were Petunia and Snapdragon, who used to hand out the sparks to children who were coming home from school.

These children, by the way, used to get on my nerves. They'd look in at the open door to hear my bellows roar, and as my bellows wouldn't drive them away, and even shrieking had no effect on them, I threw sparks at them.

I was flinging a horse over the fence one day when a goofy-looking bird wandered in and said that he wanted his nail-file retreaded. We got talking after a while, and I found out his name was Longfellow. He said he was a poet by trade, and that the poetry business had gone to the dogs and was going from bad to verse.

"If you like," he said, "I'll dash off a line or two about yourself. It'll be good publicity for you."

Well, I told him he could have a stab at it, but that fellow got me all wrong. He said I loved to hear my daughters sing at church. That I used to actually go to church to listen to them. Buddies, I ask you!

Geranium, I'll admit, had had a fair voice — she was a caricatura soprano. But the other two used to frighten the horses if they only hummed. I could knock out better tunes on the bellows. And as for going to church . . . if you've ever been a blacksmith you know that Sunday is the only day in the week that a man can get a bit of exercise. And another thing, I was overworked. Day in, day out, from morn till night, I'd be bellowing or hammering or something, and when I wasn't doing that I'd be ringing my anvil, which is no mean feat and not to be undertaken lightly. And on top of all that, when I wasn't toiling I had to do a bit of sorrowing and rejoicing, so you can see that I had my hands full.

One dirty crack that Longfellow brought off had a certain amount of truth in it. I'll admit that I had a handy habit of looking people brazenly in the face and telling them that I didn't owe them anything. It is not true, however, that I looked the whole world in the face, as I never had the time nor the money for travel.

I will say, though, that looking your creditors in the face and denying all knowledge of the debt works on ball bearings if you're a blacksmith. I used to just wave my muscles at them and they'd regard themselves as paid.

My daughter Geranium married the village butcher, which narked this poet Longfellow to such an extent that he wrote a poem about him. I only remember the first verse. As near as I can remember, it goes:

> *Under the village poplar tree*
> *The village butcher sets,*
> *The butch, a poplar man is he*
> *For he takes S.P. bets.*

Of course they tarred him, feathered him, put icing sugar on him, and ran him out of the village on a rail.

Petunia, my youngest, has got a job as a foghorn on a lighthouse, and is doing well. She writes to me regularly, inquiring about the church and one thing and another, and sends me a brace of seagulls every now and then.

Snapdragon had the luck to be kicked by a horse, and it made such an impression that she is now showing as "Lucky Lydia, the Girl with the Horseshoe Embedded in Her Face." Coining money, I believe.

Well, well, I suppose I've earned the usual night's repose. Onward through life I go.

PS. — You will all be sorry to learn that since writing this I have passed away greatly mourned. The village hearse was decorated with flags and bunting, the occasion was made a public holiday, and a good time was had by all. It is believed that I died as the result of a cold caught while shoeing draught horses. Old Casper, who was sitting in the sun as usual, when interviewed, said that it was a famous victory for the draught horses. He also said that if I had sat in the sun telling lies to my daughter, Wilhelmine, instead of fooling about with draught horses, my funeral would never have occurred.

Seeing that I never had any daughter called Wilhelmine, I consider this most unsporting. Anyhow, if I did have a kid anything like that brat I'd put ground-up glass in her porridge.

You can't get really fond of a child that's always bowling skulls about the place. The whole family were inclined to be a bit morbid. Casper's son, Casperbianca, was the village idiot who went away to sea and set fire to the boat. The mutt then stood there on the burning deck when all but he had made a bolt for the open spaces. Casper used to say that he stood there as if rooted to the spot. He should have been booted off the spot, as I told Old Casper. That reminds me; just before he left the village, Longfellow wrote another poem. Something like this:

> 'Twas evening, and the setting sun
>   Was sinking in the West.
> Old Casper sat outside his door
>   Mopping gravy off his vest.
>
> Up came that headache, Wilhelmine,
>   With the bones of some old soldier,
> And asked old Casper what they were,
>   And Casper said, "I told yer!
>
> "It was a famous victory,
>   Get that into your brain.
> And take those blasted bones away
>   And don't come here again!"
>
> 'Twas then the village blacksmith
>   Picked up a horse and cab,
> And aiming it at Casper's bean,
>   Stonkered the rude old crab.

Come down to the family vault and see me some time.

Lions Will Swallow Anything

When I was a lion-tamer, a job I had to give up after I got married because I couldn't do two jobs at once, I had a most arduous time.

And what, pray, is this apropos of? (Apropos is a word I have taken to my bosom these last few weeks.) It is apropos of circuses. (*Latin.*) Two circuses is circi; three circuses is circum. Hence the term circumnavigate, to go to three circuses or circi.

One of my lions got lockjaw, and when my act of putting my head in the lion's mouth came on, we had to prise the lion's mouth open. I won first prise. We had to use blasting powder at the finish. Then we couldn't get the animal's mouth shut when the show was finished, and we were prosecuted for being open after hours.

Then there was my celebrated act apropos of diving from a two-hundred-foot tower, enveloped in flames, on to a performing seal.

We had quite a variety of exhibits and turns in our circus. The chap who did the most turns was the acrobat. We had a white negro and a black white man, and a bearded lady who didn't smoke. I frequently had to double for the other artists. I shall never forget the time when I had to be the strong man, he being in bed with anaemia.

He used to tear cars apart with his naked hands, just like a garage mechanic, and bend tram-lines around his wrist and chew hundred-pound weights with his teeth and spit them out of his ear, and all that.

I only had three hours' notice, so I didn't have time to do much training.

Well, I bent a couple of tram-lines, and caught a 200-pound weight on the back of my neck, and a very ripe tomato on the chest, and a few odds and ends, but I'm afraid I overdid it a bit. I lifted up the circus pole as a sort of crowning achievement. And it was. It brought the the house down — all over us.

I also had to train an elephant to count. It was rather marvellous the way that animal learnt things.

He was what is known in the show game as a furore, which is another name for a successful elephant. When he put one foot down, that was one. Putting the other foot down made it two, the third foot being three, and so on. He could only count up to four. I have since thought that if he'd had crutches, he could have counted up to six. One always thinks of these things too late.

Bare back riding was another act which was very apropos of me. *(I don't think I like that — start over again.)* Apropos of bare-back riding, I was extremely proficient at it. It is really quite simple when one gets the hang of it. All that is needed is a bicycle.

I did have a go at being a real live American cowboy, but was not so good at it. I was wearing my chaps, having forgotten my lanoline, and twirling my lariat splendidly for the first half of the act, but something happened, and I lassoed myself so splendidly that they had to get the fire brigade to unloose me. Benefiting from my experience, I have been leading a loose life ever since.

The lure of the sawdust ring, the tinsel and glitter, the spangles and grease paint, and elephants and that sort of thing, have led many a young girl away from home — which is wrong. Never run away and join a circus — it's bad for you.

Hoping this finds you as it leaves me, I remain — which, my wife tells me, is the best thing I do.

Burning Memories

I don't think I've told you yet about the time when I was a fire-engine. Anyhow, I've got to tell *you*. I nearly told a friend of mine a while ago, but he got away from me.

When I was young and carefree and just about to launch myself on a startled world, my mother wanted me to become a doctor because it was such a refined occupation and she knew a lot of friends who would gladly get sick just to help me along a bit, but my father said there was a great future in electricity.

The head school-master was dragged into the discussion and he said that I should be in gaol. Mother smacked his face. The other scholars were so delighted they all chucked in one day's play-lunch money for a brass tablet to be screwed alongside the other brass tablets in among the Rhodes scholars and other distinguished people.

Anyhow, after the whole family had decided that I should become a doctor, electrical engineer, an admiral ("The navy will make a man of him, Flo. His great grandfather was——" . . . "Yes you told me before.")

I'm coming to the fire brigade part any minute now. Almost immediately.

I was sitting out in the wood-shed smoking a cigar-butt, which I had found in the house, and it occurred to me that my future was in the balance. *(We can't go on like this.)*

I was on duty this night. Some of the boys were playing euchre; some were just resting. I was polishing my helmet.

The Super. came in and said: "Men; there's a fire on! Get shaved and dressed!"

"I have just finished polishing my helmet," I protested. "Am I going to get my helmet all wet and charred and sooty, and be a disgrace to the brigade?"

"You will carry the ladder!" he snapped. He was like that.

"Stand back, there!"

"Why?"

"For your own safety."

"Lower!"

"Yessir!"

"The eighth floor. There's a woman there." There was, too!

We were short of ladders. I had to pull up one ladder and put it on top of the next — but you wouldn't understand.

I got to the window.

The woman was on fire. It's marvellous how calm one can be on such occasions. I said, "May I put you out?" She said, "No. I live here. And what's more, it'll take a better man than you to put me out. The dirty, greasy caretaker has had a go, but I pay my rent, which is more than that old hag downstairs does, and if I liked to tell all I know about what goes on in this building on Saturday nights — mind you, I'm not a nark. Everybody says I'm a good sport. That is, nice people, I mean. Not twerps. Personally, I wouldn't have a twerp in the place. I was only saying to a friend of mine——"

"Madam," I said, "do you realize that you are in imminent danger of being burnt to the ground and lost with all hands?"

"It's people like you," she *glickered* (that's a good word. It means when a woman talks and tries to gnash her teeth at the same time) "who make people like me dislike and despise and detest people like you!"

"Listen!" I growled, grabbing her by the throat. "Do you want to be saved? — or don't you!"

I saved her after a lot of mucking about. She still hangs around the fire station in an honorary capacity as a siren.

Me And The O.A.A.M.C.N.O.C.

I have long felt the need of a really impregnable excuse for having a night out with the boys. All my excuses are worn so thin that my wife, when I get half way through, finishes them for me. Which is humiliating to a fellow who earns his living solely by his imagination.

I thought of joining a lodge. I did not know whether to join the Hibernian Society or become a Mason. And, being in doubt about some others, I decided to form my own society.

My name not being Murphy or O'Brien, I was a non-starter for the Hibernian Society, but I was rather attracted to Masonry because of all the little hammers and trowels, and spades and gold-plated things. Still, the goat-riding part of the initiation ceremony perturbed me.

I was informed by a very exalted Mason (I think he was the Chief Rock-Chopper and Honourable Foundation Stone Chiseller) that the lodge goat was a nice animal which had been donated by Mr. Skuthorpe from his buckjump circus as he was unable to control it. This rather put me off becoming a Mason.

The Antediluvian Order of Buffaloes did not attract me much. I know a few buffaloes, personally.

Then there was the Ancient Order of Foresters. Well, you can't go home late at night and tell your wife you've been out planting trees, or chopping wood, or whatever the Ancient Foresters do.

The Ku-Klux-Klan seems to be a back number these days, and anyhow, there is no scope for an energetic member in this benighted country. What's the use lugging a rope around when there's nobody to lynch?

So I was driven to forming a society of my own. It is The Old and Ancient, Antediluvian, Moth-Eaten, Cobweb-Covered, Neolithic Order of Complainers.

It is a secret society which has an annual meeting once a week, its object being to stay out as late as possible and assist charity by buying State Lottery tickets. All members of the Order are pledged to save up their old razor blades which will later be melted down into a battleship, thus helping towards the defence of the country.

The signs and countersigns are rather complicated. If you see a man with his vest on back to front, and wearing his wristlet watch around his neck, you will not be far wrong in guessing him to be a member of the O.A.A.M.C.N.O.C.

The fist must be clenched when shaking hands, after which the member must turn around three times and then yell in a loud voice, "WHACKO!" They then exchange bootlaces.

After that they make a moue. I am not quite sure what a moue is, but Phillips Oppenheim is always making people do it. I read only last night where "The bewitching young Countess made a little moue, and tapped Sir Edward lightly on the arm with her fan." It must be some kind of knitted thing, because I can hardly imagine the Countess wandering about the ballroom with a hammer and nails. However, I digress. I'm afraid that my passion for literary research work overcomes me at times.

One good thing about my lodge is that you can get buried free. Any time you like. We have a lodge doctor who will give you a medical certificate for a small fee so that you can stay away from work for a week. The fee goes into the Sick and Accident Fund so that any brother of the Order who wishes to have an accident merely notifies the Secretary to the Grand Canyon, who gives his official permission.

The Supreme Hooded Terror (me) has the last word in all disputes. Such a change from home life; I'm sure I'm going to enjoy it.

I am inviting tenders for the headquarters building. The bar will be on the top floor. On the next floor will be the meeting room, then the second (or novices) bar. After that comes the horizontal bar, where you can lie down to drink. Then the swimming pool and an ambulance station in the basement. Thus one progresses by easy stages towards home and mother.

One of the most important positions in the lodge will be that of Grand Chief Sympathizer. Last week I injured my wrist. I wrapped it up in most impressive bandages and put it in a sling and went around the town with an agonized expression. Did anybody rush up to me and say, "My poor chap! How dreadful to see you so frightfully maimed, and what a blow to literature that it should be your right hand! I'm sure you're being tortured with pain, but I see you are bearing it with a gallant smile"?

Not on your life! They just said: "Hullo! Been playing up again?" or "You ought to take more water with it," and "How's the other bloke look?"

All this will be altered when the O.A.A.M.C.N.O.C. gets going. Brothers with sore wrists will go to see the Grand Chief Sympathizer and be sympathized at and with so thoroughly that they will go home and take to their beds for weeks, complete with medical certificate and free burial chart.

Don't miss these benefits. Rip out a coupon!

That's Life Among The Billionaires

I note that a representative of Carnegie, who goes about the place endowing libraries, is having some trouble in giving away money. He finds it very difficult. That's my worry, too! Do you know that at the present moment I couldn't give away two bob? Of course, I wasn't always like this. Once I was known as the "£uxurious £ennie £ower."

I would rise about eleven and be carried into the bath, which was filled with champagne or sometimes rum. Meanwhile the shoes, suit, hat, etcetera, which I had worn the previous day, would be thrown away and a fresh lot laid out by my valet.

A footman would then hold me up while the valet dressed me. One of the under-footmen would then go for a brisk walk for me. One morning he overdid it, and walked two miles. Boy, was I tired when he got back!

Then the fleet of cars would be got out. The one with the orchestra in it went in front. Then came the limousine with my hat and stick in it, then the one with the eau-de-cologne sprinkler to lay the dust, closely followed by the armoured car with my pocket-money in it, and the next car held ME.

On either side of me was a limousine, one to carry my cigars and one for the matches. Spare chauffeurs, mechanics, messengers, secretaries would follow on in the rear. Should I be held up at an intersection, I just bought that particular street and went on my way.

Arriving at my destination the car would be peeled off me, the red carpet put down, and I would make my leisurely way into my offices.

Seating myself, I would press a button and immediately a secretary would shoot through a trap-door in the floor.

"Why is there no one here to press buttons for me?" I would inquire coldly, "You're fired. Take twenty-five years' salary in lieu of notice."

Another one of my secretaries would enter.

"Sir, the Prime Minister has been waiting for three hours, and he won't go away."

"Send him in."

The Prime Minister would enter timidly.

"Hello, Bob! Sit down, man! Sit down! Don't stand there like a great woolly-headed oaf!"

"Thank you kindly, sir," Bob would say, seating himself gingerly on the edge of the chair, "I was wondering, sir, if you wanted any more laws passed this week?"

"Ah! Trying to get round me, eh? Want some more battleships, I suppose. Didn't I pay the national debt last week? You don't mean to tell me you've gone and run up more bills! Speak up, man! Don't cringe!"

"Well, sir, it's about the new Governor-General . . ."

"What about Haile Selassie? Looks as if he's going to be out of a job shortly. Pretty hot stuff on progress and enlightenment and all that bunk, too, if you can believe the newspapers."

"But, sir, he's black!"

"So were the Murada and the Orungal and the Moruya. Get him bleached! See to it. Shut the door gently as you go out."

"Oh, sir!"

"Well, what is it!"

"When I was in London the King particularly asked me to thank you for the gold-mounted stamp catalogue you . . ."

"That's enough. Get out!"

More button pressing.

"The Governor of the Commonwealth Bank to see you, sir."

"Haven't I told you before that I don't wish to be bothered with these tinpot concerns? Isn't there a notice on the door, 'Hawkers and Canvassers Not Admitted'? How did he sneak in?"

"I understand, sir, that he secreted himself in the lift-well last night."

"Sling him out. And tell my footmen that I wish to be carried to my car. I have finished here for the day."

Leave The Honey To The Bees

An American department store has discovered that women customers resent being called "dearie" or "honey" by the salesgirls.

Quite right, too! If and when I go shopping all I want is service.

The ideal store would be where the customer slams her fist down on the counter and says, "Do I get served here or do you think I'm part of the furniture?"

"Say what you want and you'll get it. Think I'm a mind-reader?"

"I want a hat!"

"I'll say you do! I wouldn't be found dead in the one you're wearing. Try this for size, if your head's clean."

"You're going the right way for a slap in the teeth, my girl!"

"Say that outside, you frump."

"I'll fix you later. How does this hat look from the back?"

"A great deal better than it does from the front. Try walking backwards in it. The hat's all right. It's your face."

"You'll eat those words shortly, my dear. How much is this relic from the scrapheap?"

"Two guineas to you."

"Rot! They've got the same thing up the road for nineteen and eleven."

"Phooey! If you could get that hat cheaper elsewhere do you think you'd be wallowing around here wasting my time? Snap out of it. This is not a rest-home."

"Don't try me too far, sister. Let me see another one. There's a blue one in the window I rather fancy."

"You would. Suitable for a nineteen-year-old girl, and you must be forty if you're a day. And if you think I'm going to upset the window display just to let you make yourself look a bigger boob than you are, you can forget it."

"I want to see the manager!"

"So that's the game is it? Come in here pretending to buy a hat and all you want is to see the manager. A married man with five children, too. You ought to be ashamed of yourself."

A woman would enjoy shopping under those conditions. Men are different somehow. Nobody calls me Honey.

When I go to buy a pair of socks the salesman says, "Yizzer?"

"Socks."

"They do?"

"Oke. How much?"

"Two eleven."

"That's robbery."

"Yes, isn't it? Wrap 'em up or will you stick 'em in your pocket?"

"In my pocket. Keep the change and buy a house with it. Know anything for today?"

"Rosie Morn in the Juvenile."

"I've seen better horses on merry-go-rounds. See you some more."

"I hope not. S'long."

That's fair dinkum shopping with no honey in it. As any schoolboy knows—where have I heard that before? Even a half-witted numbskull like yourself—that also sounds familiar. Anyhow, it has been said that politeness costs nothing, a soft word turneth away wrath, and a kindly glint in the eye is as dew on the rose. That last one is my own. What is needed in all shopping transactions is a helpful and understanding attitude to be taken up and stood on by both parties.

I have recently had some experience of shopping in a country store. It goes like this:

"Goo-day. Hot enough for you?"

"We've had it worse. How's the water out your way?"

"We're buyin' it. Still got a bit of grass around here, I notice."

"It won't last. It's the dust that worries me. Gets on everything. There's a line of women's singlets I got in about eleven years ago all practically ruined as you might say."

"I thought we might get a drop of rain this morning by the look of them clouds."

"You can't take any notice of 'em. I believe Hogan's burnt out."

"That's right. If he'd have burnt a break between his joint and the place where the creek used to be, he'd have saved a lot of them sheep."

"It just goes to show. We might have a good season next year."

"That's right. How's the missus?"

"Oh, same as usual. Always complaining about something. You know how they are."

"I suppose you can't blame 'em. Have you got any flour?"

"Might have a bag out the back. Do you want it now?"

"Aw, later on."

"I mean to say, that blue kelpie of Scotty's has had pups out the back there and I don't want to disturb her."

"That's all right. Ounce of fine cut."

"Want me to put it down?"

"Might as well. You don't mind me leavin' the mare on the veranda, do you? The flies worry her."

"Terrible weather for horses. Even the stationmaster feels it."

"Him! He couldn't feel his way out of a diamond necklace!"

"And that's the sort of bloke who calls himself a public servant. We pay for the likes of him. There was a train here last Thursday and he didn't know where it came from."

"Where did it come from?"

"I dunno. It came in the nightime. Old Fred said his ulcer woke him up about four o'clock and it was there then. Save me one of,them pups."

"You might as well have a cup of tea while you're here."

That's real service. Leave the honey to the bees!

Down Among The Wombats

People who think that there are no more thrills to be had in our great open spaces have not heard anything. Why, only the other day a man was attacked by a six-foot kangaroo in the bush near Corinda, and fought with it for ten minutes. I have had similar experiences with wombats. Not dingbats—wombats!

While camped on the edge of a small nullah-nullah or waterhole I was startled by a loud roar. With true bushman's instinct I fell into the waterhole, and, on looking around, observed a huge wombat devouring one of my dogs. From tip to tip, its antlers were about eight feet across.

My rifle was on the bank, and I had broken my sheath-knife off at the hilt trying to cut a damper I had made. I knew I was safe so long as I stayed up to my neck in the water. Unfortunately I had not foreseen the cunning of this wombat.

Stamping its feet with rage, it approached the edge of the waterhole and commenced to drink. Rapidly the water level went down. from my neck to my armpits, then down to my waist.

Every now and then it would pause and glare at me with its little red eyes. This gave me an idea. Next time it glared at me I glared back at it. This seemed to disconcert the beast and it looked away and hiccupped.

It resumed drinking after a while, but without any great enthusiasm.

The water was down to my ankles, when the wombat gave me one last pitiful, frustrated look and rolled over on its side—full.

I splashed towards it. "Come on now," I said, shaking it by the antlers. "Pull yourself together. I'll get you a taxi. Where do you live?" (This, of course, was sheer force of habit.)

"Brr-hup! Groo," he answered.

"Don't give in to it," I said. "Do you think you can walk? Lean against me. That's the way."

Well, it was just the sort of thing you'd do for anybody, but you wouldn't believe how grateful that wombat was when next I met it. Of course, things don't always work out that way. I could never get on with goannas—or iguanas, as you city folk say. They have a nasty habit of turning up at the wrong time. This would not be so bad if it were not for their penchant for climbing up trees.

I recall the time when I was leaning against a gum-tree talking to the squatter's daughter. We were getting along famously, and I had even got to the point of shyly asking her what she thought of the price of fat lambs at the saleyards.

I could see the faint glow in her cheeks, her dewy, downcast eyes and tremulous lips as she replied: "You really want to know? You are not one of those—those men who——. Oh, you wouldn't understand."

It was then that the goanna missed his footing and fell down the back of my shirt. If I had been wearing a belt all might have been well, but as I was wearing braces the thing went right down my left trouser-leg. Its beady eyes looked out from just above my left boot and its tail waved frantically about the back of my neck.

"Are you in the habit of indulging in this horse-play?" she asked in icy tones. All the spirit of her ancestors—both of them—was in that steely glance.

I tried to explain. "You see," I said, "I'm wearing braces——"

"I see," she said haughtily. "You usually keep your trousers up by sheer willpower, I suppose?"

I wanted to tell her that if I had been wearing a belt the goanna couldn't have gone all the way down. But she spurned me. She wheeled her horse with a look of utter loathing and gave it a slash with the whip. Surprised and indignant, the horse leapt in the air and the squatter's daughter landed on a hard portion of one of her father's many acres of grazing property.

"Serves you right," I said.

Chivalry did not permit me to laugh out loud, so I contented myself with a quiet smile.

"Are you in the habit of indulging in this horse-play?" I drawled. Then we walked away—me and the goanna.

But for that goanna I might now have been a squatter's son-in-law, pushing sheep about the place and picking the flies out of my ears, with a trip to the city once a year when the Show was on.

No, one doesn't have to go abroad for thrills. In one day on an outback station I was—

(a) Kicked by a horse.

(b) Chased by a bull.

(c) Savaged by a dog.

(d) Lacerated on a barbed-wire fence.

Also, in some mysterious fashion, I managed to put the lighting plant out of action.

You can't tell me anything about bush life. I am fully qualified to put an advertisement in the "Positions Wanted" column containing the words, "Do anything. Go anywhere."

Address all communications to Lantana W. (Wallaby) Lower. I'm equally good as a horse-breaker, tutor, or native companion.

Peeping At A Modern Pepys

Whether it was Capetown or Newtown perhaps will never be known. Our instructions were to bring back films of wild life in the jungle which would make the hair stand on end, sending clouds of dandruff into the air.

We struck the fringe of the jungle about Wednesday, travelling with twenty-six bearers in charge of four shikaris and a ramadan who was driving the howdah. Matted growths were matting monotonously on every side. A glance at my diary is very illuminating.

12th Sept. Saw boa conspirator of great length. Party held up for two days while it passed. Have issued quinine to bearers and beaters. Lions bawling all around us. Have instructed whole staff to bawl back, thus upholding supremacy of white race.

10th Nov. Have been travelling three months on hands and knees. Bearers have deserted. Beaters have beaten it. Shikaris on the shikar. They have taken camels, field glasses, corkscrew, mules, and other portable goods. Saw five lions.

11th Nov. Lions following. Am well in front approaching the three-furlong post.

14th Nov. Lions getting closer. Have taken close-up of tonsils of front lion.

15th Nov. The four rear lions have eaten the front lion, photos of whose tonsils I have taken. Jealousy. Four remaining lions have now lined up to have photos taken. Have taken photos and asked lions to call back in three days for proofs.

20th Dec. Running short of water. Will have to go easy on the hot baths. Think will throw bath away. Sick of carrying the thing.

22nd Dec. Gave last drop of water to Voodoo rain-maker. Used remainder of quinine for shaving. Very weak, being scarcely able to push the rhinoceroses from my path.

23rd Dec. Struck Umbookoo River. Water dirty, too many fish in it. Have to boil water, and hate boiled fish. What to do? Probably will die of thirst. Who cares in these wild regions? Thin red line. Playing fields of Eton.

1st Jan. In hands of cannibals. Have told cannibals that if harm hair of head, Great White Chief will send Atlantic fleet play brass bands at them. Also A.B.C. wireless programmes.

2nd Jan. Have cannibals cowed. Today had a House of Parliament erected and put all cannibals on dole. Excelsior!

4th Feb. Choked my first puma. Have trained fifteen baboons to carry luggage. Getting short of citronella and elephants very troublesome.

5th Feb. Came upon Kaffir kraal today. Shot it. Will have skin tanned and sent back, if I live. Natives very friendly. Offered to guide me into local volcano.

9th Feb. Lost! Baboons deserted, taking camera and equipment. Will have to memorize scenes and take them when I get back to the studio.

11th Feb. Have been captured by hostile natives. Am writing this on piece of bark. Am trussed by hands to hundred-foot tree, toes barely touching the ground. Have great difficulty getting bark into typewriter.

13th Feb. Have been visited by chief of tribe. It seems that I am on their bread-fruit tree and am attracting weevils. Am bargaining.

14th Feb. Have uprooted tree and escaped. Will take canoe down the Umboo Rapids if can untie myself from the tree. Fearful privations. Mosquitoes, leeches. Lost back stud.

15th Feb. On our last tin of boot-polish.

29th Feb. Alligators bar further progress. Will have to turn back. God help us all.

Here the thing seems to end. I am probably still there.

A Crotchety Musician

I don't think I'm getting senile, but I feel all crotchety & quavery. I think it must be all these eisteddfods that are going about. What with lugging home gold cups & shields & belts & diplomas & ribbons & illuminated addresses & things I am just about worn out.

I won the Senior Yodelling Contest from scratch. The Swiss Consul, who was present, burst into tears and said he wanted to go home to his Alp. I tell you I created a furore. I still have it at home somewhere.

Quite a number of interesting things happened during the competitions. In the Whistling Contest one of the competitors was disqualified for unseemly behaviour. In trying to emulate one of my high notes he blew out one of his front teeth and stunned the adjudicator. I was awarded the verdict on a foul.

In the Electrocution Section I was so good that they gave me a handicap. I had to recite, "Oh, Save My Mother's Picture From The Sale", with a billiard ball in my mouth.

I followed it up with "Don't Sell My Father Rum". You remember the part where the little child is pleading with the scoundrelly publican, and the publican got a bit fed-up with it?

> And he hit her on the jaw,
> And she fell upon the floor,
> And he threw her out the door,
> And said, "I WILL sell your father rum!"

I had most of the women sobbing towards the end. The adjudicator awarded me first prize and said I ought to get a good job broadcasting auction sales from one of the B Class stations.

But it was at singing that I really distinguished myself. You should have heard me sing "Now the Moon Shines Tonight On Pretty Redwing"! I brought the house down—or part of it. A considerable amount of plaster fell from the ceiling during the rendering, and the vibration jolted the eggs out of all the pigeons' nests on the Town Hall till the place looked like an omelette.

I was paid a unique compliment by the judges. They stopped me when I was half-way through, and said that they didn't want to hear any more, and that they were greatly impressed. One of them said that never in his life had he heard such a voice. They then said to help myself to any one of the cups I fancied, and let me out the back door.

A diversion occurred during the judging of the instrumental

music. One of the competitors was playing a French horn—you know, one of those things that go round and round, and fit over your shoulders, and you wear it like a life-saving belt.

Well, the poor gentleman must have swollen somehow. I don't think he took it off when he had his lunch. Anyhow, they had to get a blacksmith to get him out of it. When the blacksmith had finished cutting the instrument away he had enough spare parts to make two cornets, a bassoon, three whistles, and a trombone.

Then there was another fellow who went mad with a sliding trombone. He played on for hours and wouldn't stop. They tried hanging on to the sliding part, but it made no difference. All they got was the ride. At the finish they had to shoot him to stop him. He was buried underneath the organ loft with his trombone beside him.

Still, we don't want to dwell on these sad things. As I frequently remark to my grandfather, always look on the bright side, and if there's no bright side, don't look.

I am sorry to say that I failed in the instrumental music. I was playing a piccolo, and the test piece was "Asleep In The Deep", which had some very low notes. As a matter of fact, the whole thing is so low that anyone playing it ought to be pinched under the Consorting Act. Well, you know how hard it is to piccolo note on a piccolo? (*Listen, I thought you'd reformed and given up that sort of thing?*)

I endeavoured to get over this difficulty by using a bass drum, and every time I got to the low notes I'd just kick the drum, but it didn't seem to go over too well. Still, I suppose one can't win everything.

I am now practising on the bassoon, and I will be ready for the next musical festival when it comes along. Let's hope it'll bassoon.

Bucking The Buccaneers

AVAST!! (*Eh?*) I said, AVAST!! (*A vast what?*) Shut up! Yo, yo! And a bottle of gum! I've just received my income-tax assessment and it reminds me of the good old days when I, too, was a pirate. Yes, girls, little Lennie was once a pirate and sailed the high seas. The seas were much higher in those days than they are now.

Many's the galleon I've sunk. Galleons and galleons of them.

The moment I sighted a Spaniard I'd board him—thirty shillings a week and soft washing.

The loot I used to get! Gold plate, doubloons (they're not worn now), pieces of eight; sometimes I even got pieces of nine.

One day I was sharpening my cutlass when the look-out man cried out, "Rot me for a land-lubbering wowser if I don't see a galleon in the distance, Captain!"

"Heave to!" I shouted. "Belay! Whoa!" Which was done.

Every man took a cannon and was given orders not to shoot until they saw the whites of their eyes. "What if one of 'em's got bloodshot eyes?" said one of my merry men. "Don't shoot him," replied my bosun, Long John Saliva, "he's probably shot already."

Long John Saliva was one of the best pirates I've ever worked with. He was tattooed all over. Even his tonsils had "I love Maggie" on them in three colours.

We were nearing the galleon. "Bait the grappling irons," I said in a tense voice.

BOOM! (cannons). BOOM! BOOM! (more cannons). TINKLE! TINKLE! (very inferior Spanish cannons).

We boarded her, cutlass in hand and fighting like reckless demons, little devils that we were. A proud Spanish Don, espying me from the bridge of his crippled ship, said, "By Crikey! It's Bully Lower!" in Spanish. Then he gave in.

We got fifteen chests of doubloons and things, and four fair maidens, which I threw back because I already had an island full of them, and a couple of wristlet watches and a lot of odds and ends. It was very troublesome dividing the two wristlet watches between the crew. Being the captain, I got a main spring, but there was a lot of heart-burning and jealousy for some time afterward.

Well, after hanging a few prisoners from the yard-arm we hoisted sail, and the men, who had been served with a tot of rum, were in high spirits.

I smiled as I gazed down at them from the poop. They were singing that rousing old song, "Now Drake Was an Animal Brave and Bold". You know, the one where he beats Von Tramp, or Vin Blanc, or whatever his name was.

After a while they became quarrelsome, so I said to myself, "I shall deal one of those oafs a buffet which will sort ill with his liking, begad!" Just like that. Then I waded into them. They were a sorry crew when I'd finished with them. When I coughed, they leapt into the air and whimpered.

I got home covered with glory and green parrots. But not without some trouble, mark you. There were always arguments about burying the treasure. The idea was simply to bury the treasure, make a plan of the spot, and then lose the plan. Sounds simple enough, but you've no idea of the complication that arose. I used to have a mutiny three times a day, and the last time I got so fed up I said, "All right! If you won't behave yourselves I'll take my share and get off the boat and walk home." That quelled them.

I got tired of the life after a few years. It was too monotonous. I left the sea and retired to my little cottage in the wolds with my trusty henchman, Long John Saliva, there to end my declining years in peaceful contemplation of the long, long ago.

I have a few old, blood-stained maps for sale, very cheap. Make good New Year presents. All the places on the maps are far away. Give one to your time-payment collector.

Lower Away For The Landing

Just fancy! It was way back in 1788 that Governor Phillip and I landed in Botany Bay. How time flies!

As we sailed into the bay we got a whiff from the boiling down works. "My goodness, this country smells!" said Phillip.

"I told you we were landing in the wrong place," I replied. "Why couldn't you land in some genteel place like Rose Bay?"

"Who's Governor of this colony?" he replied heatedly. "All right! All right!" I said. "Don't do your block in front of the convicts."

So we landed at Farm Cove. Thus is history made.

It was a pretty wild spot, and the natives were a bit suspicious. "Blime!" said one convict. "Tike me back to Dartmoor!" We put him in irons.

"I think we'll build a gaol first," said Phillip. The first sign of civilization was the gaol. Then we built the barracks.

After that I said to Phillip: "What about lunch?" "Good idea!" he said.

"Lunch ho!" I bawled, and there was a great clashing of leg-irons as the convicts collapsed in their tracks.

"I'm glad you thought to pack some sandwiches before we left England," I said. "There doesn't seem to be much to eat in this place."

"I think of everything," said Phillip, somewhat boastfully, I thought. "I've even brought a couple of rabbits and a potted prickly pear which I intend to plant shortly. They ought to do well in this country."

We were sitting down munching our sandwiches when Sir Joseph Banks came rushing up with a piece of lantana in one hand and a sprig of Bathurst burr in the other.

"Look what I've found!" he cried delightedly.

"How quaint!" said Phillip. "We must plant a lot of that, too. Come and have a sandwich, Joe."

We had just finished the last of our sandwiches when a soldier came up, saluted, and said, "Sir, one of the convicts has just bitten a piece out of his pick. Did it deliberately."

"Hang him," said Phillip.

"Yessir."

And that was that.

"You're a bit drastic, aren't you?" I asked, when the soldier had gone.

"We can get plenty more convicts, but we're a bit short of picks."

"I suppose you're right."

"Of course I'm right!" That's the sort of man he was. Bombastic.

"What's this track they're cutting here?" I asked him.

"That's George Street. I called it after the ship's parrot. Holy Moses!"

"Wasser matter?"

"It's all right. It must be the heat. I thought I saw a big brown thing standing upright on two legs with a long tail and it jumped fifteen feet and disappeared into the bush."

"You want to lay off that rum," I told him. We found out later that they were real. Kangaroos—not rum, after all.

All this time, Blaxland was away in the hills with Lawson and Wentworth. We were beginning to get a bit anxious about them. However, they came back after a while and said that they had discovered three railway stations. They had had the effrontery to name them after themselves. Phillip immediately named a street after himself. He was very annoyed. He even went so far as to name a whole bay after himself and called it Port Phillip in order to make it sound more important.

He was a man who was inclined to bicker about trifles. One day when he found me fraternising with the aborigines he was quite furious until I told him that I had learned a number of real good names for towns, such as Wagga Wagga, Coonamble and Wantibadgery. That soothed him a bit.

After a few months, when we had the town pretty well fixed up and had imported a few bushrangers to liven things up a bit, darn me if Macarthur didn't arrive with some merino sheep he'd picked up somewhere.

"You fool!" said Phillip, bitterly. "They'll eat the grass and then how will my rabbits get on?"

"I never thought of that," said Macarthur, biting his nails.

"A fine team of colonists I've got," went on Phillip.

"You must admit," I said, "that we have made progress. When we first landed here there was nothing else to see but scenery. Now look at it. We've put up two new scaffolds, we've got a street, planted a whole lot of prickly pear . . ."

"Yes! Yes! I know all that, but nobody is ever here when they're wanted. There's Bass and Flinders gone off in a boat somewhere, fishing, I suppose. They can get somebody else to be Governor. I'm fed up."

It was a very nasty scene and has rightly been left out of most history books.

Still, when I look around today and see the result of our labours I say to myself, "Well, we certainly gave the town a good start."

I'm still able to give the town a bit of a start when I've got the money. The old pioneer spirit lives on.

Me And Richard One

It has occurred to me that I should speak of war and battle, of grim happenings of long ago when you were muling and puking, as Shakespeare so indecently puts, in your little cot.

I fought for Richard the First.

I shall never forget the time when King Richard came along with the Chief Armourer and assisted to rivet a medal on to my breast-plate.

"Egad, man 'twere well that this fair land hath men of mettle, such as thou!" he said, hammering on the medal.

That's the sort of bloke he was. My memory is wilting a bit, but, if I remember aright, the boys called him Richard the Lyin' Ba——. No. Richard the Lion-Hearted.

We were booked up for a battle with the French next morning. I was locking myself into my suit of armour when the King pushed his head into my tent, and said, "Zounds! Aren't you ready yet!"

"I'm looking for my helmet, sire."

"There it is, under the bed. No. That's not it. Did you leave it in the canteen last night?"

Just then a fair maiden knocked on the side of the tent.

"Enter!" I said, grabbing my battle-axe. You had to be on the up and up all the time in those days. A nice piece of luggage she was, too. I put my battle-axe back into its folder. "Well, wench?"

"Noble sir," she said, dropping a curtsy. "Your helmet you left at Howdowie Castle last night in the Lady Ermentrude's powder-closet. I have it here."

"Ho! Ho!" guffawed Richard.

"Ho-ho your ruddy self, with all due deference, Your Majesty," I replied coldly.

I donned my helmet, snapped down the visor, and said to Richard, "Now, where's this ruddy battle? My charger awaits me!"

With my armour on I weighed close on three hundredweight, but, luckily, I had a horse which could take it. It seemed no time before we were in the thick of the fray.

"Stick by me!" said Richard.

What we did to the enemy was a shame. *We routed them.*

Don't misunderstand me. What I mean is that we put them to flight.

In the midst of the battle the King's horse went too fast for the King and left him a bit behind. And you needn't get any vulgar ideas about that, either.

"A horse!" he bawled. "A horse! My kingdom for a horse!"

Of course, all the boys knew that the kingdom wasn't worth a horse at the time.

The King grabbed my off-stirrup and ran alongside.

"The enemy is fleeing!" I shouted above the din.

"I'll be doing that myself when we get back to camp," said Richard. An oaf at heart. One of the people.

I was sorry to leave Richard's service. He wasn't a bad sort of cove, but we had a quarrel.

Such a trivial thing. After we'd won the war he wanted to beat my sword into a plough-share. At the time, plough-shares were a drug on the market, and operators at the Stock Exchange were unloading before the crash came. You may have noticed that swords make a helluva difference to shares.

I refused to turn my sword into a plough-share. After all, you can't, in your old age, point to a plough-share hanging above the mantelpiece, and say to your assembled grandchildren, "And there you see the—er—whatsis, with which I hacked my way —"

"Aw, pipe down!"

"Give yerself a rest."

"Let 'im go. He's gettin' old."

I may, perhaps, organize a conducted tour of the head office of a museum known as the Mont De Piété, where many relics are preserved for the nation—among them my medals.

Anon, I ask you to charge your glasses and drink to the health of King Dick. What a person!

All At Sea

You should have been at our fleet manoeuvres last week! We had a wonderful time. We fired off about half a million pounds' worth of shells and only hit two seagulls.

I was Front Admiral of the Fleet, which is higher up than a Rear-Admiral. That's me standing on the bridge with the second-hand telescope. The telescope got bent like that while we were using it as a baseball bat in the officers' mess. The battleship in the background got bent like that while swerving too quickly to avoid a torpedo.

The position of Admiral carries a lot of responsibilities. One has to be so careful. Last time we had battle practice we set off with ten ships and came back with two.

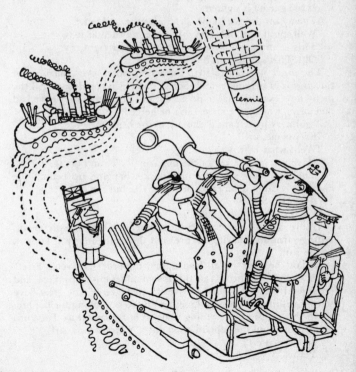

"Where's the rest of them?" asked the Minister for Defence when we got back.

"Sunk," I said proudly.

"Struth!" he exclaimed — rather coarsely, I thought. "Do you know those ships cost about two million quid each!"

"Well, what did you want me to do — miss them?" I replied heatedly. "Fine practice that would be. Teaching the gunners how to miss!"

"Hmm. I suppose you're right, but it seems frightfully expensive. I dunno what the Prime Minister will say when he hears about it."

That's gratitude for you. Yet in time of war, if I was to sail about, missing everything about the place, they'd grumble just the same.

The ordinary civilian does not realize the intense strain on an Admiral during fleet manoeuvres. He has to think of everything.

Take a typical naval engagement. I'm standing on the bridge when the enemy is sighted.

"Enemy on the port bow, sir!" cries the lookout.

"Well, push him off! The ship's overcrowded as it is."

"This is an enemy fleet over there on our right, sir."

"Oh! That's different."

The order is given to strip for action. Soon, every member of the crew is in his singlet and shorts. There is no confusion. All the men know exactly what to do except in cases where they have bad memories, which, of course, can't be helped.

A gunnery lieutenant dashes up to the bridge.

"Excuse me, sir!"

"Well, what is it, you slob!"

"Have you got the key of the magazine? We can't get in."

"They're in my spare trousers pocket hanging up behind the door of my cabin. Don't take anything else but the keys."

"Aye, aye! Sir!"

"Yi-yi, yourself. Get going."

You've got to be stern with them otherwise they dawdle about, telling yarns and playing euchre, and the next thing you know is you're sunk.

At last the guns are all loaded, and the order is given, "Fire!" With an inexperienced crew this is sometimes misinterpreted, and on several occasions when I have shouted "Fire!" the crew have started rushing about with hoses and buckets, looking for the fire.

On this occasion, everything went off fairly smoothly. The guns crashed out, and the captain cried out, "A direct miss, sir!"

"Signal-master!"

"Yessir!"

"Signal to the enemy to come closer."

"Yessir!"

"Tell the Master Gunner not to shoot till we see the whites of their eyes."

"Yessir!"

"And wipe that gravy off your singlet. Where's the crew from No. 2 gone?"

"Down below, sir. They said it was too draughty on deck. Shall I speak to them, sir?"

"Aw, let 'em go. It'll be lunch-time shortly, anyhow."

"Excuse me, sir. I don't know whether you've noticed it, but if we don't fire shortly they'll bump into us."

"Goodness gracious! So they will! FIRE!"

You've no idea the shudder a ship gives when all its guns go off at once. It stopped my watch.

"Hey!" I yelled from the bridge. "Can't you do it a bit quieter than that? I've got a splitting headache already."

Just then a shell from the enemy whistled across our bows.

"Signal to the enemy to cut that out," I roared. "It's not their turn. FIRE!"

"Got one, sir!" said the lieutenant. "She's sinking by the stern. I'm afraid there'll be trouble about that, sir. You know what happened last time."

"Well, if you shut up and say nothing about it, there's no need for anybody to know. We can say that some discontented vandal pulled the plug out of it."

"But that would be an untruth, sir!"

"Well, just don't say anything."

"Excuse me, sir. There's a torpedo coming our way. Don't you think we should shift the ship?"

"Certainly! Excellent idea. I'll recommend you for promotion when we get back. FULL SPEED SIDEWAYS TO THE LEFT!" You have to think pretty quickly when you're an Admiral. The torpedo just missed us.

"Signal-master! Signal the enemy to knock off for lunch."

"Aye, aye! Sir."

And so back to the officers' mess.

"I must congratulate you, sir, on your masterly handling of the ship. So far we have lost only one funnel," said a young officer, as he seated himself at the table.

I blushed, slightly, hardened old sea dog though I am. "It's just a matter of practice," I said, gruffly.

Jack The Dragon-killer

Jack Gudgeon, the highly unrespectable hero of Here's Luck, *wants to make it up with Agatha, his wife, who has fled to her mother's house in Chatswood, on Sydney's highly respectable North Shore. Jack's mother-in-law, in zoological terms, is an extra-virulent specimen of female dragon, and Jack, as you will see, a rather ineffectual St. George . . .*

Chatswood is one of those places that are a stone's throw from from some other place, and is mainly given over to the earnestly genteel. Here, respectability stalks abroad adorned with starched linen and surrounded by mortgages. The clatter of lawn-mowers can be heard for miles on any sunny Saturday. Sunday evenings, the stillness of death descends on the place, but if one listens very attentively one may hear the scraping of hundreds of chewed pens as they travel the weary road of principal and interest and pay-off-as-rent.

Agatha's mother's home tucked its lawns about its feet and withdrew somewhat from the regular line of houses in the street. It had been paid for. My mother-in-law's chief occupations were writing letters of complaint to the municipal council, and calling upon God to look at our so-called democratic government and blight it. She also laid a few baits for the neighbours' dogs, kept a strict eye on the morals of the whole street, and lopped off any branch, twig or tendril which thrust itself from the next-door garden over the fence and so trespassed on her property. What spare time she had left was used up by various communings with God about the water-rates, and the only really light work she indulged in was when she seated herself behind the window-curtain and watched for small boys who might be tempted to rattle sticks along the front fence. Altogether, she was a busy woman. And then, of course, there was the parrot. The parrot was also an opponent of governments, cursed the municipal council, squawked miserably over the water-rates and was withal highly religious. Whether this spiritless subservience to local opinion was due to force of example or merely a desire for a quiet life, I do not know. In this description of my mother-in-law's mode of life I think I have written with a certain amount of tolerant restraint. She is an old lady and the age of chivalry is not dead while a Gudgeon lives. Perhaps a different son-in-law might have described her as a senseless, whining, nagging, leather-faced old whitlow not fit to cohabit with the rhinoceros beetle. But I wouldn't.

Arriving at the house, I paused. The lawn needed mowing. I crossed the road and stood regarding the place. That the grass of the front lawn needed mowing may seem a very little thing and not sufficient to make anyone pause, but I had bitter memories of my infrequent visits to this place in my earlier days. I would enter and be given a cup of tea, then— "Ha! Now we have a man in the house."

In other words: "Ha! Here is a work-beast. Let him paint the tool-shed; let him mend the wheelbarrow; bring out the hedge-clippers and the lawn-mower and point out to him the location of the axe and the woodheap."

That, of course, would be when I was comparatively welcome.

And now?

As I gazed across at the place, a window-curtain quivered. I had been seen. I could not now retreat with dignity so I crossed the road, took a deep breath, and knocked at the door. Wiping my feet industriously on the mat, I waited. I could imagine the scurrying and the whisperings that were going on inside. I knocked again. I had expected this sort of thing, and after waiting a few moments longer I turned and made for the gate as though about to leave. The strategy was successful. The door opened a few inches and the hideous beak of my mother-in-law protruded from the gap.

"Well," she snapped, "what do *you* want?"

I doffed my bowler.

"I've come to see my wife."

"You've come to see your wife, have you?"

"Yes, ma."

"S'nmmph!"

Just like Gertrude.

"Supposing I don't allow you to see her? Supposing I forbid you to enter my house. Supposing I set the dog on you!"

"In that case," I replied, taking another step toward the gate, "I think I'll go."

"You just come inside here!" she whinnied, flinging the door open.

"Come inside at once, my fine gentleman!"

I went in, like the fool that I was.

"Sit there," she commanded, pointing to a chair at the drawing-room table.

"Now then," she said, seating herself opposite me; "explain to me, please, if you can—*if* you can, why my daughter comes to me in tears for my protection. Who are these low women whose company you prefer and why is it that after being drunk for practically every day of your life and ill-treating and starving

Agatha, my daughter—my daughter, mind you, who has had a better upbringing that the whole of your common Gudgeon relations put together and the Lord God on high who watches over His lambs knows what it cost me to bring up my girls, the sacrifices I have made, the money I've spent; me, a poor lone old woman who has had to struggle and pinch to keep a roof over my head and paying for this and for that, and the council wanting me to pay for the drain—me, mind you; an old woman who has hardly enough to keep body and soul together, paying for their filthy drains. I never asked for drains. Why should I? What do I want with drains at my time of life? Calling themselves aldermen——"

"They'll never get a penny out of me! They'll never get a penny out of me!" shrieked the parrot scuttling into the room excitedly. I sank back into my chair and fumbled in a hopeless manner for my pipe as the bird fluttered on to the table.

"And you," continued my mother-in-law, recovering from the interruption. "*You* have the audacity, the impudence, the—the——"

"Hyperbollicality?" I suggested. It was the best I could think of at the time.

"The brazen impertinence to come here and ask to see my daughter. I'd rather see her dead and in her grave!"

The parrot scuffled feverishly up and down the table.

"Call this a government!" it demanded hoarsely.

"Look here, ma," I said. "It's this way——"

"Don't 'ma' me! Don't try any of your soft snivelling ways with me, my soft-soaping gentleman!"

"But listen——"

"Listen! Oh, yes, listen to him! Just listen to him!"

"I came here to see Agatha!" I shouted, thumping the table. I was becoming annoyed.

"Don't you raise your voice to me!" squeaked the old lady, clawing the air.

The parrot was almost frantic with excitement. It staggered drunkenly up and down the table between us, shrieking of governments, of municipal councils, of poor, lone women, and the mercy of God.

"Where is Agatha?" I shouted, rising and jamming my hat over one eye."

"Not a penny!" shrieked the parrot. "Call this a government! Take that back. I won't have it! This is your council for you! Milko! Call this——"

I swiped it off the table and it struck the floor and lay prone, frothing at the beak.

"Gertrude!" screamed the old woman. "Police! Gertrude! Unchain the dog! He's killed my parrot!"

She picked the parrot up, and it croaked weakly, "This is your council for you," and ceased to flutter.

"You drunken beast!" hissed my mother-in-law.

"That's all right," I replied. "You like your little drop, you old sponge."

"Get out of my house!"

"I'm going," I said.

As I made for the door I noticed for the first time that Agatha was in the room, regarding me with horrified amazement.

" 'Lo, Agatha," I said, nodding pleasantly.

She covered her face with her hands and dashed out of the room.

Almost immediately after, a dog dashed in with Gertrude bringing up the rear. I decided that it was best to leave and would have managed it easily only for getting caught on the front fence. I vaulted it all right but my coat caught on one of the pickets. The dog leapt the gate and came at me with all external appendages streamlined and its teeth bared for business. Just in time, I wrenched the picket off the fence and swiped it in midleap. It never yelped but fell back on the pavement, breathing calmly. The three women screamed on the front lawn. I threw the picket through the largest pane of the front window and hurried away. One dead parrot, one unconscious dog, one busted fence, one broken window. Not bad for one visit, I thought, as I bounded into the waiting taxi.

I was calm, but I felt sickened with life. With the very best intentions I had come, and in a shower of broken glass and dead parrot I had gone. And not through any fault of mine had the sweet spirit of forgiveness turned to ashes in the mouth. The proffered hand of friendship had been spurned, and Charity was even now feeling her bruises and sobbing in the arms of her disillusioned sisters, Faith and Hope. I am a man of vast experience and worldly knowledge and perhaps I should have passed over this rebuff with a shrug and a smile; but my better nature had been wounded. The iron had entered my soul and no faith-healer could help me unless he was also a blacksmith.

As I jolted along in the taxi, too dashed in spirits to smoke, I felt that I understood why men burned their boats behind them, sold up their homes and went to Africa to hunt elephants.

2 Bloodhound Lower Of The Yard

The Man Who Cut His Head Off . . .
The Case of the Five (5) Strangled Butlers . . .
The Mystery of the Yelping Goldfish . . .
You need nerves of rustless steel to follow super-sleuth
Lower, the hoodoo of the whodunits.

A Slight Case Of Axident

I shall always look back with pride on my career in the detective force. Bloodhound Lower they used to call me, and I can truthfully say that I deserved it. No one looks more like a bloodhound than I, unless it's a bloodhound.

I must tell you about one of my cases. I was called to a house in the city where I was told something serious had happened. Hastily donning a false beard and a limp I called at the house disguised as a bee-farmer. On disclosing my identity I was let into the house, and conducted to the scene of the mishap by the wife of the victim, Mrs. Panky. On the floor of the study was a sight to put you off your haggis. In one corner of the room lay the legs of Mr. Panky; in the other corner, on top of the wireless cabinet, was his head, and his arms were under a chair. I examined the pieces.

"I'm afraid, Mrs. Panky," I said, "that your husband is in a bad way. I shouldn't be surprised if he was dead."

I was right, as it turned out. The only clue I could find was one fingerprint on the desk. I scraped this off and placed it carefully in an envelope. I then searched the room for a hair. Not one solitary hair could I find. I could find no cigarette butts in the grate either. I had then to look for a man who had only one finger, was bald, and did not smoke. The table was three feet from the floor, showing that the miscreant must have been at least two feet high in order to reach up and leave his fingerprint on it. The description was circulated to all stations.

After that I went through the house with a fine toothcomb, which I invariably carried for the purpose. My colleagues used to say to me, "Why do you always carry a fine toothcomb, Bloodhound?" I would reply, "I keep it to go through houses with," and they would say, "Houses like that ought to be fumigated," but I would just smile my slow, inscrutable smile, and go on my own inscrutable way.

While combing the chimney in the study I found a bloodstained axe half-way up. I again examined the body. It had soot on it!

In a flash I knew all. While toying with the axe in his study Panky had accidentally cut his head off. The bloodlust had gripped him, and he proceeded to cut his arms off and then his legs. Sanity returned, and, horrified at what he had done, and afraid of the stigma of suicide being attached to his hitherto honourable name, he had then hidden the axe in the chimney.

43

But what about the fingerprint, you ask? I will admit that at first this had me puzzled. I took the thing out of the envelope, and tried it on everyone in the house. It didn't fit one of them. Then I had another flash of inspiration. I tried it on myself and it fitted!

I was aghast. Could I have done this foul thing in a moment of abstraction? I hastily turned up my diary. No, my time was fully accounted for. At the time the thing happened I was in an hotel bar ordering the customers out because it was after closing time. I remembered distinctly that I was in that hotel ordering people out for about four hours. I decided, after long consideration, that the best thing to do about the fingerprint was to say nothing about it. Let them, I said to myself, cling to their myth that no two fingerprints are alike.

I put in my report, and some days later a verdict was returned, "Wilful Suicide by Some Person or Persons Unknown." So ended the Panky case.

Ghastly Ghosts In A Haunted House

I was invited by the Hon. Howe-Orvil to stay the week-end at Ghastleigh Towers, the country seat of Earl of Drefful, the last time I was in England.

Having missed my train I arrived late and there was no one to meet me at the station. The night was dark and stormy. The wind was blowing the lightning in all directions. I would have been struck a couple of times only I saw the flash coming and ducked.

When I reached the castle the door was opened by Miss Terious, the housekeeper. "The butler has been strangled," she explained, "or he'd have been here to attend to you. That's the fifth butler in two weeks. It's getting quite monotonous."

"I'm sorry to hear that," I said, dumping my bag and billy-can in the hall. "Is the Earl about?"

"He's been strangled, too," she replied.

"How annoying!" I replied. "Who strangled him?"

"There is a theory that the butler first strangled Earl Drefful and then, realising that he was becoming dangerously insane, strangled himself in self-defence. I'll show you your room."

She led the way along a gloomy corridor and flung open a door. "This is the least haunted of the lot," she said. "I'm sorry about

44

that bloodstain on the floor, but we can't get it out." Just then a frightful shriek rang through the building. "My crikies!" I gasped. "What was that?"

"Must be ten o'clock," said the housekeeper. "I didn't know it was so late. It always shrieks at ten o'clock. Oh, by the way, it's no use locking your door because they come in just the same. I hope you will be comfortable. Goodnight!" And she left me.

Hastily undressing, I got into bed and switched the dark on. Immediately there was a low moan from under the bed. My hair stood on end and my moustache stood out like a cow-catcher. Then I heard stealthy footsteps outside my door. There was something standing at the foot of my bed.

"Go away!" I said.

"I want to tell you the story of my life," it said in a low, moaning voice. "Have you met the rest of the boys? Come out from under the bed, Alfred."

A figure crawled out from under the bed with its head under its arm. "Do you mind me putting my head on the mantelpiece?" it said. "I'm sick and tired of carrying the thing around. Half the time I'm mislaying it, and when I want a smoke I've got to search all over the house for my mouth."

"Alfred was a politician in his lifetime," explained the first ghost. "His head was never of much use to him."

By this time I was becoming more composed. "Did you strangle the Earl?" I asked the first ghost.

"Dash it all!" it replied. "A chap doesn't strangle his own relations. I was his great-grandfather. I suppose that Terious woman has been spreading tales as usual. I'll admit I garrotted a couple of butlers, but a man must have a hobby of some kind."

He turned to Alfred. "Go and tell Leslie he's wanted on the ground floor. Poor old Les," he added, laying a clammy, phosphorescent hand on my forehead. "He's a lift-driver with a curse on him. Whenever he wants to go to the top floor he immediately finds himself on the ground floor. He spends all his time pressing buttons and waiting for himself."

"Who is that who keeps on saying, 'M two Oh eight one. Hello! Hello!'?" I asked.

"Oh, that's Oscar. Very sad case. He's got a curse on him, too. When he was alive he was one of those people who go into telephone booths and stay there for hours keeping people waiting. Now he has to carry the booth around with him and get on to wrong numbers for eternity."

"And how long have you boys got to stick around here?" I asked.

"Until we find the secret document," it moaned.

"What's it like?"

"It starts off something like this: 'Ye Prosperity Club, Faith, Hope and Charity. Thif chaine waf ftarted in ye hope of bringing profperity to you. Within three dayef or fooner make five copief of thif letter . . .' I forget the rest.

"You broke the chain!" I exclaimed.

"Yes," he moaned. "It was started in 1720, too."

"You cad!" I said bitterly. "Leave the room."

It uttered a loud, piercing wail, and disappeared. I had had enough. I dressed myself, picked up my bag and billy-can, and left the accursed spot.

I have since heard that the Hon. Howe-Orvil was found in the moat—strangled.

Keep your fingers crossed.

Murder Most Fishy

I think I will write a mysterious detective story. You won't believe me, but I write them at home as a hobby, and throw them away. It's your throw.

This is how it starts: Speeding along the wet, wind-swept road which led from Katoomba to the County of Shropshire, Inspector— I always have a stab at the telephone book for this—"Frankston Bros., Funtre Mfr., LM5523" is the man.

Inspector Frankston made sure that his automatic was in his right-hand pocket. The rain beat a monotonous tattoo on the windscreen. His destination was Chartres Towers, an old mansion which had fallen into decay with the passing of the years. Eleven bodies had been found in the grounds surrounding the house. They were all dead.

It was Constable Thomson who first sighted the strange figure furtively barging through the hedge surrounding the fishpond and told Frankston.

Alighting from his car, he walked to the front door and rang the knocker. The door was opened with suspicious alacrity. Most doors open with a key, but this had been so fitted that it opened with a suspicious alacrity, a device which had been fitted only recently.

"You the butler?" said Frankston to a man standing in the hallway.

"Yessir. You are the police, I presume. Step this way, sir. The master is in his study."

They followed him till he came to a door and knocked. Hearing no reply, he opened it.

"Goodness gracious!" he said. "The master has met with an accident. The top half of him is missing!" It was indeed a strange sight.

"Was he in the habit of doing this sort of thing?" asked Frankston.

"Not to my knowledge, sir. But then I've only been here a few weeks."

"Noticed any strangers about?"

"Well, sir, there was a strange, club-footed, lop-eared, left-handed man about here a while ago."

"How do you know he was left-handed?"

"I observed how he swung his axe as he was chopping the master in halves, sir."

"You were present? Why didn't you stop him?"

"I had other duties to attend to, sir."

"And what about those other eleven bodies outside?"

"I intend to phone the Salvage Commissioner, sir."

"Good man! Excellent! Where are the other servants?"

"In the fishpond, sir. The master drowned them one at a time last night. He said they were getting too old for their jobs."

"Hm! Couldn't he have rung the R.S.P.C.A. and got them to send a wagon around?"

"Probably never thought of it, sir. What I want to know is where is the other half of him?"

"We'll see about that later. Why is there no blood? That's what I want to know."

"The master was very anaemic, sir."

"I see. Constable, peel off all the fingerprints you can find in this room and put them in a bag."

"If you don't mind, sir, I'll go and feed the goldfish," said the butler.

The detective watched him go.

"He seems very fond of those goldfish," he muttered. "I wonder?"

He paced back and forth, back and forth, back and forth, then stopped suddenly. No. Wait a minute. That leaves him forth when he should be back. He paced back and then stopped suddenly.

"By Jove!" he cried, "I see it all now. Constable," he said, as the policeman entered the room, "go and arrest the butler."

A few minutes elapsed before the butler was dragged, handcuffed, and screaming, into the room.

"So you've been feeding portions of your master to the goldfish, eh?" said the detective.

"He starved them," sobbed the man, suddenly breaking down. "I used to hear them moaning and yelping at night. There was no meat in the house because the foul fiend was a vegetarian."

"I see," said the detective, his expression softening. He had goldfish of his own at home.

"Is meat good for them?" he asked.

"Oh, yes, sir! It builds bony babies—I mean bonny goldfish."

"Well, I didn't know that. Constable!"

"Yessir!"

"Release this man and then go and stack a couple of those bodies in the back of the car."

"What are you going to do when your stock runs out?" he said, turning again to the butler.

"I intend to start a guest house, sir. People who live in guest houses are hardly ever missed. Being mostly a collective pain in the neck."

"True," muttered the detective, reminiscently. "I trust you'll let me have a couple of carcases now and then? I'm fond of goldfish, myself."

"With pleasure, sir!"

"Very well. Come on, Constable. We're finished here."

"Ain't we going to arrest nobody?" asked the constable.

"If you'll pardon me making a suggestion," said the butler, butting in, "there's a man at the local inn who does a lot of S.P. betting. I can never win off the cow. If you can put him in the cooler for a couple of years, you'll do me a great favour."

"Certainly! We've got to show something for the day's work. Well, good-bye, old man. Let me know when you get the guest house going and I'll send my mother-in-law up here for a rest. You and the goldfish do the rest."

"Thank you for your kindness, sir. Rely on me."

That's about all. And about time, too.

Memoirs Of A Painless Detective

When I read the back pages of some of these American magazines I always get mad ideas. So far as I can make out, I owe it to myself to become a Diesel engineer. I should also have a powerful, accurate, economical, practical air-pistol and fight germs. But, most of all, I must be a detective.

Already we have one detective in our family, but I'm used to all her methods. So much so that I can scarcely get a kick out of any of my domestic crimes now. There's none of that feeling of suspense when you begin to feel that she mightn't find out about whatever it is you've done.

It's so long since I did any active detecting that I feel that I will have to brush up my knowledge.

Nowadays, all the smartest detectives carry two or three sets of fingerprints with them when they're on a job, thus making certain that if the worst comes to the worst they can fasten the crime on somebody. I'm not like that.

Supposing somebody's been murdered. Gruesomely murdered and dismembered, and there is no sign of the weapon, no motive, no fingerprints, and the victim was a wealthy, friendless, paralysed orphan.

You send for me when everybody else is baffled. I arrive with my grim, inscrutable smile and a small, shabby leather bag.

The local constable says, "You will notice, Mr. Lower, that the legs and arms are missing from the deceased."

"I noticed it," I reply, glinting at him. "Tell me—was he a recluse?"

"No, sir! He was a staunch teetotaller."

"Hmm."

"We found his left leg under a culvert on the main road, sir."

"Yes. Of course. Where else would you expect to find it? Leave me. I want to think."

I then pace up and down. Something catches my eye. Merely a speck of dust. I pick it up and place it in an envelope, and smirk. I have the aged housekeeper sent for.

"You have been employed here for sixty-eight years?" I say to her, brusquely.

"Yes, sir. Sixty-eight years come Michaelmas—though how you know, sir, being a stranger to these parts . . ."

"Enough! When you last saw the deceased Mr. Bancroft—did he have all his legs and arms on?"

"Oh, yes, sir! He was very tidy that way, he was. Everything had to be in its place. He was very good to me, sir . . ."

"Arr, shut up!"

"The cat has been gone ever since . . ."

"What's that! The CAT! Out with it, woman! The whole thing hinges on the cat. I see it all."

"This cat, sir, hasn't got hinges."

I have another smirk and, sitting down at a desk in the fine old library, I spread out a clean sheet of paper and place on it the envelope with the speck of dust in it, three cigarette butts, two hairs, and a footprint. I ring for the butler.

"Welks," I say to him, "was your master ever in Burma?"

"Not to my knowledge, sir."

"Did your master suffer from St. Vitus's dance to any extent?"

"Strange that you should mention that, sir. He was a martyr to it."

"Nothing is strange where I am concerned, Welks."

"I can quite believe that, sir."

"Did he shave himself or go to the barber?"

"Shaved himself, sir. Very finicky, he was, sir."

"That will be all, Welks."

"Thank you, sir"

I jot down a few notes, close my leather bag and send for the constable who has been on guard in the pantry all this time.

"You've solved it, sir," he says in his ingenuous way.

"Yes, my lad. Suicide. Or perhaps it might be kinder to call it an accident. He was shaving. Suffering from St. Vitus's dance as he did, he inadvertently sliced one of his arms off."

"Lawks-a-mercy!"

"Then, having to use his left hand to continue shaving, he clumsily cut one of his legs off at the hip."

"Well I never!"

"The housekeeper will tell you that he was a very tidy man. What more natural than to carve off the other arm and leg in order to preserve a certain amount of symmetry?"

"Fancy me not thinking of that, sir!"

"Child's play. You can fix up the details. Don't mention my name in your report."

It's all so simple. Or at least it seems simple. Just at the moment I have lost my matches. Do you think I can find my matches? No. I can't find my matches. Even the greatest of us slip sometimes. Anyhow, I'm not sure whether I had any matches in the first place. Turn to the next page while I concentrate.

The Return Of Sherlock Lower

I had long retired from active criminology and was devoting myself happily to my hobby of classifying blowflies by their cries, when one day the loud baying of my bloodhounds told me I had a visitor.

It was Inspector O'Grady from the C.I.B. The Inspector looked worried. "Mr. Lower," he said, seating himself, "we're baffled again. We want your assistance, if you will be so good."

"Well, what is it this time?" I sighed.

"Murder, robbery, and arson," he replied, miserably.

"Ha! the Montgomery affair! Very interesting case. No clues?"

"Not a thing."

"Well, I've got a quarter of an hour to spare before lunch. Got a car outside?"

"You'll come!" exclaimed the Inspector, trembling with excitement. "Oh, goody, goody!"

I calmed him and departed for the scene of the crime. It was an old brown-stone mansion set in its own grounds, and as the butler opened the door a feeling of nausea swept over me. I'm psychic.

"Where's the body?" I said to the butler.

"In the study, sir. This way."

We followed him to the study, where poor old Montgomery lay on the carpet in a pool of blood. "Where's the weapon?" I said tersely.

"There is no weapon," said the Inspector.

"Hmm," I hmmed, and knelt down to examine the body.

"That's strange," I said after a while. "No wonder you couldn't find the weapon. He's been stabbed with an icicle and it melted. Very ingenious."

"Marvellous!" gasped the Inspector.

"Phooey!" I replied. "Elementary. This is an inside job. Is there a cocaine addict in this house?" I asked, turning to the butler.

"Well, sir, we strongly suspect poor Mr. Montgomery's grandmother of giving the gin a bit of a clout occasionally, but it might be cocaine."

"Send her to me," I rasped.

The old lady tottered into the room, quacking loudly.

"What makes her quack like that?" I asked the butler.

"Someone told her in her early youth that she was his ducky-wucky, sir. She's been like that ever since."

"Do you think you can stop quacking long enough to answer a few simple questions?" I asked her.

"Too right!" said the old lady. "Quack!"

"Where were you when your grandson was bumped off?" I asked kindly.

"If you can tell me the precise moment when the murderer put the skids under him, I can tell you where I was. You don't expect me to give you a ball-to-ball description of my activities, do you?"

I glared at her. "You can screw that stuff down," I said sternly. "Don't get flippant with me or I'll give you a belt in the teeth."

"What a man!" she sighed. "I think I could learn to adore you, you ruthless brute. Quack!"

"Take her away!" I gritted.

The next to be interviewed was the housekeeper. "Have you noticed if Mr. Montgomery has been behaving strangely of late?" I asked.

"He's been muttering a lot lately, sir. Something about the walls."

"I thought so," I muttered softly. "Inspector, look at the wall-paper in this room. Does it mean anything to you?"

"Not a thing," he replied.

I went over to one of the walls and licked it. "Arsenic," I muttered.

"How long has this paper been up?"

"A week, sir."

"Was the deceased ever in Greenland?"

"Yes, sir. That's where he made his fortune."

"Thank you, you may go."

"Well," I said, turning to the Inspector, "that's that. Arrest the butler."

The butler was hanged some few weeks later. He protested his innocence right to the last.

I was not surprised at this. Old Mrs. Montgomery had told me in secret that her son had impaled himself on an icicle when he fell into the refrigerator while endeavouring to get a bottle of sherry. To save the family honour she kept silent. The arsenic on the wallpaper was to keep flies off. As for the arson and burglary, she had done that herself just to make it harder.

Anyhow, he was a rotten butler.

3 Husband Lower Of The Back Yard

Does your wife bark at strangers?
When you are asked to pass the butter,
do you pass the plate as well? Do you
know how to clean a window with a
Pomeranian? Then you're a social misfit,
mister. So read on and be the Life
of the Party.

Model Husband — For A Day!

That's the worst of these New Year resolutions—they get you into so much trouble. I think it is much safer to give some harmless order to yourself, such as resolving not to drink out of horse-troughs on Sunday. But I wasn't satisfied with something simple like that. I made a grand, sweeping gesture and resolved to be a model husband. And the result: The resolution split up the sides the first day.

For the first few hours I was so good that the wife thought I was sickening for something. Then she came to the conclusion that I wasn't cranky enough to be sick, so she decided that there was another woman in the case, and I was trying to allay suspicion. Following this she searched the house to see what I'd smashed or burnt.

It had her completely puzzled, and when I actually offered to help with the washing-up, she had to sit down for a while to recover.

Having managed to smash the cake-dish which was a wedding present from her mother, and apparently the only one of its kind in the world, I volunteered to do the shopping and go to the butcher's, and I even went as far as to say that I didn't mind carrying flowers.

She gave me the money to do the shopping in a kind of daze, and when I came back with the correct change she swooned away and I had to rally round with the smelling salts. When she came to, she inquired feebly whether I'd called in at the hotel on the way, and I said, "No."

"Do you mean to tell me you didn't meet that old school-mate of yours this time! You know, the one you haven't seen for years—the one who insisted on having a drink with you and you couldn't very well refuse?"

"No, dear," I replied, "I didn't meet him and, even if I had, I would have told him that you were waiting for me at home and I couldn't leave my little wifie all at home by herself. Now, darling, I'm sure you want me to go visiting your Aunt Jessie. You know, the one with those two blasted brats . . . I mean those two dear little children. I'd love to romp on them. I mean romp with them."

"Listen, you half-baked hypocrite," she said, pushing me into a chair, "what have you done that you're trying to smother up? Tell me, because I'll find out, anyhow."

54

I then explained to her about my resolution to be a model husband. She didn't congratulate me—just said it was about time. That's gratitude for you.

After having mowed the lawn and taken the dog for a walk, I rather overstepped the mark when I said I was going to paint the house. I had to withdraw this alarming statement and explain about the high cost of paint and ladders and brushes and things.

All the time I was looking forward, pretty gloomily, to the prospect of afternoon tea at Aunt Jessie's with the confounded kids crawling all over me, eating cake and nursing their filthy lap-dog. And not being allowed to smoke. And listening to Aunt Jessie's complaints about her back.

I was walking about the house, glooming over things and conquering my evil inclinations by not going up the road to see a man about a dog, and wherever I went the wife moved me on with a vacuum-cleaner or a broom or a mop or a duster.

At last she said, "For the love of Mike, can't you keep out of the way, you clumsy, useless oaf! Why don't you go for a walk or something? Hanging around the house with a look on your face that's enough to make a woman burst into tears!"

"I wouldn't think of going out while you may need me for something, darling," I said. "And I don't think it's very nice of you to call me names when I'm only trying to help you!"

"Help me! Yes! Tramping dirt all over the floor just after I've polished it. Hurling cake dishes about. I believe you did it deliberately. And another thing! Take that long-suffering, martyred look off your face. If you're going to keep this up I'll finish up in the asylum. Now get out, and don't come back till lunch time!"

Very reluctantly and slowly I left the house. I mean to say, I was pretty slow and reluctant until I got around the corner out of sight, and then I ran like mad to the S.P. bookmaker, and had two shillings each way on a horse, and then had four pints of beer, and came home and burnt a large hole in the carpet, and knocked the ashtray all over the floor; kicked the wife's dog, criticised the lunch, and asked how a man could be expected to keep alive on stuff like that; complained about a button being off my trousers, and wanted to know why the devil there never seemed to be any matches in the house.

"Well! Well!" exclaimed my wife, gazing at me almost affectionately, "Back to your old form, eh? Well, I must say I much prefer it. And for Heaven's sake don't do any more reforming. I couldn't stand it!"

Can you beat it! Anyhow, I'm happy again.

Etiquette Without Tears

There has been some talk about the deplorable manners of the present-day male. Also the lack of etiquette displayed in Australia. I intend to rectify all this. If the ignorant and boorish reader will get these few points off by heart, he or she will be able to hold his or her head or heads up in any company.

It is the little details that count. At table, for instance, it is not good form to jam the lid down tight on the golden syrup after you have used it. Someone else may have to struggle with it later.

The careful hostess will see that the jam is tastefully displayed. A little crêpe paper around the tins will easily fix this. She will also avoid having peas for dinner if possible. Peas are very annoying, and, if they are a bit hard, one can only fork two or three at a time, and the mental concentration necessary and the monotony spoils a good dinner. If one is dining out, and one is given peas and mashed potatoes, one is fairly safe. Give the peas a good coating of mashed potato before forking. They stick much better. Take care, however, not to run out of potato before the peas are finished.

Many people are confused by the multiplicity of knives, forks, and spoons set before them, and are inclined to make a haphazard selection, thus making goats of themselves. Remain calm and do the thing systematically. First of all, use up the spoons; secondly, go through the forks; then wind up on the knives. In the case of wine glasses and so forth, select the biggest and stick to it. I do this myself invariably, and have never been tossed out of a dining-room yet.

If you are asked to pass the butter, always remember to pass the plate as well.

When eating fruit, such as watermelon, the seeds should be removed from the mouth with the hand and placed in the pocket or handbag. At important functions it is best to swallow them, as it saves mucking about.

At the conclusion of the dinner the hostess gives the signal to rise. I am not sure how this is done, but I should think that a green flag waved two or three times above the head should be sufficient, or at an informal affair, just a cheery remark, "Now, come on! You've had enough," would suffice.

I forgot to mention that where the guest of honour is a man, he should take the hostess's arm when entering the dining-room. If the hostess is very far gone, another gentleman may hold the other arm, a third gentleman going in front with the legs.

Rum should not be drunk with fish, as it spoils the taste of the rum. (Not that I've ever had a drink with a fish—don't run away with that idea!)

Now for the other odds and ends of etiquette. A gentleman should not talk to a lady with his hands in his pockets—unless she's his wife, in which case it's unavoidable.

Nowadays it is hardly necessary to ask permission of a lady to smoke, unless it's opium; but be careful, if you do ask, not to use the phrase, "May I smoke?" You are simply asking for the correct answer, which is, "I don't care if you burn."

A gentleman should always remove his hat in a lift when ladies are present. If the gentleman is bald, he can walk up the stairs. Makes no difference to me—I'm just telling you.

Ladies, when filing their fingernails in the tram, should be throttled by the gentlemen sitting nearest to them. This is important. Crossing the knees is extremely unladylike, and, what is more, in the tight frocks that are worn now, one is liable to get a hump on the shoulders while doing it.

Of course, our manners and customs are varied by popular usage, and according to the latest ideas, if a gentleman rises and gives his seat to a lady in a tram, she should first grunt at him, then take a step forward with the left foot, planting it firmly on his right foot, glare at him for having his foot on the floor, flop into the seat, and look out of the window.

I think that ought to be enough for the first lesson. Practise diligently, and let's know how you get on and I'll come and bail you out. Adieu! *(French.)*

Mr. Justice Lower Issues A Warning

I want to issue a very solemn warning. For the nonce I am Public Warner Number One.

Some time ago I read about a Court of Domestic Relations operating in the U.S.A., with the idea of settling little differences between husband and wife instead of having recourse to the Divorce Courts. There was a male president and a woman referee. This, I said, is a job that is cut out for me and the ball-and-chain. We had no difficulty in persuading the Government to allot us a suite of rooms to domestically relate in.

The first day there was such a queue outside that people mistook the place for a totalisator. I was sitting on the bench and my wife was sitting on my right hand. She should have got over that a long time ago. I arranged my glasses, unscrewed my fountain pen and said to the usher: "Right. Send in the first bunch."

"Mr. and Mrs. Blathersplosh," he announced, and in they came.

"Well," I said to them kindly, "what's wrong with you mugs?"

"Well, it's this way," commenced the husband.

"It's a horried lie!" shouted his wife.

"Now, wait a minute! Wait a minute!" I said.

"You leave the poor girl alone!" said my wife. "What's the matter, dear?"

"He never takes me out," sobbed Mrs. Blathersplosh. "And, besides, I found two tram tickets in his pocket. And he was one and six short in his pay envelope last week, and I know for a fact that he's meeting another woman because I found a piece of paper with 'Pretty Dora' written on it."

"That's a racehorse," said the husband.

"Racehorses don't have blonde hair!" snarled Mrs. Blathersplosh.

"Some·have," I replied gently.

"You shut up," said my wife. "That's all you can talk about. Racehorses and beer."

"He waits until I've got the house all cleaned up," continued Mrs. Blathersplosh, "and then deliberately throws cigarette ash all over the floor."

"Just like mine," said my wife. "They're all the same. Does he pinch the matches off the gas stove?"

"Never misses," sobbed Mrs. Blathersplosh.

"Just because he had two tram tickets," I interposed, "is not to say that he is meeting another woman, and being one and six light in the pay envelope is nothing. He might have met a friend and had a beer."

"Ho!" said my wife. "Would he want two tickets for himself? And as for being short in his pay, oh, that's nothing! Oh, no! You never think of your wife slaving her fingers to the bone, stuck in the house from dawn to dark, while other women are out enjoying themselves. Self! Self! Self! That's you!"

"Blathersplosh," I said, hastily, "speak up! What have you got to say for yourself?"

"She makes me go out visiting her old Aunt Aggie on Sundays," he said in a dull voice. "She finds everything I hide. She keeps on saying things like, 'Why aren't you like Mr. Yeast? He can take his wife away to the mountains twice a year, and look how she dresses, and you don't see him in a hat like you've got, which is a disgrace, and you ought to leave your breath outside before you come in . . .'"

"I know," I said, "I know."

"Of course, you know everything, don't you?" said my wife.

"You can't even drive a nail. Do you know, Mrs. Blathersplosh, the last time we moved . . ."

"Ah, cut that out!" I said. "I've heard that ninety-nine times."

"He's got the manners of a pig, Mrs. Blathersplosh," said my wife, gently.

"It would be a relief to live with a pig after being married to my husband," sobbed Mrs. Blathersplosh.

"I dare say it would," said my wife.

"Don't you dare to talk about my husband like that!" exclaimed Mrs. Blathersplosh. "Take a look at your own before you criticise another's."

"What do you mean?" demanded my wife in cold, society tones.

"Now, don't be silly," I said.

"You mind your own business!" snapped my wife. "You're the cause of all this. Meddling, interfering, incompetent . . ."

"She opens my letters," said Mr. Blathersplosh, suddenly remembering a fresh one. "She remembers thing away back ten years ago and throws them in my teeth."

"That reminds me," said my wife. "What about that letter I gave you to post? Still got it in your pocket, I suppose. That's the perfect little business man. Card indexes. Filing cabinets. Can't post a letter. Bah! You make me sick."

"Now, listen. I was just walking up to the post office when all of a sudden who should I bump into but . . ."

"One of your pothouse acquaintances," suggested my wife. "One of your so-called friends. Huh! You can't tell me!"

"This is a fine way of conducting a court, I must say," said Mrs. Blathersplosh. "Strikes me we'd have done better if we'd never come here."

"You're at liberty to leave whenever you like," snapped Mrs. Lower. "And although I'm not a woman to talk, I could tell you a few things about yourself which would make even a woman like you blush. And what would make you blush would tip a bullock-waggon over."

"Don't you talk to me like that!"

I got down off the bench and went over to Blathersplosh. "Come on," I said.

We got as far as the door when they both yelled out at once, "Where are you going?"

"Out," we replied together.

And that was the end of the Court of Domestic Relations.

And the warning? Ah, yes. I'd forgotten it. Don't marry whatever you do, and then there'll be nothing to settle—relations, domestics, bills, or anything else.

The Court is adjourned *sine die*, whatever that means.

Alone With A Tin Opener

I am a sort of orphan. My wife has gone away on a holiday and I've been left with a lot of instructions about not burning the house down and be sure to shut the door when I go out, and don't forget to water the pot-plants and all that.

I am now down to my last tin of sardines and one of these days, perhaps next Sunday when I can spend the day on it, I am going to make up the bed.

On Saturday I think I will wash some socks. If I put a dish on top of the wireless cabinet I will be able to wash the socks and listen-in to the races at the same time.

In the meantime I am looking around for a couple of dozen stray cats to get rid of the surplus bottles of milk which seem to be piling up all over the place.

And that's not all. This morning, just as I was having a last look around to see if there were any taps running, the door-bell rang. I opened the door and a bloke smiles at me and said, "Good morning." So I said, "Good morning," too. We looked at each other and he said that it was a nice day. I agreed.

Then he said, "I'm the insurance man."

"So what?" I asked.

"Isn't Mrs. Lower at home?"

"No," I replied.

"It's four shillings," he said.

"What's four shillings?"

"Perhaps I'd better call back later."

"Okay. Good morning."

"Good morning."

And that was that. There's some queer people about.

There seem to be the germs of an idea in this insurance business. You just wait till the housewife goes out and then go and tear four shillings off the unsuspecting husband. I might have fallen for it myself if I'd had the four shillings.

I have now put a notice on the door, "Please do not leave any milk." Another notice reads, "Please do not leave any bread." I think I will take these down and just substitute one large placard, "Please Do Not Leave Any —— Thing." This should save a lot of unnecessary mucking about.

Of course, I know what's going to happen. The missus will come home and find the gas cut off, and the bailiff with his feet up on the table eating his lunch.

One consolation is that I don't have to shave on Sundays. That, however, is about the only bright spot.

I have taken precautions about losing the front door-key. I have it tied around my waist underneath my singlet. It means getting partly undressed each time I want to open the door but it's better than sitting on the doorstep all night. Or is it?

When I look around the place it looks a bit like cocky's cage and maybe the doorstep would be a bit more tidy and aesthetic like.

Anyhow on Sunday—not this Sunday, the Sunday after next—I am going to give the place a thorough doing over.

I have found out that by making a few adjustments, the vacuum cleaner may be made to blow instead of suck. By blowing all the dust and stuff from room to room and so out the front door, I shall avoid the drudgery of having to empty the bag thing on the back. It's strange that women never seem to think of these little labour-saving dodges.

On the other hand there's a possibility that one of the wife's friends might pop in for a cup of afternoon tea and a chat. I will explain the situation and invite her in. If she's any sort of a woman at all she will take one look at the place and say, "Oh! You poor thing!" Then she will proceed to take charge and clean things up. I hope.

Failing that, I think a direct hit from a fair-sized bomb would exonerate me from all accusations of untidiness and not looking after things.

Although I'm not sure. The wife might come home and survey the wreckage and say, "So! You've been having another one of your bachelor parties, eh? I might have known! The moment my back's turned——." And so on. It's all very difficult.

I could engage a nice housekeeper for a while, perhaps, but you know how people talk. Certainly the touch of a woman's hand seems to make a slight difference in the home, I mean.

For instance, I have made myself some junket but it won't junk. I will give it another two days and if it doesn't set by then I will mix it with some mashed potatoes that I have left over from last Thursday.

Meanwhile, I think I'll go to the club and see if I can win a tin of salmon or something on the poker machines.

Where do they get this "bachelor gay" idea?

Trials Of A Male Domestic

Men are being employed in domestic service in Western Australia because of the scarcity of female domestics. I've done housework

61

plenty of times, but I never got paid for it. Last time the wife was sick I did all the housework. It's child's play once you get used to it. The difficulty, however, is in getting used to it.

Take scrubbing floors, for instance. You start off with a bucket of water, a scrubbing-brush, and some soap. After you've scrubbed a couple of yards of floor you find that you've left the bucket behind. That means going back on the soapy floor, slipping on your back, and knocking the bucket over. To scrub the floor of, say, a kitchen, one wants to start somewhere about six o'clock in the morning so that one can have it finished before midnight.

Dish-washing is easy. I only had to wash the wife's dishes because I regard it as a waste of time when you can put your plate on the floor when you've finished and let the dog clean it up.

Then there's putting clean paper on the cupboard shelves. It's remarkable the number of interesting things you find to read when you're folding up the newspapers to put on the shelves. About half an hour to a shelf is fair going. One need only do it about every St. Swithin's Day, but it's a nice, restful job. Just lie on the floor and fold up the papers and then throw them on to shelves.

I don't like window-cleaning much. I found that the easiest way to clean windows was to throw buckets of water at them and then polish them with our Pomeranian. The dog used to yelp a bit, but it was really a good idea, as by this simple procedure I polished the windows and cleaned the dog at the same time. A woman would never think of a simple thing like that. They're too set in their ideas.

I got on well with the tradesmen. The baker was an awfully nice man. He used to come into the kitchen and have a cup of tea with me most afternoons, and we'd have a good old talk. Believe me, I never knew we lived in such a scandalous neighbourhood. The things that man told me would make your hair curl.

I didn't always have time on my hands to chat, though. There was the baby to look after. I really don't know whom that child takes after. It must be his mother; I'm sure it's not me. Mind you, he's a dear little thing, but the temptation to wring his neck became so terrific at times that I had to go and lock myself in the bathroom and count a thousand — sometimes two thousand.

And the darn muck he lived on! Warmed-up milk with soggy biscuits in it. Gruel, and stuff like that. That was his official menu, but when he found out how to open the ice-chest his diet became considerably varied.

A bit of raw chop, followed up with half a pound of butter, and the contents of the milk jug poured all over himself was just a sort of snack.

My wife used to call me into her bedroom, and say in a weak, suffering voice (all put on, of course): "Is Willie all right? What's he doing now? He's very quiet." That's the sort of kid he is. If he's quiet, you immediately suspect that he's dead. Either that or trying to burn the house down.

On one occasion we found him pouring tomato sauce on the dog. The dog, when released, raced through the house, rolled all over our best carpet and then crawled under the sideboard. I had a good mind to crawl under with him.

Needless to say, we had callers. I'd answer the door bell, thinking that it might be one of the boys with a bottle of something. Instead of that it would be someone with a jar of calves' foot jelly as entrance fee.

"How is poor dear Mrs. Lower? I am so sorry to hear she's ill. I was only saying to my sister the other day, 'I'm sure that poor little thing is ill.' Do you know, I was always like that — right from a little girl. Sort of psychic, if you know what I mean."

"Yes! Yes! Of course. Go straight through into the bedroom. I'm sure my wife will be delighted to see you." (Oh, yeah?)

Then you go out into the kitchen and say to the kid, "Here's a piece of bread and jam. Go and talk to the nice lady inside." Pretty sinister move, that. If that woman doesn't leave this place glaumed from head to foot with jam, I'm a very bad judge.

Now one of these male domestics wouldn't have to put up with all that. What's more, they'd get their twelve and six. ME, if I was to go and ask for as much as two shillings I'd be questioned for a quarter of an hour as to what I wanted it for.

Thank goodness on these occasions I'm in the box seat. "We're out of butter, and flour, and sugar, and I've got to get the meat for tomorrow — I suppose I'd better make out a list."

"Bring my bag from that drawer over there. Let me see; two pounds of sugar, that'll be sevenpence . . ."

When it is all worked out to the exact halfpenny, and you have been warned to come straight back and not dawdle, the escape is made.

I think these male domestics are going to be cured pretty quickly.

How To Remember To Forget!

I have been given a memorandum book. I'd have given it straight back if I'd known what it was at the time. I've had memorandum books before. The idea is to jot down things that you otherwise might forget. Having jotted them down in the book, you may then (a) Forget to look at the book; (b) Lose the book.

Those pocket diary things are not much good either. By the end of January you find that you've filled the book up as far as November, and you've got about three pages to last you for the next eleven months.

And another thing; what is more maddening than to turn over the pages of your little book and see, "B.W. 5/-" in it? Does B.W. owe you five shillings or do you owe B.W. five shillings, or is it a bet? Anyhow, who is B.W.? Or it might mean "Both ways, five shillings."

Then there's phone numbers — my especial bane. Perusing the book, one comes to "Ring OB 2468 urgent, Wednesday." The question arises — why? And which Wednesday?

Inexperienced people would say, "Why not ring up and find out?" Oh, no! I've done that before.

"Hullo. Is that OB 2468?"

"Yes. Who's speaking?"

"Lennie Lower."

"Ho! It is, is it! Well just you listen to me. If you think you can get away with the kind of thing you're trying to put over on me you owe yourself another think — see?"

"But listen . . ."

"I'll give you another two days. That's final!" *Click!* And there you are.

Abbreviations are another source of bother. Gazing at the very latest memo one sees staring one in the face the stark demand, "Bring home six D.N.'s." D.N.'s? Ah! Door knobs! But what would she want with six door knobs? Better get them to be on the safe side.

When you get them home she says, "What on earth are these?"

"Door knobs. Don't say you didn't ask me for door knobs? There it is in my book. Look!"

"You fool, I said doughnuts!" What can you do?

Also secrecy is essential in memorandum books. An entry such as "One lb. behind P.F." simply means that you have secreted a pound behind a picture frame. Secure in the knowledge that you have one lb. behind a P.F. you go gaily through the day and, coming home at night, start taking all the pictures down off the walls.

In the midst of it the wife says, "What are you doing now?" in that end-of-the-tetherish way she has.

"I was just wondering, dear, if there were any silver-fish doddering about behind these pictures. They eat the paper off the back, you know. Destructive little devils."

"A woman was asking me only today what was it like to live with a raving maniac. Oh! What do you think? I had a wonderful piece of luck today. I was rearranging the pot plants, and guess what I found? It must have blown through the window. It was behind that potted fern — a pound note!" That's when you give up examining the picture frames.

A simpler system is to fix an image in one's mind which will stick. Supposing you have to meet a man called Brown outside the Post Office at 3 o'clock. You say to yourself: "Post! Every time I see a post I'll think of Post Office." That's an easy one. Then the name Brown and the time. A brown man climbing up a post with three clocks on it. That's the whole system in a nutshell.

The net result of this complicated method is that you spend all day looking for a Hindu watchmaker carrying a telegraph-pole.

A wife is a good aid to the memory, if you feel like going to extremes. Just say, "Remind me to meet Brown tomorrow, will you?"

From then on life becomes grim. At bedtime she says, "Now, don't forget that appointment with Brown tomorrow."

"All right, dear. Thanks for reminding me."

About midnight she says, "You haven't forgotten about meeting Brown tomorrow, have you?"

"All right! I haven't got to meet him in the middle of the night, have I! Go to sleep!"

And next day, after you've forgotten the appointment, you remember his name was White.

But whatever you do, never keep a memorandum book. It is like living in the same room all the time with your wife, your boss, your S.P. bookmaker and your creditors. It is a pointing finger, a prodding thumb. It is a loud-speaker attached to the voice of conscience. In short, it is a real nuisance.

Now, having been thoroughly cured of memorandum books and the like, I can look the whole world in the face and say, "Oh, *that!* I forgot all about it. I'm awfully sorry."

The Dean On Dish-washing

The Dean of Canterbury has made a suggestion for communal dish-washing centres. This sounds very jolly, but I doubt if it would work in our suburb.

We could have the local church hall or the School of Arts fitted up as a dish-washing centre, but there would be some dissension on the matter. I mean, who is to carry the crockery, cutlery, pots and pans a mile and a half to the dish-washing centre.

Even if this difficulty were overcome by stacking the lot in the perambulator there would still be difficulties.

"Mrs. Jones, if you will kindly move over a little I could get my frying-pan into the trough."

"You're not putting that greasy frying-pan into the trough with my cups!"

"Your cups!" snorts the woman on the other side. "Those are my cups! And, please, leave my dish-rag alone."

"Your dish-rag, is it? I thought that was it you're wearing."

"Do you want a slap in the face?"

It would be much worse after the evening meal, when husbands would be dragged along to help with the drying up.

Green would say: "Are you going to the smoke-o tonight, Brown?"

"What's that you said?" says Mrs. Brown.

"I just said they'll be over Tokyo tonight. The R.A.A.F., you know."

"Oh, well you shouldn't! You know what a lot of gossips there are in this place. I wouldn't trust some of them an inch."

"Oh!" says Mrs. Green, grabbing her dish-cloth. "If you're referring to me——"

"Dear me, no, certainly not. But I dare say you know who I mean."

"Oh, that one! My dear, you're perfectly right. If I told you some of the things she's told me——"

CRASH!

"George! You clumsy lout! Do you know that basin was a wedding present! Not that you'd care. Oh, no! Nothing is sacred to you. To think after all the time——"

"It just slipped out of my hand."

"Pah! Count those forks before you put them in the pram. There should be eight."

"Only seven."

"I thought so! Mrs. Robinson, please return my fork."

"Is this the one that's branded 'N.S.W. Railway Refreshment Rooms'?"

"Certainly not! How dare you insinuate such a thing, you — you——"

At this point the helpful husband puts his foot in it as usual. "Yes. That's it! I remember I got it at Penrith station when there was a bit of a rush on. There should be another one there marked 'Cosy Cafe'."

For this piece of unsolicited information, the poor blighted husband gets a kick in the shins which would maim a horse and is glared at with such ferocity that he cracks a couple of saucers in sheer panic.

No. I don't like the idea. The same goes for communal cooking, if it ever comes off.

"Do you mind if I put a couple of eggs in to boil with your onions, dearie?"

"Too ruddy right, I'd mind!"

I'm sure the Dean of Canterbury meant well with his suggestions, but it is easily seen that he has been nowhere and seen nothin'. Certainly not on the home front! Even if the dish-washing was conducted in an amicable spirit, what with all the conversation the process wouldn't be finished until about midnight.

I have seen enough of this get-together business in our block of flats on wash-days. Somebody has taken up all the space on the clothes lines by pegging things lengthways instead of sideways. Somebody takes them all down and re-pegs them. Then the clothes-line falls down in the dirt. Three women immediately yell for the caretaker. The caretaker goes and hides at the back of the incinerator. The husband comes home and gets an ear-bashing about it all and is told that if he wasn't a spineless grub, he'd immediately go and seek out the caretaker and smash him to the ground.

The only place where this community washing-up works is in the army. You clean your tin plates with a bunch of grass, dig your knife and fork in the dirt, and then wipe them on your trousers, knock your tin pannikin on a tree or brick to get the dregs out and there you are — set!

But maybe the Dean of Canterbury has never had to do his own dish-washing. If not, he should start now. He and the Archbishop could do their washing-up in the font.

He's not the only bloke who can make suggestions.

Hot Tips For Cold Days

Why doesn't someone in a position of authority declare a new season? I'm getting tired of winter. I wouldn't be a bit surprised if a certain person started knitting another woollen jacket for me. I have noticed a glazed, fish-like look in her eye lately, and it's nearly always a sign of a knitting bout.

Still, I can take it. I used to be a bit self-conscious about the cardigan jackets and things that were knitted for me for the winter, but now I have become hardened.

Once, when people said, "Have you seen Lower lately, wearing that untidy-looking door-mat with the buttons on it?" I'd get all hot and bothered.

Even when the conversation went on: "Yes! I hear that his wife did it to him."

"What a vindictive woman she must be!"

"That's nothing. She knitted him a scarf once and they're using it as a ceremonial carpet on the Town Hall steps now." As I said, once that used to peeve me. Now I'm unpeevable.

What grieves me most is that for the next four or five months I will be unable to bathe. A man should always have a thoroughly good wash late in autumn, but I always forget.

Still, one thing about the cold weather — it's so healthy. On a cold winter's morning you can't beat a brisk walk before breakfast. Just put on everything except the wardrobe mirror and go for a hike, breathing deeply the while. It's the best way of annoying people that I know of.

Be sure to come back home blowing clouds of steam and slapping the hands together. Stamp around the house singing. Walk into any bedrooms that might be about and say, "Ha! There's a wonderful nip in the air this morning. You don't know what you're missing. The keen wind on the face — the crispness."

They say, "You're not getting back into bed with your boots on!"

You reply, "Too right I am."

A cold plunge is bracing. Have the bath about three-quarters full of cold water. Lock the bathroom door. Slap the water a few times with the open hand and sing "D'ye Ken John Peel" in a loud voice and say, "Phoo! Hah! Phow!" This means that you are actually having a cold bath. Stay a reasonable time in the bathroom and then pull the plug out of the bath and emerge, prancing slightly. I have done this every winter for years and have never been found out yet. But be sure to wet the soap.

Grizzly bears crawl up hollow logs during the winter. That might be all right for bears, but I don't recommend it. There is always the possibility of emerging after hibernation riddled with white ants. Then you'd have to drink creosote and, believe me, creosote is one of the worst drinks I've tasted. It's all right when you can't get anything else, but I advise you to put up with the white ants rather than take to creosote.

I think I told you once before how I spent one winter snowed in, in a lonely cabin in the mulga country! I had to burn a hole in the snow-covered roof to get water. Even then it tasted just like boiled snow.

Still, there's one thing about the winter time that's cheering. When the wind whistles through the keyhole and the rain batters monotonously on the window-panes, and the cat is singeing itself in front of the radiator, and you're trying to dry your boots in the gas stove and all that, it's nice to have a roof over your head.

It's also nice to sit in one's cosy little domestic nest and have chats. I mean cos-ey talks.

"Shut that door! Were you born in a tent? That's right! Stand there like a big oaf and drip water all over the carpet. DON'T HANG YOUR COAT UP THERE!"

Of course, living in the city, I don't get such a great deal of fun like people do in the country. I used to live in the country once, and in the winter time there was never a dull moment. Wood to keep the fire going. You take your boots off and go out to the back yard with an umbrella and an axe. Hours later you come back with three pieces of waterlogged wood and throw them on the fire. The fire goes out immediately. The best thing to do is just let yourself go when shivering. If you can shiver hard enough the exercise will warm you up.

Look on the bright side. If your teeth are chattering, at least you've got something to listen to. Think of the North-West Mounted Police stuck fast in the frozen wastes. Crochet a rope singlet for your husband. When you're trying to file a piece of butter off the plate — sing. Wear wool next to your skin. Sheep do. And don't forget to slice up an onion and put it in an old sock and wear it across your chest.

See me in spring and let me know how you got on.

Kindness To Animals And Husbands

Owing to the lack of elephants in Australia, our divorce courts have not had to deal with a case like that of Mrs. Marie Jacobs, of New York. Seeking a divorce from her husband, an animal trainer and circus proprietor, she is asking for the custody of their twin sons, three elephants, and a horse.

I imagine that she might have some difficulty in getting a flat. I don't know whether there are any elephants in the flat above mine, but I have often suspected it. I don't mind a horse about the place. A well-trained horse can be slid under the bed during the night and turned out to graze on the aspidistra during the day; but elephants are another matter.

Anyhow, it just goes to show the lengths to which some women will go — just from sheer spitefulness. To have a wife walk out on you merely calls for a shrug of the shoulders. If she takes the twins, well, perhaps, they would be better in a mother's care. But to take a man's last three elephants as well as his horse is a sign of deliberate and heartless malice. Surely these things can be arranged amicably?

I remember the time when I came home with a camel which I'd won in a poker game after a race meeting at Bourke. You'd think that a woman would be glad to have a camel about the place for company. A husband can't be home all the time and I am sure that many wives will agree that a camel, with its well-known habit of going without a drink for weeks at a time and not answering back and kneeling when ordered, should be an ideal beast to have about the place in the absence of a husband. But, no! Not in my case!

"You take that filthy beast out of the house at once!" she said.

I pointed out to her that the camel hadn't done any harm; that she never gave him a chance to prove his value about the place.

I also explained how we could hire him out to the neighbours as a lawn-mower and hedge-trimmer. She was still anti-camel.

"You could take him out with you when you went shopping. He'd carry the parcels and he'd also save tram-fares," I explained.

"Either that animal goes, or I go!"

I looked at the camel and the camel looked at me. I said to my wife, "I don't want you to go because of us. After all, this is your home."

"Showing a bit of sense at last, are you?"

"Yes. Don't you go. You stay here. *We'll* go!"

You'd think that a chivalrous, unselfish gesture like that would have been enough to melt any woman's heart. But it wasn't.

"So! You'd hold me up to public ridicule! I can hear them now: 'He left his wife and now he's going about with a camel!' "

At this stage the camel grunted disgustedly. He said: "If this is the sort of ménage you've brought me to, I'm going back to Bourke." He then spat into the empty aspidistra pot and walked out, taking most of the front door with him.

"Now look what you've done!" I cried.

That happened a long time ago and it's all over now; but occasionally I awake in the night and seem to see that camel gazing reproachfully at me from the other end of the bed.

The last time he came back, I leapt out of bed and cried, "He's back! He's back!"

"Who's back?" mumbles the wife, testily.

"The camel!"

"What camel?"

You see how it is? She won't even recognize him. That, I reckon, is the very depths of female snobbishness.

I may yet arrange with the R.S.P.C.A. for a divorce. Costs against the camel, I suppose; but that's the way it goes.

There is no justice for husbands, camels, elephants or horses.

Sad Saga Of Savage Silkworms

Although I have given up keeping domestic pets since my divorce, my vast experience entitles me to drop a dash of advice here and there. Among the domestic pets I have had are wives, goldfish, cats, mice, guinea-pigs, half-guinea-pigs, parrots, tortles and turtesses, silk worms, barbed-wire-haired terriers, carrots and pockatoos, camels . . . you've no idea.

Goldfish are very interesting. In the winter they should be kept in warm water. A drop of rum added to it helps the fish along tremendously, although it should not be overdone.

One of my goldfish leapt out of its bowl and bit me on the ankle last winter, the drink having gone to its head. However, as I had had one or two drops of the same rum I was able to bite back, notching a victory in the second round, and that goldfish is now in the same place as anyone else who tries to thwart me.

One of my silkworms turned on me, too. It was in the autumn of 1902, or it might have been '03. Anyhow, I was shovelling the mulberry leaves into its den when it snapped savagely at me and barked in a most ferocious manner. I could see that one of us had to go. As usual, I won.

I was sorry to lose that silkworm. When you come to think of all those silk frocks and things they are responsible for it makes you do a bit of marvelling. Though how the devil they manage to stitch around the buttonholes has got me tricked.

Now, about dogs. I am rather good on dogs. I really should have been an inveterate surgeon. The main trouble with most dogs is fleas. If there were no dogs there would be a lot of unemployed fleas about, and you should bear this in mind next time you feel like whanging your dog one over the muzzle. A dog should be taken out into some open space and thoroughly shaken.

On washing day, if he is a white dog, put him in the copper with the rest of the things, or if he is a coloured dog put him in with the coloureds. Stir him frequently and, when finished, run the heavy roller over him and he is then fit for his Sunday parade.

Cats are very easy to handle if you can get close enough to them. There are two kinds of cats. Male cats and female cats. One is worse than the other. I have not yet decided which. So long as a male cat has plenty to eat, can sleep all day in some soft, warm place, and howl all night, he doesn't worry. You do that. Female cats are practically the same only for their careless habit of foisting kittens on to you at odd times.

Camels are not very popular in this country yet. I only had one camel, called Cedric. He used to wait at the gate for me when I came home from work. The only trouble I had with him was that when he lay down in front of the fireplace there was no room for anyone else in the place. Many's the night I've spent out on the veranda.

Birds are inclined to be temperamental, especially canaries. Sometimes they refuse to whistle. That's when they want a good smack across the beak. Spare the birch and spoil the bird has always been my motto.

The best thing to do is not to have any pets in the house at all. But if anyone wants a real nice little boy about five feet eight in his socks and thirty-nine around the chest in his singlet, quiet, broken into harness, non-abstainer . . . well, here I am. Much better than goldfish. Open one week.

Poultry Farming On The Lay-by

I have been requested to write a short treatise on poultry farming.

As an ex-poultry farmer, I am in a position to review this industry from all angles but will restrict myself to the actual farming and will leave other details until a later date.

Firstly, the farmer will decide upon the breed of fowls he intends to use. He has a wide range from which to choose, but I would suggest that he make a selection of the following:

Buff Orphans, Rhode Irish Reds, or White Legirons.

The more exotic breeds, such as Spotted Whynots, are unreliable.

Personally, I prefer the White Legirons.

It is desirable to keep the fowls out of the house if possible. If space is available, a shed should be erected in the back yard and fitted with perches.

It is not necessary to measure fowls for their perches, as they have an astonishing facility for hanging on to a pole with their feet, and going to sleep.

If you have ever tried to do this yourself you will realize how difficult the feat is, but fowls seem to thrive on it.

As for nests, I think they are a waste of time. You could have the most elaborate nests, but the hens would lay their eggs under the house or in the dog's kennel just the same.

They can be trained to use the nests by giving them a sharp slap on the back when found laying elsewhere, but this takes time and patience.

A solution of the problem is to raise the house about eight feet off the ground. This saves a lot of grovelling on the hands and knees when collecting the eggs, or cackle-berries as they are called in the trade.

In the matter of feeding, the farmer has a wide choice. Bran mash is the usual thing in the proportion of two parts of bran to one of mash. Shell-grit is also necessary as roughage, but the shell must be selected with care.

It is possible to produce unbreakable eggs by using iron filings, but it is not a commercial proposition. People object to cooking their eggs in an expensive blast furnace.

The psychology of the hen is worth studying. The keen student will notice that when eggs are one and a penny a dozen the whole fowlyard starts laying like mad. When eggs are two and eleven-pence a dozen they seem to knock off laying.

This is one of the crosses the poultry farmer has to bear.

If the farm is situated near a main road much used by week-end motorists, all crook eggs which have been found after many months in unsuspected corners should be displayed on a roadside stall with a notice, "Straight from the Farm," attached to the stall.

By the time the motorist gets home it's too late to do much about it.

This is a profitable little side-line.

A modern incubator is a necessity on all poultry farms, but great care must be taken with them. Eggs which have been baked a dark black and contain incinerated and cremated chickens lose a lot of their market value.

The incubator must be carefully watched. Patience is necessary. It is futile to go slicing the tops off the eggs just to see how things are going.

The newly-born chick must be kept warm. It is not necessary to knit a layette for it, but just shove it in the gas oven and turn the burners on full.

People have asked me which was the better — poultry farming or dairy farming.

Well, you've got to milk a cow, but a hen does her own egging.

Mind you, there's a lot to be said for dairy farming. A lot of dairy farmers say it, too. I don't blame them much, although I never did approve of bad language.

I have never had much to do with cows. It is hard to know how a poultry farmer would get on with cows as a side-line. I will leave that aspect of the matter to someone else more fitted for the job. I am first and last a poultry expert.

Incidentally, I don't think a rooster is necessary on a poultry farm. He's going to be bumped off, anyhow, so why make his brief life miserable with a heap of hens all around him, day and night? I've seen roosters who were so hen-pecked that they went and laid their heads on the block and pleaded dumbly for the axe.

What pleasure do they get in life, apart from yelling out at sunrise and waking everybody in the neighbourhood?

When I look in a shop window and see a rooster all plucked and tied, I think of me. Nobody wants to eat me, I'll admit, but I'm tied, and am I plucked? I'll say.

There is one thing about poultry farming which appeals to me and should appeal to all other dyed-in-the-wool loafers. A poultry farmer doesn't have to get up in the middle of the night to milk. And then do it all over again at sunset.

No. He merely waves his hand towards the fowlhouse, with an imperious gesture, and says, "Lay!" He can then go and lie down and read a good book and leave the rest to the birds.

I have yet to work out some method of persuading the hens to lay their eggs straight into the egg boxes, and then all one would have to do would be to get someone to nail the lid down and take the things away and bring me back the money.

Poultry farming is all right for people who think it's all right, but I'll stick to my silkworms.

4 Hints For Young Home-Muckers

Can you take a hint? Do you collect wrinkles? There are hundreds of them given away here, from the art of making toast under the bathroom tap, to the science of preserving cigarette butts.

Why Be A Flat And Live In A Cottage?

Housing Committees have decided that people would be better off in small cottages than in flats. This is a matter open to discussion. Flats have no lawns to mow for a start.

Having lived in both cottages and flats, I know what I'm talking about. If ever I live in a cottage again it will have a nice green concrete lawn and sweet-peas will be permanently painted on the fence.

In order to have a peaceful week-end in a cottage with a lawn and a garden it is necessary to send the lawnmower to be repaired on Friday and tell the repairers that there's no need for any hurry whatever. Any time within the next six or eight months will be quite suitable.

A drawback to flat life is that you're always having arguments with the caretaker and the outcome of it is that your wife says, "There you are! I told you those people upstairs would complain. Doing the Lambeth Walk at this time of night!"

Cottages are much better. Sometimes the people next door come and say they've got a patient in bed who is dangerously ill — the liars — "and would you please step on the soft pedal." But mostly they leave it until next morning over the back fence.

"I believe you had a party last night?"

"Yes, we had a few friends in."

"Many Red Indians among them? Oh, and do tell me who was the person who was jumping up and down on the piano. Is there much of the piano left?" Catty stuff!

The general thing, however, is just to wait until they throw a party of their own with bagpipes and tom-toms and cracked tenors. Next morning you look over the fence.

"Good morning, Mrs. Simpson. I was shocked to hear about the murders in your place last night."

"Murders! There were no murders in my place last night!"

"What a pity! Oh, well, better luck next time, I suppose. It sounded like murder to me."

Another thing about cottages is that the kids can hold mysterious meetings in the woodshed at the bottom of the yard.

"They're very quiet," says the wife. "They must be up to something. Go and see what they're doing."

"They're probably chopping each other's feet off with the axe and pelting lumps of coal at the fowls. Leave 'em alone and let's have a bit of peace."

Even such perfection is liable to be marred. When the wife is elsewhere a deputation from the woodshed approaches for a ration of bread and jam. I ask them what they've been doing down there. It seems that nothing that passes in the Temple of the Brotherhood of Blood can be divulged to a non-member on pain of instant death. They depart with a tin of jam and a loaf of bread. They don't need a knife because every member already carries one to defend himself from the killer, Wang Ho, the Chinese fiend, and his hordes.

The cry of "Dinner!" is shortly afterwards heard and the members of the Brotherhood of Blood swarm up to the house.

"Holy Mike!" exclaims the wife. "Look at them!"

They're worth looking at, too. Each is smothered with jam and coal-dust and has a mysterious sign marked on his forehead with the wife's lipstick.

"You go straight into the bathroom and wash yourselves!"

In the bathroom the peaceful harmony of the Brotherhood is suddenly shattered by an argument about towels. No mention is made of soap. Soap, it seems, is banned by the Brotherhood.

At the table mysterious signs are made with conversation such as "Pass the butter, Number Seven."

"The password, Number Three!"

"By the Sacred Block!"

"'Tis well!"

After the meal — back to the Temple.

Now, you couldn't do that in a flat. The only thing a child can do is get sticky with toffee and then pull all the books out of the bookcase to see if he can find one with pictures in it. Or perhaps kick the cat.

Therefore, I am heartily in favour of cottages for most people. But not for me. I'm getting a bit too old to stand the strain.

Nightmare Of A Dream Home

I've always wanted to live in a modern home — they seem to be much in the boom these days. I don't mean one with wall beds and folding book-cases and all that. I mean a real modern home such as I have pictured in my wistful moments.

There would be sliding panels in the house so that you could press a button and find that you were no longer there, but in some other place. This for emergencies only, of course. And St. Bernard dogs would do the shopping.

But let us describe this little nest in detail.

There would be cold needle showers in the bathroom. Don't shudder! There would be no cold water laid on to the showers. Celluloid soap and bath-salts would be provided and scattered here and there would be bath-mats of various hues and a small table in green and cream. Of course one would wash in the kitchen sink as usual, but a bathroom like that would be a nice place to look at.

Then there is the kitchen. A most important place. There would be a machine for washing up the dishes. This machine would also dry the dishes, put them away, and sweep the floor after folding the tablecloth, and then say in a loud mechanical voice, "Well, thank goodness for that." Then there is the boiled-cabbage-smell remover. But that is much too complicated to discuss here.

The front door of the house would automatically open when you fell against it. Or if you came home from a shopping expedition laden with parcels you would just kick it and it would fly open.

As a matter of fact, we've got a door like that at home already. *She* insists that I had the key last, but I distinctly remember putting it in the gravy tureen, where it always goes. However, we still have the back door key.

The laundry would be a home from home. Just toss everything into a machine, turn the switch, and carry on reading your book. All being well, everything comes out of a spout, washed, starched and ironed — although I don't know how this would go for socks.

I forgot to mention that television will be applied to the front door. When the door-bell rings there will be no necessity to go and hide or say, "I wonder who the devil that is?" or say to somebody, "You answer it. I'm not in." Nothing like that. You just peer into the screen. If it's the landlord, you switch over the high-tension current on to the door-knob and electrocute him.

At the back door where the tradesmen and hawkers call there will be an automatic gramophone which will say in a harsh voice, "No, thank you. Nothing today. Call some other time. The wife is out. Good-bye."

The mechanical bedmaker will be a boon. You know how, when you're making up the ordinary double bed, you walk about a mile and a half around it, tucking things in here, and straightening things there? Well, with this thing you just kick all the bed-clothes down to the foot of the bed, and pull a lever and the whole lot shoots back again and folds your pyjamas up, all in one go.

Returning to the kitchen once again we come to the built-in bean-stringer. When, in an effort to atone for some misdemeanour,

I offer to help peel the beans at home, I often think that it would be much more economical to cook the strings and throw away what's left of the beans. With the mechanical bean-stringer, all that will be necessary will be to measure the bean carefully, adjust the machine according to the size of the bean, insert the bean, pull the lever and rush around the other side of the machine and catch the bean as it comes out.

It may sound complicated, but you put your husband on to stringing beans. It'll be a lesson to you. I'll bet he goes about six beans to the hour. If he does more than that he's a goat.

Now, as to the general lay-out of the home! Has your husband a den? A man's den is where he keeps all his old pipes, and books, and private correspondence. It is a room which is all his own and he tidies it up himself. He retires there to commune with his soul, or sulk. It is his own, his very own. When he goes to work you can have a lot of fun searching the place for information which might come in handy when the next domestic fight is on.

Lastly, in any home there should be a spare room. Into this room you bung all the old furniture and pictures of your great-grandmother and the bed that sags in the middle. This is the guest's room. It's a sure cure for people who want to park themselves on you.

Our spare room at home is a huge success. Nobody has ever stayed more than two nights in it. It has everything. The window won't open, the bed's full of lumps, the wardrobe door won't shut, a draught comes under the door, and the electric light switch is out of action. Indian fakirs couldn't stand it. The mother-in-law sleeps in it when she calls.

A home, to be a real home, must be a haven to which one can return with a sigh of contentment and relax amid cheerful, soothing surroundings.

Something like a lounge bar of the better type.

The Handyman Puts His Foot In It

If you've got a wall that needs papering . . . and who, after all, hasn't got a wall? What is home without a wall or two? As I was saying, if ever you have any odd jobs to do about the house, send for me.

The ceiling of our bathroom was dreadful before I fixed it up. It's not so hot now, but it looks different, and that's something. Of course, we won't be able to have a bath for a couple of months, but as I told my wife one can always have a bit of a flounder in the kitchen sink.

I was so successful with the bathroom that I decided to do all my own plumbing, and gas-fitting, and draining, and carpentering and painting, and general repair work about the house. I'd asked the landlord about it, and every time he'd say: "Yes, all right. I'll send a man along." After a couple of years he had cards printed with, "YES, ALL RIGHT. I'LL SEND A MAN ALONG" on them.

Being a man of literary tendencies, which means that you'd rather lie down and read the turf guide, I at first doubted my ability to cope with the work of a mere tradesman. I gained confidence, however, when I fixed up the gas pipes and the water pipes all in one day. It has made life much more interesting in our place. We have to lie on top of the gas stove to have a shower, and we make toast under the tap in the bathroom.

My wife is a most adaptable woman. When I papered the lounge room she had all the furniture painted paste colour. I had a bit of paper left over so I used it on the wireless. It was a pretty flower design and you've no idea how handy it is. The third petal on the left is 2BH, and the pink streak on the right is 3KO and so on. Saves a lot of fumbling.

I darned the wire door leading from the kitchen and from a friend learned how to stonker the gasmeter to such an extent that when the meter-reader calls he owes me something.

I also put up some shelves. It saves the linoleum putting up shelves. You have to walk very softly past them. Visitors approaching my shelves are told to shhh! They say, "Baby?" I say, "No. Shelves. Don't breathe!"

The wireless set went bung one day. The head of the house said: "I told you not to go fiddling around with the thing. Now, look what you've done! You and your wrestling matches." Of course I knew what was wrong with it. I just took the valves out and reground them and put in a new screen grid-wiper and now we can't hear anything. Am I any good!

Then there was the day when the sink got clogged up. I unstrangled the plug thing where the pipe turns around underneath and poked it with a wire. Nothing happened, so I decided that the fault was somewhere else.

Well, do you know, by the time I had the backyard dug up and all the drain pipes laid out on the front veranda to dry, the sink just gave one gurgle and it was fixed. All I had to do then was to put everything back. When I'd done that I had four drain pipes left over, which I intend to bury in the ground and let out as flats to rabbits. Angora rabbits. *(Haven't you got any dam sense?)*

I made a bad mistake when I was fitting a new side into my bookcase. I made my own foot rule, and, always the generous lad, I made it about eighteen inches long. You should see our bookcase now! Anyhow, we've read all the books in it, and we only keep it for show (which is more than Wep, the notorious sculptor, will admit) so who cares. But all the same, if ever you want a few repairs, amendments, or alterations about the house, send for me and my little hatchet.

And my wife says, if you've got a wireless set, dig a deep hole and hide it until I've gone, or I'll fix that, too. And, don't forget, I'm good at bathrooms. Any time you're having a bath. . . .

Housepainting As An Abstract Art

This is about the time when people start painting the house, if they have a house. I am cured of such madness, having had a go at it once before. What I say is that if a house can't hold together without being glamoured up with paint every now and then you might as well live in a dug-out.

The last time I painted our place the landlord supplied the paint. He's awfully generous that way. I had to supply the brushes and ladders and things. The ladders were the hardest part. It's surprising how many miserable skinflints there are who don't own ladders.

While I was trying to borrow a ladder, Mrs. Lower packed up and left home. She left a note on the kitchen table saying that she refused to be smothered in paint, have all her meals tasting of paint, and get about reeking of the stuff. That was a bit of a blow. You can imagine how I felt. There was I left with no one to hold the ladder for me. Still, I was determined to carry on.

The first thing I did was to have a look at the outside of the house. It was then that I realized how big our place was. It looked as big as a cathedral. Still, a start had to be made, so I put the ladder up in front, climbed up it with the brush between my teeth, and then found that I'd forgotten the paint. I went back and got the paint and by this time a couple of neighbours had strolled along.

"Going to do some painting?" they asked.

I did not answer. Instead I got up the ladder again and started.

"That's not the way to do it," said one of the spectators. "Don't dab at it like that. Put it on with long, even sweeps of the brush."

The other said, "Looks as if he'll be a very old man before he's finished."

"Doing a tradesman out of a job, that's what he's doing."

"Quite right! No wonder there's so many workers on the dole."

I stood all this and kept on painting steadily. I found that you can only reach a certain distance each side of a ladder. What I really needed was some scaffolding. I put this thought out of my mind as quickly as possible. There's a limit to everything.

My arm was beginning to ache a bit, so I decided to splash it on unsparingly. It was a good scheme, too, because I found, as I worked my way down the ladder, that the lower half of that side of the house had practically painted itself.

When I ran out of paint I was extremely grateful. And I thought, as I got to the bottom of the ladder, "The labourer is worthy of his hire. Lower, you deserve a glass of milk."

So I went to the local shop and had what is commonly known as "one."

The next day there were two Press photographers taking pictures of the house. I thought it best to leave the front part and start painting the back, where I could have some privacy. I started on the window-frames, which is rather a delicate job. One gets so much paint on the glass. Anyhow I painted the lot, glass and all. I found it much easier.

The landlord must have read something in the newspapers, because he came to see me and was very rude until I pointed out that his property was rapidly becoming the show place of the district and if he cared to go out in front and announce himself as the sponsor of the new modern art of exterior decoration he would probably get a big publicity boost. He was somewhat mollified, and we had our photographs taken together. That brought Mrs. Lower home. She wanted to have her photo taken, too.

By this time I was sick of the taste of paint, and, having fixed up most of the front of the house and part of the back, I decided to leave the other parts.

I've retired from house-painting now. Hitler was a house-painter and look how he turned out. I am now a stove-polisher. Not voluntarily, of course. My wife and I have decided that a man should always help in the home — blast it.

Department Of The Exterior

I think I have dealt pretty thoroughly with interior house decoration. We will now carry on with the exterior. Home owners only are included in this treatise because, as we all know, a landlord doesn't care if the front wall falls in so long as he gets his rent.

We will start with the gate. If it has rusty hinges and the latch won't work, just tear it off and throw it away. It's useless, anyway. Anybody can open it.

A front lawn is only a week-end penance, and should be dug up and cast aside.

All cracks in the outer walls should be filled in. Soap is not bad, and it is easy to work, although the house during wet weather is likely to froth a bit. Still, I think this is rather picturesque, especially if you use scented soap.

The roof should be gone over thoroughly, preferably in the daytime. One is liable to render one's self conspicuous crawling about the roof with a hurricane lamp in the middle of the night.

The first thing to do when inspection of the roof is contemplated is to go somewhere and borrow a ladder. This takes about three days. Always get your wife to hold the ladder, so that you have something soft to fall on in case of accidents.

Having reached the roof, examine the guttering carefully for birds' nests, tennis balls, stones, and empty rum flasks.

We then come to the roof proper. If it is a tiled roof it is better to stay on the ladder. This also applies to slate roofs. Corrugated iron roofs may be inspected with a fair amount of impunity, and you can always get someone to call the local fire brigade to get you down again.

If the roof needs painting, paint yourself all over first and then paint the roof. Then, if you get paint on you while painting the roof it won't matter.

Having finished the roof, wipe your hands on your hair and go to the nearest hotel and have three pints. I make this an invariable rule when painting roofs.

When (and if) you get down off the roof, the front and back doors are the next things to be examined. You will probably find that all the paint is scratched off around the keyhole and that the lower portion is dented in various places where you have been kicking it when you have lost your key.

If the door is very bad, take it off its hinges and turn it around so that the outside is on the inside. This may be a bit confusing at first, when you think you're going out when you're coming in. But you'll get used to it in time. After all, appearance is everything.

Windows should come next. Good taste dictates that a window with a busted sash-cord should not be propped up with an empty sauce bottle. Replacing sash-cords is a ticklish job, and I have found it easier to punch a hole in the window when fresh air is needed and paste a piece of brown paper over it when you feel that the window should be shut. This method may seem unconventional, but it works.

People who nonchalantly raise and shut windows would be astonished if they could see the inner works. Pulleys, ropes, and lead weights are necessary to open a window. Brute strength is necessary to shut it. I wonder what sticky-beak invented windows?

Verandas, if you have any, should be inspected for white ants and borers once a month. It is embarrassing for any home-owner to invite his guest out on to the veranda and see him plunge through the floorboards into the cellar.

Have you a cellar? People without cellars don't know what they're missing. When our doorbell rings and we don't know who it is we always go into the cellar.

For a while, we practically lived in it. It was a bit damp and I think that's where I contracted my pneumonia. But it was worth it.

Now that we have risen in financial status, we are living in the attic. We are not so troubled with the rats, but we occasionally have bats.

I would like to tell you about tuckpointing and dampcourses, but I haven't the time. This is a pity because the dampcourse is particularly fascinating. I speak as one who has been over the course. Strangely enough, there are no water jumps.

I now have an important appointment to avoid. EXCUSE ME!

Bungling A Bungalow Job

Expert carpenters are dark handsome men with small toothbrush moustaches and a secret sorrow which adds to their already romantic aspect, and they are simply crawling with sex appeal. *I am an expert carpenter.*

Wep is not. Wep is a bald-headed, skinny chap who would have driven Freud mad. (I hope I'm not boring you? . . . *Oh, no! We're not even reading the darn thing!*)

It was Wep's idea to build a week-end cottage on a piece of land that some diligent salesman had hung on to him in one of his particularly dull moments, and it was my suggestion that we build it ourselves.

You know those weatherboard cottages that you buy all ready cut with the pieces numbered and directions how to slam it together and all that? Well, we thought it would be easier to get one of those.

All the fragments arrived on a couple of lorries and the only things I could recognize were the doors. Wep, in the meantime, had lost the plans and recipe for building the place. We decided to start by erecting the doors. The beautiful part of having doors with no house wrapped around them is that you can walk in and you're still out. I wish I had thought of it before I was married.

The next thing was to get the sides of the house up. This is much harder than it sounds. A wall has got to have something to lean on, and believe me, Mr. Ripley, I had the devil's own job holding up one side of the house while Wep was building the part that joined on. Complaining all the time he was, about there being no holes bored in the wood to put the nails in. By the time we'd got it nearly finished, it was dangerous to go near it.

We had a long argument about the roof. I wasn't going to risk my life climbing on top of a structure which was liable to collapse any minute. Wep at the finish admitted that we could do without a roof and said that we could sunbake without going out of the house on fine days. Wet days, he said, if we had a roof it would be bound to leak, anyhow, and if it got too wet inside the house we could go outside.

That sounded reasonable to me, but when he discovered that we'd forgotten the foundations and wanted to pull the house down again, I got annoyed. It was only a matter of days before the thing fell down, so why go to the trouble of yanking it apart for the sake of a miserable foundation? We'd have to go to all the trouble and expense of hiring a politician to lay it, then we'd have to listen to his rotten speech and present him with a gold-mounted hod, or whatever the thing is you give them.

I explained all this to Wep, but he was adamant. *(What did you say?)* I said, adamant. It's not often I use foul language but it's no use just calling a man an ant. One thing led to another, and I said that I hoped that the first shower of rain would shrink his fool house until it was the size of a dog-kennel, and he said in that case it would be just about fit for me to live in, and anyway it was his house and I could go and live in a tent, or a barrel, which might make me feel more at home.

Then I told him that I had paid for the nails, and if I wasn't going to be allowed in the house, I wanted my nails back. He said, "Take your rotten old nails!" So I took all my nails out of the house and the place fell down, and I said, "There you are! I told you the thing wouldn't last," and he said, "You put that house back where you found it or you'll hear from my solicitors!" I said that if he felt like that, I'd pay him for his heap of junk just for the pleasure of making a bonfire of it.

Well, at the finish we agreed to take half each and I've got the door and two windows at home, half a roof and two sides of a house and if any of you girls are thinking of home-building or anything like that, now's your opportunity. You'll find, when you're married, that you only need half a house, because your husband will be out most of the time.

I'll be outside the G.P.O. all next Tuesday. I'll be wearing a white carnation.

Heaven Preserve Us!

The old household art of preserving things seems to be neglected these days. Once, every kitchen had its pantry, with rows and rows of glass jars with all sorts of things in them. Now, the space is given over to hooks and nails for tin-openers and bottle-openers and the like.

It's astonishing how you can preserve things — from moths and silverfish. For the benefit of those who wish to know, I can preserve anything from big game to mango chutney and blankets.

Take carpets, for instance. All you have to do is to give them a liberal coating of tar on each side and then roll them up and stand them in a corner. They last for years that way.

The same with woollens. Just put them all in a heap and pour kerosene over them. They'll smell a bit, but if anyone remarks on it you just tell them that you like them to smell that way. That will put them off the scent, so to speak.

Pickles, if left bottled too long, develop a green fur on the top, you may have noticed. It is not generally known that five or six cakes of camphor put into the mixture just before bottling will prevent this. You will find that the pickles will last for years and years. You won't even be able to give them away. That's what I call *real* preserving.

Now, speaking of silverfish! You know how they chew pieces out of the pictures on the wall? There is an easy remedy for this. Take a pillow-slip or a chaff-bag for a larger picture. Place the picture in the bag, fill with mothballs, and re-hang. So simple— yet how many people do it?

Furs may be preserved during the summer months by taking them along to the local butcher and asking him to put them in the refrigerator. Of course, there is always the danger that he'll mistake your fur necklet for an ox-tail, and treat it accordingly. Another thing is that when the winter months come on and you get your fur back from the butcher you may smell like a couple of pounds of dripping. That, however, is only a slight drawback.

Butt-preserving is highly economical. You throw all your cigarette butts into a box for a month or two. Then one wet Sunday afternoon you sit down and cut all the charred ends off them, remove the paper, and place the tobacco in a pouch. You don't smoke it yourself. You keep it for your friends. It's amazing how soon they will give up what seemed a fixed habit of asking you for "the makings".

Pipe-smokers are not so particular. Some of them would smoke cut-up boot soles. That, by the way, is a use for old boot soles.

Pieces of string should be saved, no matter how small. When you get enough, you can make yourself an onion bag; then, if anyone ever gives you an onion, you've got a place to put it.

And now, before I go, I must tell you how to make pickles. Get all the vegetables in the house—especially the onions—and put them in a pot with vinegar and mustard. Some people peel the onions but for this particular kind of pickle it's just a waste of time. Test from time to time with a fork. When the fork turns a bright green and the prongs start to drop off, the pickle is cooked. Allow to cool and put in bottles. Cork tightly. Arrange bottles on shelf and then go for a week's holiday. This recipe is guaranteed to blow the bottle to pieces in three days.

But still, I suppose I'm wasting my time telling you all this. The woman of today is not like the dear old housewife of the past, who used to live in the kitchen and sleep in the wash-house.

So far as I can make out she never seems to do anything right. You ask your grandmother. She'll tell you. "Think of nothing else but gadding about with their high heels on, and their permanent waves. When we were girls we all had to be in bed by seven and be up with the lark."

"What lark, grandma? I've heard a lot about this lark you all got up with. Why didn't you get rid of the thing?"

"Merely a figure of speech, my dear. And then there was the baking and jam-making and preserving."

"You weren't preserving every day, grandma!"

"Oh yes we were! Sometimes we didn't have the time to get the preserves into the jars. We were a very large family, my dear. People used to have large families in those days. Of course we had our little pleasures. We used to have a dance every six years.

"My, how we used to look forward to it! That's where I met your grandfather. He won the prize for guessing the number of beans in a bottle, and the prize was a jar of my jam. After your grandfather had tasted it he proposed, and I have been making jam ever since.

"That reminds me. Now that oranges are so cheap I think I'll make some marmalade."

87

"Sure! That's a swell idea. Go right ahead. I'm going to the pictures."

"You don't want to do any preserving?"

"Sure I do! That's why I'm going to the pictures. I'm preserving my youth. So long!"

And quite right, too. Carry on with the tin-opener, girls!

Moving Story Of An Anti-removalist

This is a story about moving. But before I start I'd like to make it clear to landlords, butchers, milkmen, and other people that there is no need to get panic-stricken. It's all about the last time I moved—a very moving story.

Of course, any sensible man will have nothing whatever to do with moving. He will just pack a small bag with enough socks, shirts, and handkerchiefs to last him a couple of days, and go and book a room at an hotel until the riot is over.

Unfortunately, I have a strong sense of duty. Furthermore, my wife says that there should be a man in the house to reprimand the removalists when they smash legs off chairs and things like that.

It is a bit difficult to reprimand a man who is used to walking up a flight of stairs with a sideboard under one arm and a piano under the other. Kindness is the thing.

The last time we moved—or it might have been the time before— I had a couple of bottles of whisky in the house in case of sickness. You never know when a bout of typhoid or malaria or measles or something might swoop on you, and even if you haven't got typhoid, malaria or measles it's good to have something to ward off typhoid, malaria or measles in case typhoid, malaria or measles break out.

Well, there were three of these chaps and I said, "It's a hot day. Would you boys care for a whisky and soda?" They were half-way out the door with the piano, but they dropped it immediately, making a not-unpleasant jangling sound.

After they'd finished the second bottle they became extra-ordinarily enthusiastic about the job. They even unscrewed the gas-fittings and electric light switches. They also wanted to know if I wanted to take the wallpaper with me.

Mark you, it's not the furniture itself that matters. It's the odds and ends.

"There's half a bottle of tomato sauce here. Not much use packing that. I wonder if Mrs. Jones would like it?"

"Aw, leave it there."

"I certainly will not! Couldn't you drink it? And there's three eggs. You can put those in your pocket. Now come here and help me get these curtain rods down. There's a screwdriver in the drawer of the sewing-machine."

"Sewing-machine's gone."

"Well, get a knife or something. Of all the useless—— Anyway, see who's at the door."

"Do it yourself. And I hope it's the police."

"Well, if it's not Auntie Ethel! Come in, Auntie!"

"You're moving, are you?" says Auntie Ethel, falling over a roll of linoleum.

"Oh, no. We're just taking the stuff out to dust it. We do it every Wednesday. Won't you sit down? There's a chair outside in the street."

"Did you find the place too small for you, my dear?" asks Auntie sweetly.

"No. It's not exactly that. Of course, we do a lot of entertaining" ("Bunk!") "and, another thing, I thought it would be better if Lennie was living closer to his office. Such a saving in fares, you know."

"Oh, of course. Marvellous how it mounts up, isn't it?"

"I don' wanna live closer to the office! I wanna live hundreds of miles away from it!" That's when you fall off the step-ladder with the curtain rods.

"Temperament," mutters Auntie. "All these writers are the same. Your uncle, my dear—rest his soul—a marvellous man on the flute. But temperamental. Many was the time after he'd come home from a concert when I had to pour cold vinegar over his feet. The only thing that soothed him."

"I must buy a keg of it Lennie, have you finished now?"

"You said a mouthful! Where's my hat?"

"But you can't go out——"

"Can't I? Watch me."

And when, after an hour or so you've got yourself soothed, you're confronted with the stark, grim realization that you're homeless and hie yourself unto the booking clerk in the hotel and book a room.

I shall never move again. No. That sounds a bit drastic. I'm not as tired as all that. I mean that I shall not shift from my present place of abode unless I am flung out holus-bolus. You know Holus-Bolus, of course? One of the greatest wrestlers of all time.

Now, getting down to important matters. If you find a fountain pen, it's mine. You can easily tell it. It's got a gold nib in it and it's black.

Highlights Of The Lower System

I don't know whether you know Maudie and Bert? Well, it doesn't matter. They're getting married! (*You don't say! What on earth can he see in her? He's not much chop, either. They tell me he drinks. Mrs. McOven told me . . .*) SHUT UP!

So, of course, they had to buy furniture and things. A home with no furniture in it becomes extremely monotonous after a while. They asked me to come along with them and advise them. I'm an expert shopper.

Last week I went out to buy the winter wardrobe, and although I had only ten shillings I got some astonishing bargains. Seven and ninepence for rum, a shilling each way on Whittingham, and threepence for a pair of shoe-laces. I lost the shoe-laces on the way home, but that doesn't matter. I just want you to realise that sales managers grit their teeth when they see me coming.

We started off with the dining-room suite. I recommended a table with removable legs so that they wouldn't get in the way of the polishing mop. The store had none in stock, so we had to get one of the old-fashioned ones.

"You want," I said, "extremely hard chairs in the house so that visitors will not stay too long. You can use cushions for yourselves, and all you have to do when the door-bell rings is to hide the cushions."

They thanked me, and agreed.

"About the kitchen?" said Maud, blushing.

"Ah! The kitchen! First of all, you don't want one of those kitchen dressers with glass doors so that everybody can see that you've got only two cups. I've got one, and it's been a continual source of embarrassment to me.

"Get one of those good, sturdy, Japanese oak ones with three-ply tacked on to the back. The handles come off. but you can always get the drawers open by not shutting them. Don't get a kitchen table that's too white. Get a dark, soup-coloured one, then you don't have to scrub it."

"You think of everything!" exclaimed Bert.

"My boy," I said kindly, "when you've been married a few years you'll be so quick-witted you'll find yourself making excuses for things you haven't done. I'm always a week ahead with my excuses. Of course, I think of everything."

"You won't have to make any excuses to me, will you, darling?" said Maud.

"No, my sweet," replied Bert.

I ha-ha'd silently. "Now," I said briskly. "I'm a busy man. Australia's foremost mechanical churn. We've fixed up carpets and curtains and so forth—by the way, make sure to get a house that will fit the linoleum, Bert. It's much easier. We will pass on to the bedroom furnishings." They both turned a deep pink, and tittered slightly.

"Twin beds or double beds? That's the question." They both looked away from each other.

"Come on! Come on! Make your minds up!" I exclaimed. "You'll find twin beds handy when Bert's been eating garlic, my girl, although with a double bed you only have one bed to make in the morning . . . even if you do have to walk miles around the thing to make it."

"Couldn't we have twin double beds?" asked Maud in a small shy voice.

"Excellent idea!" I said. "Wish I'd thought of it myself. Bert, you'll want a lowboy for your wife to put things in that she can't find room for in her wardrobe."

"I suppose we'll need a bookcase for the lounge-room?" inquired Bert.

"Well, if you're going to live in one of these society suburbs, a bookcase would add tone to the place. Of course, you'd have to have a book."

"What kind of a book?" asked Maud.

"You've got a green carpet for that room so I think a yellow-covered book would harmonise nicely."

"You literary men!" said Maud admiringly.

"Well, now I must be going," I said. "I'll leave you to buy your own crockery. My wife is thinking of buying a cast-iron dinner-set for our place, but please yourselves. All you have to do now is to pay the deposit and the balance in easy weekly payments for the rest of your life. Good-bai!"

The poor devils!

5 Bearding Grandpa In His Den

Lower's grandfather was just a dotty old man.
His name was Cedric or Arburthnot or Alfred or Harold.
He got his first start in life when he was kicked by a
horse and his last when he was assassinated by the
umpire of a croquet match.

From Oxygenarian To Nonentity

There seems to be a great deal of interest taken in my grandfather, and I have been asked to provide some further particulars of the old gentleman. Well, for a start, he is a nonentity. That is to say he is in the nineties. When you're eighty you're an oxygenarian, and when you're seventy you're a vegetarian, and when you're sixty you're a sexegenarian, and so on.

As a boy he was extremely brilliant at school, so brilliant, in fact, that the rest of the class had to wear smoked glasses, and they used him to light up the school on dull winter evenings.

Grandpa got his first real start in life when he was kicked by a horse. "It gave me the start of my life," he told me. But his active commercial life commenced at the age of fourteen, when he got a job as assistant hole-borer in a whistle foundry. His work was not arduous. All he had to do was to hold the hole while the chief borer bored it.

It was while he was on this job that he invented the Family Whistle. It was shaped like a cross and had sixteen holes in it, and four people could play it at once, two blowing and two sucking. By spreading a board across the middle you could play cards on it and whistle at the same time.

The invention was an instant success and the works manager was so pleased that he granted my grandfather the right to be tired in office hours whenever he felt that way, and transferred him to the mouth organ department as efficiency manager.

An efficiency manager is a man who gets a big salary to go around upsetting the routine of the business and giving the staff the jitters. My grandfather did his best, but he wasn't such a success as he was in the whistle foundry.

He started by putting the bundy clock on half an hour fast and then fined everybody for being late. This would have been all right if the whole staff hadn't claimed overtime at the end of the week.

Nothing daunted, my grandfather set to work and invented the Automatic Mouth Organ. It was in the form of a windscreen wiper which clamped to the forehead. On the other end was the mouth organ. When the wiper was set going, the mouth organ went to and fro across the mouth and the player blew on any particular hole he fancied as it went past, leaving his hands free to play billiards or get on with the knitting. You could play it while eating your lunch, but you had to be pretty slick. Very few people could do it without getting their mouth organs clogged up with beetroot or something.

Having learnt from past experience with the Family Whistle, my grandfather patented the invention himself and made a small fortune. With this he bought a bicycle.

Shortly after he had learnt to ride the bicycle he had the astonishing good luck to be knocked down by an R.S.P.C.A. waggon which was rushing to stop a dog fight. After eight months in hospital he was awarded damages and compensation by the Full Court. They were all full. Even the constable on the door was a bit full.

It was then that my grandfather decided to get married. He married my grandmother. Of course, he didn't know she was my grandmother at the time, or, as he said, he would never have married her.

My grandmother was an ambitious woman and was always urging my grandfather on to higher things. Like painting the roof and cleaning out the attic and all that.

Just to please her, grandpa built a saxophone factory. He was undecided whether to go back to his old profession of whistle manufacturing or to start work on the newer models of saxophones. Eventually he decided on saxophones. As he explained to me, it was saxophone and half a dozen of the other. (Hotcha!)

The venture was a failure and at the finish my grandfather was left with 10,000 saxophones on his hands. It almost broke his spirit, and day after day he used to pace the streets feebly blowing on a handful of saxophones.

Then came the Crimean War. The Lowers were ever a proud race, and after my grandfather had been handed 36 lb. of white feathers grandmother stuffed the bed with them and grandfather joined the colours and sailed away.

The rest is history. After he had been eight months away, they caught my grandfather and sent him to rejoin his regiment. He was treated for shock and allowed to go home. My grandmother was very proud when he walked off the boat covered all over with medals. Some of them he had won twice—with a double-headed penny.

Well, after a while he settled down and, naturally, being a returned soldier, they gave him a job on relief work. He got only one day a fortnight, and somehow his day always seemed to fall on a Sunday, when there was nothing doing.

My grandmother, a resourceful woman, went to the Dead Letter Office and collected all the socks she had sent to my grandfather while he was away at the war, and set up a sock shop. They were those real home-knitted socks that you don't have to wear boots with. As a matter of fact, you can't wear boots with them.

Of course, he has retired since then, after seeing to my education. He wanted me to be a water diviner, but I could think of a lot of things diviner than water, so I just loaf around the office here and get roused on. Somebody's got to do it.

About Being A Very Greengrocer

I think I'll have to disown my grandfather and cast him out into utter darkness. A disgrace to the family, that's what he is. "Cedric," I said to him, "do you know anything about the greengrocery business?"

"My boy," he replied, "I have it from an authoritative source that I was found under a watermelon by my mother, who was looking for snails."

"And was she disappointed?" I asked.

"No," he said. "She found a snail, too, but it was delicate, and it died on her. Were you thinking of opening a greengrocery?"

The upshot of it was that I engaged him as a floor-walker; a foolhardy and reckless deed.

We opened the shop auspiciously. You got a halfpenny back on your empty passionfruit skins. We gave a banana to each customer purchasing 10/- worth of goods.

We seemed to be in for a boom, but my grandfather spoilt it. A customer came in for three-pen'orth of soup vegetables. Cedric had a vague idea that you had a little bit of everything in soup vegetables, so he doled out one carrot, one onion, one parsnip, and one stick of celery. And then the thing got into his blood, like stamp collecting, and he went on from that and included one pumpkin, one marrow, one pea, one cabbage, one coconut.

Anyhow, there was a mad rush on soup vegetables that day, and I was too busy taking threepences at the cash register to see what was going on. We sold out in about two hours, and Cedric was delighted until after I had counted up the day's takings and stunned him with our sole remaining coconut.

The coconut incident gave me an idea, and the next morning I went to the markets and stocked up entirely with coconuts.

The coconut is a good, hard-wearing fruit, easy to handle, and amenable to discipline. Cut in half and hollowed out they make serviceable berets for schoolchildren. They make dependable doorstops and are miraculous as a missile. Boiled in their jackets they are delicious. Solomon Islanders climb trees for them. You can get milk out of them without having to get up at three o'clock in the morning and risk being kicked to death in the bails.

The coconut is the greatest all-round fruit known to civilization, and was invented by the Chinese during the Tsang Ming dynasty, and now modern science is even attempting to improve on this wonderful fruit, and is experimenting with depilatories with a view to producing a clean-shaven coconut with a hinge growing in the middle, so they can be used as flapjacks or tobacco-pouches. But I digress. The coconut scheme was a failure, and I had to go back to the usual fruit and vegetable racket.

But I still had the same trouble with Cedric. He came to me one morning and said, "What's a brussel?"

"Blowed if I know," I said. "Who wants to know?"

"There's a lady here who wants some brussels snouts." Of course, he meant brussels spouts, and I had to serve the lady myself.

Another time I was serving a customer with a pound of peas, and I was just taking a pea out of one of the pods on account of it being slightly over the pound, when he came to me and said, "This fellow here wants a pound of pumpkin."

"Well, give it to him," I snapped.

"But you know I'm no good at pumpkin," he whined. "Couldn't you do it?"

"Get on with your work," I said sternly, and he shuffled off, mumbling.

Well, just then a boy came in for some speckled fruit, and I was busy putting specks on them for him when I heard sounds of an altercation at the rear of the shop.

"If you think you can do it, have a try!"

"Why don't you get a sharp knife?" . . . "You're too weak in the wrists" . . . "You hold on to it" . . . "How am I going to cut the thing with you kneeling on it!" . . . "I'm a greengrocer, not a carpenter!" . . . "Why couldn't you order something soft, like cucumbers or something?" . . . "You wait there while I get the axe; don't let it roll away again!" Then I heard smashing noises and loud cheers. Shortly afterwards Cedric came in, wiping the perspiration from his face.

"Just been cutting up a pumpkin," he said. "Come and give me a hand to get the axe out of the floor."

I sacked him on the spot, and, later, in tugging at the axe, I fell over and broke the soda fountain, and when I came to Cedric had given away all the stock and was sitting on the scales swinging his legs and singing "The Minstrel Boy".

So I quietly locked up the shop and set fire to it. I haven't been back since.

The Mixture As Never Before

A festive air seems to be pervading the district. The peasantry are warming up in preparation for the usual bout of Christmas and New Year parties. Your poor Uncle Lennie is just getting over a cocktail party, and there is another one looming on the horizon.

I never did care much for cocktail parties, I'm all the time looking for a place to put the olive-stones. You can't park them under the table like chewing-gum. Cherries are easy; they just go down whole with the drink, toothpick, and all.

Just recently I flung a party for Arburthnot, my grandfather, in celebration of his reaching the age of discretion. Having reached the age of 95, he found that his financial resources were so limited that discretion looked the best shot on the table.

I made the cocktails in the washtubs, and we had a few cases of whisky for the teetotallers. Ever tasted an Angel's Smack? I can mix an Angel's Smack, a Horse's Neck, a Side-car, or a Viper's Breath just like mother used to make. Good stuff, too. You can get happy washing up the glasses.

I had a lot of trouble with the savouries, or horse devours, as the French call them. The average hostess's idea of a savoury is to butter a biscuit and plonk a bean on top of it. Some, I'll admit, make such an artistic mess of gherkins, anchovies, chillies, and cheese that the whole biscuit is suitable for framing, and only a vandal would eat it. But I invented a savoury composed of hard-boiled egg and sandsoap. All the guests said it was a wow.

My grandfather came forward with a suggestion for a biscuit soaked in bromide, with an aspirin tablet embedded in it. This was one of the few sensible suggestions he made during my preparations for the party.

Have you ever paused in your mad rush to the sideboard and considered what a lot of work has gone into the making of those cocktails and savouries you're wolfing like a famished greyhound? I spent hours at those washtubs, pouring in this and that: a bit of gin, a dash of bitters, a bucket of absinthe, a handful of curry, my wrist-watch—this was unintentional, but I may tell you that after

I had fished it out it has been gaining an hour every five minutes, and when I go to put it on it walks away from me—and some stale beer and boot polish and vermouth, French vermouth and Italian vermouth. I wasn't game to put in any Abyssinian vermouth. Anyhow, seeing that both the French and the Italian vermouths were made in Australia, it didn't matter much.

Then I had to boil a copper full of frankfurts, and I had to open tin after tin of *petit poisson* (French — means sardines). Tasted like poisson, too, after I'd finished with them.

When the guests arrived they all hung about like people do at cocktail parties, talking about racehorses and books and pictures and what a rotten hat Mrs. Stogers had on, and how Miss Flethers, who was always talking about quarrels with her dressmaker, usually got her frocks at the jumble sale in aid of the Sunday school picnic . . . You know.

Then when the gun went they fell upon my savouries and I was kept busy dashing backwards and forwards to the washtubs and ladling out cocktails. Fortunately, I ran short of olives and had to use nutmegs, which seemed to slow them up a bit. There are no stones in nutmegs, by the way. Just thought I'd tell you.

Then Arburthnot made a speech. We tried to stop him, but he threatened to pull the plugs out of the washtubs, so we let him go.

"Ladies and gentlemen," he said. "I wish to thank you all for coming here and burning holes in the furniture and eating us out of house and home. As you all know, I have now reached the age of discretion, when I have to live on charcoal biscuits and sterilised dill water, like John D. Rockefeller. It has taken me years and years to reach this happy state and, believe me, the happiest times of my life were spent in acquiring my present nervous debility, gout, dyspepsia, and various duodenal ulcers."

The guests then pushed him off the piano and locked him in the bathroom. Following which, one of my guests asked me what the devil I was doing hanging about the place, and why wasn't there any music or something, and I got thrown back into the wash-house and told to make more cocktails.

So I put four gallons of prussic acid in the mixture and served it out. They all said it was great, and asked for more. That's what cocktail drinking does to your system. Either you succumb after the first few weeks, or you become immune and unpoisonable.

Any of you girls who have a secret yearning for the bright lights had better be warned against cocktail parties. Many an innocent girl has learned to chew gum at a cocktail party, to the utter horror of her parents, who have hurled her out into the snow to battle through life alone and unaided without a soul to care whether she lived or died, and finished up in a squalid tenement scantily clad in filthy rags and dying neglected, with a bag of cocaine clutched in her hand.

There, there, now! I've made you cry! Uncle didn't mean it as bad as that. He just wants you to be warned, that's all. If any dark and handsome stranger approaches you and offers you a cocktail, spurn him. Stick to rum.

When The K.O. Was O.K.

It is with great reluctance and deep regret that I release the news to the sporting public that I have closed down my stadium. For the first few weeks all was well. I matched Young Dribbling, Tiger Maginness, One-hit Isaacs and the Terrible Tarantula. The gate-money was good. We even had enough after the first three bouts to paint the gate. I had two referees working night and day. As a matter of fact, we had the decisions worked out two weeks in advance.

It was when I billed Wild Wep, the Ohio Hyena, that the trouble started. I had made all arrangements, and he had to lose the first fight so we could have a good house for the return match.

The Hyena lost his head in the third round and started to fight. I could have hung my head in shame. To make matters worse, he knocked out Fred Heneggery, to whom he was opposed, and there was no chance of making it a draw, or no-fight. I advised the referee to give the Hyena the decision on a foul, but the crowd looked very ugly.

If you've ever seen a crowd at a stadium, my girl, you will agree with me that the whole lot of them have not got a Rudolph Valentino look among them. As I said before, they looked very ugly.

They threatened to smash up all the seats—both of them. I stepped into the ring and said, "Now! Now!" Then, flinging all caution to the winds, I said, "Come! Come!" This cowed them, and they filed out of the stadium sheepishly.

My grandfather, who was in the main ticket office, reported news of a boycott. "We will have to put on something brilliant!" he remarked with his usual acumen. He uses his acumen infrequently, and the wheel part of it where you turn it around needs a new screw, but still he can work it quite well if there is no one looking over his shoulder.

The next night there was a dearth of customers. If the dearth had paid to come in we could have retired the same night.

99

"What we need," said my grandfather, "is pip!"

"We've got that!" I explained to him. "What you mean is PEP!"

I decided to start a little subtle publicity.

MAN THREATENS TO FIGHT GRANDFATHER!

R.S.P.C.A. MAKES MOVE

ABYSSINIAN CONSUL HANDS IN

HIS PORTMANTEAU!

Portfolio . . . you're quite right.

Well, there was such a furore. . . .* The excitement grew so intense that there was nothing left for us but to go on with the fight. Accordingly the fight took place.

LENNIE (Uncle) LOWER, 10 STONE 9.

ALFRED (Panther) BRACEGIRDLE, 10 STONE 2.

I wore pink milanese trunks to match my dressing-gown, and when I climbed through the ropes the crowd clapped so hard that the police were not able to take their fingerprints for months afterwards. My grandfather wore spangled tights. Rather sissy, I thought.

I shook hands with Alfred, the referee warned us about going to sleep in the clinches, and the gong went for the first round.

There was a big crowd present. About two thousand, I should say. Not counting reporters, broadcasters, camera men, and friends of the management, there must have been at least twenty-five people who paid to come in.

I had to use all my best ringcraft with Alfred. He is an extremely clever fighter. He has frequently told me so, and he ought to know. I said, "OOH! Look, Alf!" He turned around to look and I feinted him fair on the back of the neck. Wasn't he wild!

I won the first round, and while my seconds were rubbing me down with a piece of sandpaper, frantic betting was going on in the ringside seats. I was five to two, and Alfred was fifteen to one, the referee was squared, an inspector of police was sitting next to the ring, the wife had taken home the gate-money, and hidden it in the lowboy, and we had a machine-gun in the cheap seats.

You'd have thought everything would have gone off beautifully. But, no! In the thirteenth round I swung a right cross at my grandfather. I did it with my left hand in order to make it harder for him to work out.

It was beautifully timed. I had a look at the clock, and said to myself, "This is going to happen at about half-past nine." I brought off the punch, and my grandfather wasn't there. He was

---

* *I didn't mean that about furore. It was just a slip and if you have a spark of humanity left in your bosom you will forget it.*

away fiddling around in some other part of the ring. Naturally, the spectators were furious. They paused in mid-peanut and gaped.

Then came that low, terrible mumble of a mob out of hand. "Lennie," said my grandfather, "we must uphold the family tradition and get out of this. You take one-half of the house and I'll take the other."

I called to the referee and seconds. "Stack them!" I said, "as we knock them." It was good exercise while it lasted, but we ran out of customers after the first twenty minutes, and there wasn't a great deal of the Stadium left. The scores were: ALFRED, 900; LENNIE, 1108.

Advantages Of The Whole Hog

Of course it's too late now, but I am convinced that I should have been brought up to be an Aga Khan. There seems to be money in it.

For instance, the Aga Khan is at present staying at a posh hotel in Switzerland. He had decided to prolong his stay, but the manager explained that his suite had already been booked by another millionaire. So the Khan simply bought the whole pub and stayed on.

That's squatting in a big way. It has given me an idea how I might win a snooker game one of these days. You buy a half-share in a billiard saloon.

When your opponent pots a ball, you say: "Sorry, old chap. Foul shot."

"Waddyer mean, foul shot?"

"I own that half of the table. Private property. That's four away. And also remember that if you score up to fifty on the board, you stop there. The other part's mine." If only I had the dough!

My grandfather, rot his soul, tells me that he once had a half--share in a racehorse.

"I was part-owner with the Markis of Queensberry, and a fine, upstandin' geldin' 'e was."

"Who?"

"The 'orse! We enters 'im for the Oaks. Well I remember leggin' Tod Sloan up.

" 'Sloan,' I sez, 'all you got to do is to get 'im started; then you can relax. The 'orse will do the rest. 'Ave you got anything to read during the race?'

" 'No, sir,' says Sloan, 'but I brought some sandwiches. Thought it might save me starvin' to death before I reached the winning post, sir.'

"Thought of everything, did Tod Sloan," said the old man, gazing into the distance.

"Where was the Marquis of Queensberry all this time?" I asked.

" 'E wus down to the ring tryin' to get a dollar on for Queen Victoria. All of a sudden—They're ORF!"

"What's going on here?" said my grandmother, coming out of the kitchen. "You been on the liniment again? Bellering out like that. Enough to wake the Repatriation Department."

"Get on with your 'ousework," replied grandfather.

"They comes around the bend and inter the straight. The Markis is jumpin' up and down on 'is bell-topper, and 'is mustarsh is stickin' out like the prickles on a porkeebine, what with the excitement and all."

"Porcupine," I suggested.

"You wasn't there," said the old gentleman. "Our 'orse goes on to win by ten necks."

"You mean lengths."

"Necks, I sez! They didn't 'ave lengths in them days. 'Orses wus 'orses. Not like that lump of dog's meat you put me on to last Saturday. Well, the Markis shakes me by the 'and, all worked up like, and sez, 'We won! We won!!'

" '*We* won?' I inquires raisin' me eyebrows.

" 'We're arf shares in the horse, are we not?' sez 'e.

" 'That may be so,' I replies, 'but I own the front arf. Your arf ran second.'

"Well, you should 'ave 'eard the language!

"Queen Victoria comes down from 'er box and sez, 'Gentlemen! What goes on 'ere!'

" 'This bloomin' no-'oper,' I commences——

"But the Queen turns to the Markis and regards 'im with a 'aughty, regal stare.

" 'E bows.

" 'Did you get my dollar on?' sez the Queen.

" 'Your Majesty, it wus like this——'

"The Queen just grunts at 'im in a lady-like way and sweeps up the lawn; and believe me it needed sweepin' up."

"Yes, but——"

"Which all goes to show that this 'ere Aga Khan 'as the right idea. Don't do things by 'arves. Buy the ruddy lot."

"That's unfortunate," I said, getting up from my chair. "I was going to buy you a couple of beers, but I can't afford to buy the whole cellarful."

"Wait, me boy!" bawled the old gentleman.

"We can buy it on the lay-by, like. A pint at a time. Where's me 'at?"

That's an idea, I admit, but rather paltry. I still prefer the Aga Khan's method.

No Gadgets, By Gad

Less attention to "new gadgets and medical stunts" is being advised by the American Academy of — get a firm grip of something — Ophthalmology and Otolaryngology. I could explain the meaning of those two and even, if driven to it, pronounce them, but I've had enough trouble spelling them. Anyhow, this American Academy of what I mentioned before has decided that our forefathers who had never heard of vitamins and calories and sulphanilamide *(by Gosh, I'm earning my money today!)* were all much tougher than people of the present time. People didn't "tinker with their insides," as the speaker rather vulgarly put it.

This is one of the few subjects on which I am not an expert, but having heard about dinners of 200 courses and blokes drinking port until they slid under the table, I should imagine that their insides wouldn't be worth tinkering with.

And if it comes to that, they did quite a helluva lot of tinkering. When I think of the castor oil I was forced to swallow in my boyhood days! Blime! And senna tea. And liquorice powder. The idea was that if it tasted lousy it must be good for you.

My grandfather, who is now confined to a diet of dry toast and barley water, has similar views to the American Academy.

"They bred 'em tough in those days, me boy! None of your newfangled gadgets and medical stunts." He started off like that. Trouble is that when he starts he can't be stopped.

"Up at four in the morning, winter and summer. Work in the fields till six. Porridge then for breakfast, with a half-pint of rum in it if the weather was cold — which it always was. Coupla plates of ham and eggs. We used to cure our own ham and lay our own eggs."

"Beg pardon!"

"We had our own fowls."

"Ah, yes."

"After breakfast the Missus would cook a couple of bullocks with vegetables."

"What for?"

"Lunch of course. A man must eat. That's what you young fellers don't understand. Dose yourself with these 'ere patent medicines and stuff. Look at me!"

"Hold on! Don't start pounding your chest. You were in bed for three weeks the last time you did it."

"And teeth! None of these here sissified anaesthetics.

"If we had a toothache off we'd go to the village blacksmith and he'd tear the tooth out with the tongs.

"I've seen the times when your grandmother was running up the main street dragging the blacksmith along with her. He wouldn't let go the tongs. He was a fine man. Finally her bottom jaw tore away."

"That must have been painful."

"I couldn't say. She couldn't tell us. Any 'ow we had a bit of peace and quietness in the house after that.

"He was a great feller, that blacksmith. I remember there was a spreading chestnut tree——"

"Break it down!"

"An' he used to stand under it and the muscles on his brawny arms was strong as iron bands. When he wasn't toilin', he was either rejoicin' or sorrowin'. Very temperamental, 'e was."

"Did he take anything for it?"

"Certainly not! When he was rejoicin' he'd tear the anvil in halves. Then he'd have a look at the anvil and do a bit of sorrowin'.

"It cost him a helluva lot for anvils. What's more his face was covered all over with hoof-marks where he'd been kicked by draught horses."

"And did he ever take out a tooth for you?"

"Me, I'm not a sissy. I used to tie a piece of fencin' wire on to the tooth and the other end on to the door-knob and then slam the door. It was a bit awkward, though.

"I mind one time when I had a bad back tooth — at the finish there wasn't a door-knob left in the house. Your grandmother was very upset about it. She says, 'What if somebody else gets a toothache, you selfish beast?'

"So I just gave her a damn good thrashin' although it was a Wednesday and she wasn't due for it till the Friday, that bein' her day. I was sorry after."

"Sorry for thrashing her?"

"No. About the door-knobs.

"There bein' no door-knobs, she tied the flat-iron to her tooth and then threw the flat-iron out the window. She was only a small woman and she followed the flat-iron out the window."

"Killed her, I suppose?"

"Oh, yair. But we got the flat-iron back. Not a dent in it. They made good flat-irons in those days. Not like the trash you get now."

"I don't buy many flat-irons."

"Well, yorta. That wife of yours——"

"Yes, but supposing she gets in first?"

"Hide it, you mug. Some place where you can lay your hands on it quick."

I have ordered half-a-dozen flat-irons. Certainly, in some respects, these old-timers knew how to conserve their health and peace of mind.

Red Tape In The Sunset

A terrible thing has happened to the Lower family. It all comes of living in New South Wales and being a civil servant. Harold, my grandfather, joined the civil service at the age of fourteen. He is now sixty-two. And all civil servants who have reached the age of sixty are now compelled to retire in order to make way for the employment of youths! Didn't the old man go mad!

He was at his desk in the Income Tax Department when his secretary shook him and told him that his morning tea was getting cold.

"What time is it?" he asked, stretching himself.

"Time to retire," answered the secretary, breaking it gently.

"Goodness gracious!" exclaimed Harold, who was always addicted to violent language from his youth up, "I didn't know it was so late."

"I mean you've gotter snatch your time," said the secretary, a coarse youth, who had only been in the service a bare thirty years. "Put your hat on. They've put the skids under you. They're wheeling out your superannuation. Scram!"

The old man was dazed. I mean to say, he was more dazed than usual. "But what am I going to do?" he moaned. "I haven't any other hobbies."

"Sit in the park and play draughts," said the unfeeling secretary. "There's a youth outside who's a somnambulist, and he's coming this way. And," he hissed, "you know that the Government is economizing? Well, this new fellow doesn't take milk or sugar in his morning tea!"

"Then I am indeed undone," said Harold mournfully. "Where is this youth?"

The secretary produced the youth, a mere lad of about forty-two.

"What is your name, my boy?" said Harold.

"I'm afraid you're in the wrong department," said the youth mechanically. "Registrar-General's Office. Fill in a form. Go to the other counter. Inquiries on the right. Put your signature here. Call in again tomorrow. The officer who deals with these matters is out at the moment."

"You'll do," said Harold. "My boy, there is a taxpayer who owes the State one shilling and fourpence. He is BM2756813. Remember that, my boy. I have been hounding him for four years. His files are in yonder safe. I bequeath him to you. Never let up on him."

The youth's eyes moistened. "Thank you, sir, for giving me a start in my career," he said.

But the old man was asleep.

"Hey!" bawled the secretary, "didn't I tell you that you're not working here now!"

". . . be payable without fine within fourteen days," muttered Harold. They dragged him from his chair, screaming.

Life at home now is hellish. As we're all living on Grandfather's superannuation, he has taken over the management of the house. He spends most of the housekeeping money on forms. If I want a drink of water, I have to fill in form XB7, and then he rings up the Water Board and inquires how things are at the reservoir, and after that he gets on to the Weather Bureau and wants to know about the prospects for rain and if they will kindly furnish him with statistics of the rainfall as from 1890 up to the year ending June 30, 1935. Then I go next door and get a drink of water.

It is rather significant that once upon a time the State's employees used to be called civil servants. The mistake has since been rectified, and they are now called public servants. Of course, Grandfather was never really a public servant. He was only a temporary employee during the whole of his thirty-eight years of service, during which he was the mainstay of countless money-lenders, and was also the champion time-book signer of his department. At one time he was signed up two months ahead of anybody else in the State and was presented with an illuminated fountain-pen.

Talking about money-lenders, my grandfather once called a meeting of creditors, and everybody thought it was an Empire Day rally. He eventually promised to pay five shillings in the pound, but nobody would lend him the five shillings. Our home is now entirely upholstered in red tape, and our bulldog answers to the name of BM529.

And Grandfather, now that he has retired, would like to meet all his old pals at the usual place at the racecourse on Wednesdays, and he expects to see them all out at the cricket ground as soon as the big games start. If he can spare the time, he may join the Navy in order to see the Melbourne Cup next November.

Tee And Sympathy

"Do you know anything about golf?" I asked Grandfather. You wouldn't think that my remark was very harmful, but then you don't know my grandfather. He started on me.

"Do I know anything about golf! My boy, I was playing golf when St. Andrew's links had only one hole, and there was only two of us that played the game — me and St. Andrew. I had to give up playing with him after he'd been made a saint, because he started ringing in miracles on me.

"In those days we used rough, three-cornered or square balls stuffed with haggis or some other non-detonating material.

"Now, of course, they use the gutter-percher ball. When I think of the golf-ball makers, perched in the gutter, winding the elastic round and round and round and round and round and round — all right, my boy. Don't go."

"And did you win any trophies, Grandpa?"

"In those days," he replied, loftily, "we didn't play for gain. We played for the thrill of it. Ah, what would I give to feel the smooth shaft of the dormy in my hands, to see the ball flying through the tiger country with the tigers after it, while the caddies cowered in the sand-box and the birdies drank at the casual water fountains!"

"I'm afraid I don't understand all those technical terms, Grandpa," I said. "Could you tell me in simple language how to play golf and what tools I would need?"

"Well, my boy, first of all, the caddy tees up the ball — hence the term tea-caddy. Then you take up your stance."

"Why do you have to tuck up your pants?" I asked.

"You take up your stance!" he bawled. "A stance is what you stand on. Rule 10 says that 'A player is always entitled to place his feet firmly on the ground when taking his stance.' This is a very important point, as you will find when you come to play. It is extremely difficult to hit a ball accurately with both feet off the ground.

"And while we're on the subject of rules, there's another one I remember. Sub-section 2 of Rule 22 says that 'If a ball be completely covered by sand, only so much thereof may be removed as will enable the player to see the top of the ball.' "

"But, Grandpa; how does he know where the ball is if it's completely covered with sand?"

"Don't ask silly questions. It's in the Rules, I tell you!"

"Sorry. What happens next?"

"The caddy hands you one of the golf bats. You raise it aloft, shout 'FORE!' in a loud voice, hit the ball a terrific smack, and it sails through the air and lobs smack in the hole. At least, that's how I do it. No use pottering about wasting time."

"But what do you shout 'Fore' for?"

"You don't shout 'Fawfaw'; you just yell out "FORE!" like that. It's an old Scottish custom. I think it is the start of 'For He's a Jolly Good Fellow.' "

"Well, what's the fairway in golf, Grandpa?"

"There is no fair way in golf, my boy. A man who plays fair at golf never gets anywhere."

"And putting, what's that?"

"Your ball is close to the hole, the caddy hands you your stymie, you give the ball a slight tap and dribble into the hole."

"What a disgusting habit! What if you run short of dribble?"

"When I was captain of the Moore Park Wanderers," he said, ignoring me, "we were unbeatable. I remember the last game we played in. There was only two minutes to go and we needed a goal to win. We were working furiously. Two men were going ahead with shovels getting the balls out of bunkers, the two wing three-quarters were bailing out the casual water, and the rest of us were slogging away at the ball. We were six feet from the hole, and I saw the referee fumbling for his whistle. With one magnificent leap I dived on the ball and slid on my stomach to the hole and dropped it in."

"Your stomach?"

"No; the ball, fool. We had won!"

"I'll bet you had more than one. Has the course got a bar on it?"

"Hazard! I'll say it haz! That's one of the main reasons for golf, my boy. Now run along. I want to polish up my divots."

I'm to have another lesson tomorrow. Meanwhile I'm learning the language.

Leaves From The Family Tree

Doubtless both of my readers will be glad to learn of the death of my grandfather, Arburthnot. He was killed at a croquet match between the Amalgamated Lead Pipe Manufacturers Wanderers and the Pestless Chocolate Vagabonds. Just after he'd scored a goal, too. Everybody said it was a shame. Even the umpire who killed him said it was a shame.

Cheering crowds and even throngs, not to say mobs, gangs, crowds, rabble, presses, and hordes, followed the corpse to the cemetery. All his life he had desired to have a little place to himself: now he's got it.

After the celebrations we all settled down to do a bit of solid mourning. We mourned to such an extent that the police were called in, and you should have seen the empties! The caretaker gets the lot. No wonder he owns a care. I mean a car.

SO: I went through his letters. My grandfather's, not the care-taker's. In this age of biographies it is well to get some of Arburth-not's letters published. All the best people do it. I quote a selected few; the rest will be published at a later date.

"Take notice that unless within seven days after personal service on you of a copy of this summons, or where service has not been personal within 10 days after leave to proceed, you file with the Registrar of this Court a notice in duplicate . . . stating the grounds on which you intend to defend this action, you will not afterwards be allowed to set up any defence to this action, but the plaintiff may proceed to judgment and execution. If you file the notice within the prescribed time the action will be set down for trial at a Court to be held in not less than four clear days after the filing of such notice."

There was rather an interesting reply to this, which I think should be passed on to posterity. "Sirs," it read, "you can go your hardest. Come and get me. Yours truly, Arburthnot Lower."

And then there was another one. You've all heard this, but I'm feeling a bit weak and I'm sure you won't mind meeting an old friend. "I desire to remind you that you have not yet paid the Federal Income Tax for the year ended 30th June, 1929. I also desire to inform you . . ." But you've all heard it.

It seems strange to me, but Arburthnot always appeared to have some kind of serious illness in his family when he was applying for sanctions against the Income Tax Department. I'm sorry to harp on this, but the Income Tax Department and myself do not get on too well together.

Then another thing I found while I was rummaging in the attic. He had had his telephone cut off. That's one of the horriblest things that can happen to a man, but Arburthnot never com-plained. He just told the Postal Department to take their asphyxiated telephone. Which they did.

There was a pathetic scene at the reading of the will. My great aunt got her teeth fastened into my grandmother, and it took two solicitors and a clerk to drag her off. The whole thing started over a glass case of waxed fruit which my grandfather left to his wife. My great-aunt Myrtle said that the fruit belonged to her, as, although she had originally given it as a wedding present to Arburthnot, it was really only a loan. She also claimed four antimacassars and a whatnot.

After the row had died down a bit and they had my grandmother bandaged up nicely, the startling discovery was made that Arburthnot's shark's tooth, which had been hanging from his watch-chain for sixty years, had disappeared.

I was immediately suspected, as it is well-known in the family that I am saving up for a shark, and when you come to think of the number of teeth sharks have you can see that it's practically a life job. I was stripped and searched, and when they found the gold band which used to be on Arburthnot's walking-stick—Crikey!

Still, thanks to the generosity of my grandfather I am now set for life. He left me a Chinese puzzle trick and I don't know how it works. I have an interest in life now. I rush home in the evenings and hurl myself on to the thing and wrestle with it far into the night.

Sometimes I hold my breath until I go black in the face and stamp my feet with rage; but I can't undo the thing. My wife is becoming hysterical and leaps at sudden noises, but I am not to be deterred, and, if necessary, will retire to a monastery, taking my puzzle with me.

I am trying to get into touch with Arburthnot, and am learning to become a medium in twelve easy lessons. Already I can go into a trance. The difficulty is to come out of it. ·

Not that it really matters, because my friends don't seem to notice any difference. They might say, "Lower's looking even dopier than usual," but little do they know that I am in tune with the infidels — with the institute. Blank! With the infinite!

I can feel myself going off now. I am possessed by the spirit of George Washington. Please hide all the hatchets!

6 Putting Curry Into the Curriculum

*From clinic to clink, from Montessori to Mont de
Piété, from toffee-apple to two-up school, the
Lower method of higher education will make
a little monster of your child or money cheerfully
refunded in full.*

Learning The Facts Of Life

Even when I was very young I had a strong suspicion that there was something wrong with our education system. Sitting right at the back of the class, I could never hear anything, and the teacher had a nasty habit of springing questions on me just when I was halfway through a green quince or fixing the handle of my all-day sucker.

Now, I'll bet you eight to one you can't remember the date of the Battle of Blenheim. . . .Thought you couldn't. That's what makes me mad with our present system of so-called education. If I was Minister for Education things would be altered a bit.

There would be none of this business of being sent to the bottom of the class and having children growing up with inferiority complexes as big as a cathedral. That's what's held me back in life. Just because a man's not too strong on his arithmetic, there's no reason for the Income Tax Department to put that stuff over in the assessments. They ought to know I don't know what it's all about.

My school would equip a child for its journey through life in a sensible manner. Who cares a hoot if the Battle of Trafalgar was fought in 1066, or whenever it was? On the other hand, isn't it better for a child to know the difference between a bad shilling and a good one?

Now, listen-in to my ideal class-room. You sit there and be a pupil. I'm the teacher.

"Well, girls and boys, I hope you've all brought your *Turf Times* with you?"

"Yes, teacher!"

"Well, now, can anyone tell me the past performances of Ooopa-doop King at Rosebery during March?"

"Yes, teacher. Third in the Welter Handicap in March, beaten by a short head on the same course in April. Won at the next meeting and was odds on. Looked a lay-down misere from the start. Hopped out from the tape and was never headed."

"Good! Now, if I had ninepence each way on a horse which won at six to four on, how many taxis could I take home at the rate of one shilling a mile? You can do that for your homework.

"Now, you girls, what is the correct thing to say when a man rings the front doorbell savagely and you rush to the door wondering whether anyone has been killed or the lottery ticket has romped home by a nose and the gentleman at the door wants to sell you knife polish?

"Well, I can see that question doesn't call for an answer. Now, are there any questions you'd like to ask, children?"

"Please, sir, is that right that you embezzled the Sunday school money to have a crack at the chocolate wheel last week and let the poor heathens whistle for their beads and mirrors what the missionaries give them?"

"You stay in after school and, what's more, you get eighteen lashes across the back, you pimp. Any more questions?"

"Please, teacher!"

"Yes, my boy?"

"If A has three Kings and B has three Kings and two Queens, what should B do?"

"That question is a bit moot, my boy. Who dealt in this case?"

"Please, sir, it was B."

"In that case B should shove a couple of Kings down his sock, declare the hand a misdeal and try again. Now, children, we will go through our limericks. No! One moment. Have all you girls done your homework?"

"Yes, teacher!"

"Gertie Hansen, read out your recipe."

"Take one measure of gin, sir, half of white curacoa, one cupful of brandy, a heaped teaspoon of good rum, equal parts of French and Italian vermouth and garnish with small pieces of gelignite."

"Very good. Now what have you done, Doris Duncan?"

"Sir, you take a gallon of absinthe with a pinch of caustic soda, a handful of brandy and one kettle full of the best chablis. Add a little molasses a drop at a time, stirring thoroughly the while, then you pour in the gin gently, a bottle at a time. Shake well and swerve."

"You're going to make a wonderful hostess when you grow up, Doris. Take a month off. Cedric Bowker! What are you doing there?"

"Please, sir, I was only rolling the bones with Joe Hennessy."

"What did you throw?"

"I threw a seven, sir."

"Hop out here and be thrashed. How do you expect to get on in life if you throw sevens?

"You can all go now and don't forget I want everyone to know the Stock Exchange reports off by heart tomorrow morning. Beat it!"

I don't care what anyone says, that's my idea of a decent modern education. And I'm sticking to it.

They Cheered When He Left The Clinic

When I was six months old and just learning to ride a bike, my mother said to me, "Leonard, my boy, I'm going to take you to see a doctor." I was polishing my rattle at the time, but I put it down and, looking her squarely in the eye, I said, "Flora, old girl, bunk to that suggestion. I have already seen one or two of them from a distance and they do not appeal to me."

I put my bootee down firmly on that idea, but now I can see it was a mistake. Had I but seen a doctor as I have served my King, he would not have deserted me in my last bout of megrims, as Cardinal Wolseley remarked at the battle of Trafalgar.

In my young days, you whippersnappers, there were no Baby Health Centres, and no Clinics. The nearest I got to a clinic was the clink.

I was brought up under catch-as-catch-can rules, and I must say that I am a credit to my parents. However, we are not gathered here today to talk about details which can be looked up in any *Who's Who*.

It's about clinics and kindergartens. Don't go away, you're going to get some information and instruction which will do you a mound of good. The first thing they do to a baby after it has been lugged unwillingly to the clinic with its shining mourning face, as Shakespeare puts it *(Crikey, ain't he cultured!)* is to weigh it.

After the baby has kicked the springs out of the weighbridge and had its weight painted on its side, it is washed and wrung out (hence the term, wet nurse). The child is then handed over to the doctor. The doctor examines it for signs of gout, spavins, foot-rot or St. John's Wort, and if everything is in order, he marks the child O.K., and it is then stuffed back into its clothes, jammed into its cart, and is pushed off, a sadder but wilder child. So much for the clinic.

The kindergarten is different. Children in kindergartens are never washed, as the egg marks and jam stains are useful for identification purposes. A child, on joining the kindergarten, is put down on the records as:

> *Jones, Maggie. Female.*
> *Egg mark on top lip.*
> *Jam stain on right cheek.*
> *One shoe lace undone.*

She is then regarded as a student and is given a lot of coloured blocks to play with. This is what is known as the Montessori method of training.

Cards are also used. The teacher holds one out to the child. "What have I here?" she says. "A card," answers the child wearily. Two more cards are then produced.

"What have I got now?" asks the teacher.

"Three cards."

"Good," says the teacher. "Now see if you can pick the Queen." When I was at kindergarten my teacher was a wow at this sort of thing, and used to win our play lunch money regularly.

You very soon learn to spell in these places. I remember the very first words I learned to spell were "KICK ME." The process was a bit painful but the knowledge has stuck to me.

Shortly after I learned to spell I was promoted from the Minus Z class to the Z, and was made a monitor. Being a monitor carries with it the right to scrounge all the chalk you can get away with, and you also dish out the beads. I got my blue for bead stringing in my second year, and I still have the string with the three beads on it at home.

When I was leaving the kindergarten at the expiration of my sentence the teacher said to my justly proud parents, "This boy will go far." He was right, too, because shortly after that we moved to Perth.

I shall always look back with pleasure on my formative years when my character was being moulded. I was the most belted child in the kindergarten, and it speaks volumes for my character that I came back in the night after leaving and burnt the place down. And now, here I am with my character all formed, and not a damn thing to do with it.

Ah, well. . . . You may go now.

If $X + Y = Z$, Why Have School Exams At All?

School examinations are now in the air. As a scholar I was never very keen on examinations. I regarded them as a low trick played on defenceless pupils. Now, of course, when I don't have to sit for any examinations, I can see what a great boon they are, and how much good they do, and how they help you to get on in the world, and all that.

The first kid I see today is going to be told all that. Why shouldn't I get a bit of my own back?

In my time, in the good old days, probably before your time, examinations were terrifically difficult. It will give you some idea of how difficult they were when I tell you that I couldn't pass in any subject. The teacher said that it was a school record.

Nowadays judging by the slickness with which pupils pass their exams, I am convinced that they are far too easy. I'll show you what I mean, and if the Minister for Education has any sense he'll start to think deeply about the school examination papers.

(1) *What is the length of the inside of a circle?*

(2) *If a man walks three hundred yards in one direction, four hundred yards in another direction, and ten yards in another direction, where is he?*

(3) *If a man pushed a wheelbarrow full of billiard balls from Melbourne to Alice Springs, how many times would he have to stop for meals? Also, what gave him the idea in the first place?*

That last one is in the realm of higher mathematics, but should be easy for a student who has diligently attended to his studies.

One more question in the maths paper and we will pass on to the next subject.

(4) *Fred has a bad two-shilling piece which he passes on to a blind fruit-seller, who gives him only eleven apples. Was he robbed?*

This one is worked out with mirrors and logarithms. I've never seen a logarithm, but I understand that they should never be kept chained up all the time. Exercise is essential to their well-being.

Regarding history, I could never see the sense in learning, parrot fashion, that William the Conqueror's phone number was 1066. However, a few sample questions which any child with a retentive memory will be able to answer.

(1) *In what year did Cromwell marry Queen Elizabeth?*

(2) *Who first planted the Spanish Armada? What is the average number of Spanish Armadas to the pound?*

That second bit is not strictly history, but it reveals whether the pupil has a thorough grasp of his subject.

(3) *When did Nelson say to the Duke of Wellington, "Kiss me harder", and why? . . .*

(4) *What kind of biscuits did they have at the Boston Tea Party?*

(5) *On what racecourse were the words "A hearse, a hearse! my kingdom for a hearse!" shouted?*

(You will note that the history questions are pretty easy. One must give the student a bit of a break now and then, otherwise he'll walk out on you and an examination without students is inclined to be rather dull.)

(6) Who discovered Latvia, and why?

That will do for history.

Geography I am good at. Always was. Although why all the countries were not made square in order to facilitate map-drawing I don't know.

(1) What is the main street in Latvia?

(2) About what shape do you think Bechuanaland will be next week?

(3) What is the principal export of the Canary Islands? (That's an awfully easy one.)

(4) What country exports most rods, poles and perches to the Canary Islands?

(5) Columbus discovered America by mistake. How big a mistake do you reckon this was?

(6) How much higher than wider is Switzerland, if any?

All these questions are so easy that I feel rather ashamed of them but geography is so unsettled lately. You've got to wait for the late final extra edition of the evening paper to find out if places are still on the map.

I am afraid I am not so hot on natural history. I've done a great deal of hunting in Borneo and Africa, and places, but as I was on the run practically all the time I didn't have much opportunity for study. Still, I have sufficient knowledge of the subject to make a few suggestions.

(1) What is a griller? How large does the griller grow, and who feeds the wild grillers?

(2) What makes prawns blush and go red all over when exposed in shop windows?

(3) How frequently does the ring-tailed possum's tail ring? And what for?

Now let me see. What other subjects have we? Geometry. Yes. One of the greatest pains in the neck ever invented by the human brain. When it was first put up to me I thought it was a joke, but when the teacher explained that it was fair dinkum my eyes popped out like headlamps.

(1) Give the inside perimeter of a circle to the third decimal.

(2) What is the hypotenuse of a circular triangle, five feet by four?

(3) Describe an arc with a trajectory of one in four and a half at both ends.

I am grateful that I do not now have to go to school and study twenty-three and a half hours a day for examinations so that I will be able to go on the dole when I grow up.

Judged by present-day standards, I may be iggerant, but I'm 'appy. Poor kids!

117

The Hub Of All Knowledge

People frequently ask me where I get all my culture and information from. If you met me and had converse with me for a few minutes you would probably ponder the same question.

If you must know, I get it at the pub. If I want to know what will win the Flying Handicap, if I want to know whether the Douglas Credit System is sound, if I wish to hear whether a certain show is worth seeing, what the position is in Manchukuo, what's a good remedy for sore feet, and the inside dope on the Federal elections, all I have to do is don the hat, tell those in the office concerned that I have an important business appointment, and wend pubwards.

I like hotels. I am compiling a brochure on bar-room tactics which may interest you. For instance, always get your shout in first; you never know who else may turn up later. The only exception to this rule is when the other party looks at his watch and says, "Just one quick one. I must get away soon." In that case you let him shout first. After having it, and as he is just going to the door, it is permissible to say, "Sure you won't have another?" Only a dirty dog would say "Yes."

When in a team, watch the soda bottles carefully. If they are still half full, it is safe to shout the whiskies. I once had to shout eight whiskies and assorted bottles of soda-water and ginger-ale. I didn't mind the whisky so much, but to be landed with eight bottles of soda-water and ginger-ale galled me. I have never made that mistake since.

If we ever had to send any ambassadors anywhere I should select a well-trained barmaid to go. Any woman who has just lost her permanent-wave money on a horse that ran last and can still bob up and greet the addicts with a hearty, "Hello, Mr. Smith. My word, you do look well!" is worthy of admiration and reward.

How they remember all the names is a mystery. You'll hear it every day. "How are you today, Mr. Whosthis? I hope your back is feeling better. Still bad? I am sorry. Why don't you try Sloth's Liniment? They tell me it's marvellous. Have a clove?" And all that stuff.

I'd never have attained my present eminent position in journalism if it wasn't for the worthy habit of visiting hotels occasionally. Only the worst reporters are teetotallers.

I remember once I was sent out to do a story on a big fire that broke out in a wharfside timber-yard. I got waylaid. The fire was out by the time I remembered about it, but was I dismayed? I just said to someone near me, "I believe there was a big fire down at the wharves today?" He told me all about it. Described it graphically. I wrote the story, was complimented by the editor, and it wasn't until the next day that I found out that my informant hadn't been anywhere near the fire. Anyway, it was a good story.

Strange, the various people you meet in various hotels. In the pub nearest to the Trades Hall you will find sturdy union secretaries slaving away in the saloon bar mapping out the next strike. There is talk of solidarity and the workers and down-troddenings.

At the hostelry where the woolbuyers forgather in their off moments the air is full of sheep and bales and length and quality and fibre in thirteen different languages.

Politicians spread out a bit. There doesn't seem to be any particular politicians' pub. I haven't discovered it, anyhow. And Lord knows I've tried. It's good to know the places to avoid.

Journalists' hotels are easy to pick out by the noise. Invariably one can get credit there. Otherwise, it wouldn't be a journalists' hangout. The conversation in these places is mostly lewd and profane, and you will hear any amount of marvellous news stories that were canned by a moron sub-editor because he had no more brains than a wart-hog and words to that effect.

The wireless has ruined hotels. A man might be just telling the story of his life to the barmaid and getting up to the point when you ask her what time she knocks off, and the confounded wireless booms out, "We are now crossing over to Randwick racecourse. There are three scratchings for the next event . . ." and there you are. Got to do it all over again.

Another thing, which I suppose can't be helped, is the supreme and exasperating difficulty of trying to tell a funny story to a barmaid. You just get up to the good part and she says, "Just a moment!" and flits off down the other end of the bar to serve someone. Then she comes back and says, "Yes? Go on." And you say, "Well, all of a sudden the fellow gets up and . . ." "Just a moment!" And she's gone again. That's when you leave the place with your drink half finished and swear that you'll never darken its doors again. Of course, if you do manage to get the yarn finished you're sure of a laugh. Whenever I get hold of a rotten joke which nobody will laugh at I just go along and tell it to a sympathetic girl behind the bar, and she laughs heartily and says, "What are you going to have?" And I say, "Nothing, thanks. That's all I wanted." Then I go away feeling a new man.

When I retire I'm going to make a gift of a hotel to the nation. There will be a separate section for all walks of life, a general forum in the centre, and a padded cell for bores with a grating so you can look through at them any time you're feeling morbid.

Parliament will be unnecessary then.

So You Think You're Clever, Huh ?

I've had a go at one of those intelligence tests, and it's absolutely astonishing the number of things I don't know.

You needn't smirk either. *From what family springs the common aspidistra? Define a volute.* You see what I mean? Fancy a man ploughing his way through life without knowing what a volute is.

All applicants for the better-class jobs have to suffer these intelligence tests. They even do it in the Air Force. I'd like to know who started it.

For instance, they lead you up to a table with a banana on it and an egg and a pencil and a golf ball and one hundred and fifty other different objects on it. You are supposed to take one swift look at the conglomeration—I left out heterogeneous; how careless of me—after looking at this heterogeneous conglomeration you go away and make out a list of everything that was on the table. It is my considered opinion that whoever thought of this footling idea must have been a bit ga-ga. Probably fell out of his pram when very young and landed on his geranium.

Ha! You noticed that? The word is not geranium, of course. It should be chromium. You've got to be quick to notice these things. That's where the intelligence comes in.

Take another test. You are led into a darkened room and seated at a table. After being there three minutes a blinding light flashes on for two seconds and a loud speaker says, "Write down Entwhistle three times!" And you have nothing to write with. So what?

Don't ask me. I don't know. Anyhow if you pass that test it shows that you are mentally qualified to become a bassoon player, or something.

Personally, I'm dead against all this intelligence testing and psycho-analysis business. The old methods, I think, are still the best.

I remember when I was leaving school (it was a no-tie school) my father interviewed the headmaster.

"Has he shown any particular aptitude for anything?" said my father, gazing at me distastefully.

"Well—er—hm! I understand that he is the best marbles player in the school."

"Is he, by Gad! Well, that's something. I was pretty good myself in my day. Blood will tell. Still, one can't earn a living by playing marbles. What would you suggest?"

"Why not exhibit him as 'The Bone-Headed Wonder. Straight from Peru.' Something like that?"

"That's an idea. But I'd have to have a tent. Anyhow, I'll think it over. Come on, son." And so I left school. Would you believe — within a week I was apprenticed to a hod-carrier, with the possibility of becoming an architect looming ominously in the distance. I suppose that's how I became a journalist. It's all done by intelligence tests. Now I ask you.

Take this for a sample. If a boy had five apples and lived in Newcastle and his uncle was a butcher, what train would he catch to Bathurst if he had a stiff leg and fourpence, and it was Tuesday? At first glance this seems to be a bit tough, but a little concentration will reveal the fact that the boy caught the five-fifteen, which stops at all stations, thus giving him time to eat his apples. Also he had no uncle. And, anyhow, he wasn't on the train. This shows that I should have been a lawyer. See what I mean?

The average youth, finding himself deaf, dumb, blind, and paralysed, would perhaps despair of gaining employment, unless he put himself on the waiting list at the Government Information Bureau.

But no! He could be a star turn in a waxworks show, and probably work his way up to a stage when he would be believed or not by Ripley or gloated over by Walter Winchell. That is fame.

No matter what these intelligence-testers tell you, never despair. Do not be disconsolate nor downcast and despondent and dreary and dolorous and dour and down in the dumps or depths of despair. (Didn't even have to chalk the cue for that lot.)

Remember, my lad, that there are lots of professors motherless broke. And there are lots of bookmakers rolling in it. I leave the rest to your intelligence.

I'm glad my intelligence hasn't been tested yet. I don't think I'd feel at home in a home.

A New Look At Cook

It is mooted by a well-known mooter that the teaching of Australian history in our schools will shortly be simplified. As a keen student of history, I am delighted and even prepared to assist. I suggest something like this:

One day in a tavern, Captain Cook was supping with a few cronies when he casually remarked, "I think I will go to Australia—hic!"

"There's no such—pardon me—place," replied one of his cronies.

"Ho! No?" cried Cook in his nautical way, "Well, hup!—I'll show you——"

He strode forth to his ship, pulled up the hook on the end of the chain, and, after buying sandwiches for the voyage, set sail.

That's the sort of man Cook was.

It was on a Tuesday morning that he landed at Farm Cove, so called because the aborigines used to go in for extensive farming round about the place.

That was the dawning of civilization in Australia. To Cook we owe our—well, whatever we owe.

Cook immediately cabled to Bligh:

"Post open as Governor New South Wales stop Natives friendly Bring some rum stop Love to all, Jimmy."

Bligh at once engaged a crew of ex-mutineers, and after sending the terse cabled reply, "Oke," shook hands with his friends—both of them—and sailed away.

At half-past four, just in time for the last race at Randwick, he beached his ship near the wool stores and met Cook.

"Now, none of your mutinies, Bligh," said Cook, sternly. "Did you bring the rum?"

"Well, I started off with it," said Bligh, defiantly, "but had to jettison it during a heavy storm."

"You ought to be speared!" said Cook, turning on his heel.

He was very fond of turning on his heel and used to do it on lodge nights when somebody was called up to do a turn. (Before I go any further, I would like to remind people who are interested in history that this is merely a practice gallop and any little discrepancies which occur are due to my absence from the scene at the time. A man can't be everywhere.)

Anyhow, Bligh surveyed the landscape, and said, "This looks like a mighty good place for convicts, egad!" (You may well ask when I am going to start on the history of this country. I must remind you that this is merely a sample. A fragment, so to speak, of a gorgeous tapestry woven by our forebears. That's not a bad bit. I must point it out to the Professor.)

We will leap, then, to the discovery of gold. No. One moment. Blaxland, Lawson and Wentworth crossed the Blue Mountains and arrived at the astonishing conclusion that there was an inside to the edge of the country.

"Look!" said Blaxland to Lawson. "Look at that glorious undulating country."

"Oh, it's the country that's undulating?" said Lawson with a sigh of relief. "I can't be so bad after all."

"We must send for Macarthur," said Wentworth.

"Why?" asked Blaxland.

"Bring out some sheep, mug," said Wentworth, testily. "Must have sheep."

"Why?" asked Blaxland, monotonously.

"For chops!" yelled Wentworth. "Blast you, shut up!"

Thus the first brawl occurred on the Blue Mountains and not in the Rum Corps, as other historians insist.

This brings us to the gold rush. Those were the days! Any nugget weighing less than five pounds was either used as a door-stop or a sinker for fishing.

The gold-digger home from his work would be confronted by his currency lass, saying, "Don't tell me you've brought home another drayload of that accursed stuff! The house is littered with it already. It's a pity you didn't go out and earn some money instead of mucking about mining."

"But a lot of it's quartz, dear."

"Quarts! That's all you think of!" Women were just the same in those days.

In the meantime, elderly ex-convicts and expatriated sons of old English squires were patting little boys on the head, breathing rum on them, and asking, "And what are you going to be, my boy, when you grow up to be a man?"

"I'm going to be a bushranger," piped the child. "There's money in it."

This was the depravity era, when the population consisted of bushrangers and mounted troopers and a good time was had by all.

Time marched on and it became possible to hire a bullock waggon at a shilling flagfall and sixpence a mile. But the service became so convenient to the public that the police stopped it. How history repeats itself!

Australia is now a nation. We are entitled to call ourselves a nation because we owe several billion pounds abroad and are among the highest taxed people in the world.

And if pioneer Macarthur could only see the price we pay for mutton these days, he'd weep tears of blood.

Hazards Of Homework

I have decided to give up sighing for those dear old school-boy days. School boys are raising a feeble protest about homework.

They knock off study at school, go home with seven subjects to explain to the dumb teacher who ought to know all this stuff, anyhow, and have to sit up till 11 o'clock at night to finish their work.

Surprising though it may seen, I went to school myself at one time. Things were easier then, due in part to my organising ability.

After school we all met in the wood-shed—six of us—and polished off our homework. It stands to reason that if six pupils all turn in the same answer to a mathematical problem, it must be right, and to hell with the teacher.

I keep trying to explain to the Department of Education that our present system is all wrong.

Who cares if A is travelling on a train in a westerly direction at forty miles an hour and B is going in the opposite direction at fifty miles an hour? Yet these examiners want to know something about the exact time the trains pass each other provided that one left at 3.15 a.m. and the other at 4.10 a.m.

The intelligent student will at once ask, "Why were these two people travelling at such an ungodly hour in the morning? Were they brewery workers? Did they travel first or second class? Where the blazes were they going, anyway?"

Of course, the student could get out of it if he liked to go to a little trouble. Just a sample of homework to help the boys along.

"Ha!" said A, as the three-fifteen train moved slowly out of the station. "Dead on time. I must remember to wave to B when we pass him.

"Let me see, now. His train leaves some unknown starting point at four-ten. Hm!"

Then all he has to do is hang his neck out of the carriage window and, watch in hand, keep a close look-out for B. But what if B has missed his train?

As the train rushed on at forty miles an hour stopping at all stations, at one of which the guard had a bit of an argument with the station master. A thought to himself as he read his morning paper, "What is the capital of Moscow?"

The thing is, does the student actually have to board the train at 3.15 a.m. or whenever I said it was in order to get all his facts right?

It would be very awkward for a lad to find himself in the shunting yards at Werris Creek when he should be turning up at school in Darlinghurst.

One way out is for the student to go to school in his pyjamas and thus get a flying start.

I see no way out of this homework business unless the pupil does all his work at home and then goes to school to relax.

It looks like we're going to have a new generation of superintellects, all nervous wrecks and not one of them will know anything about bird-nesting or how to assemble a shanghai or how to find a hole in a fence or make stink-bombs.

I'm beginning to think that some brands of education are quite unnecessary. For instance it would be very hard to find someone in the bar, billiard saloon or ballroom with whom one could carry on a light and easy conversation in Latin. Even then you'd run the risk of being interned.

Then there's trigonometry. Skip it. The less said about that the better. I believe that it was invented by a half-crazed monk in a damp, rat-ridden cell in the bowels of the Bastille during the Indian Mutiny. He had nothing else to do. He was executed eventually. Burned at the stake, but it was too late. The damage was done.

After all, education or acquired knowledge is just a matter of luck. Take Archimedes or Aristotle or whoever he was who discovered something about specific gravity. He just lay down in his bath and yelled, "Eureka! I have found it!" Years ago I thought that this meant that he had found the soap, but it seems that he had solved an abstruse problem.

Same with Isaac Newton—or was it? Anyhow, all he did was lie down under an apple tree and get hit on the skull with an apple. Hence the Law of Gravity. Or something.

Columbus would never have discovered Australia if he had not got himself lost first on account of his co-pilot going down with scurvy and rickets brought about by too much fresh vegetables.

Did Sir Walter Raleigh go to America especially to discover tobacco? No. It was a fluke.

I'll tell you what. If I had a son who was enthusiastic about his homework, I'd look very suspiciously at his mother.

Playing Dux And Drakes

Education experts say children should take an active part in their own education.

Why didn't they think of that when I was going to school? I'm sure I'd have had as many degrees as a thermometer if I'd been allowed to butt in now and then while I was at school.

For instance:

"We all know that Christopher Columbus discovered America," said the teacher to the class.

"I doubt that," said little Willie. "Have you any proof of that statement?"

"You will find it on page forty-six of your history book, Willie."

"Huh! You can't believe all you read. What about that report on S.P. betting? Anyhow, let it slide. Carry on."

"The Spanish were among the earliest settlers . . ."

"Well, my bookmaker's no Spaniard!"

"Shut up, Willie!"

"I'm taking an active part in my education. Whose education is it, anyhow?"

"That concludes the history lesson for today."

"About time, too. I never heard such bunk. And, by the way, teacher. About that sum you set us for homework last night. It can't be done."

"Oh, no? Sez you!"

"Sez me! It starts off: 'If a man had three dozen apples, four dozen oranges, and six dozen peaches' . . . Well, I ask you! Where's a feller going to get the money to buy all that stuff, apart from the fact that peaches are out of season? And another thing, if I remember rightly, he gives six away and receives two back. It doesn't say why he got them back. Probably they were rotten. But what I say is why worry about it? It's all over and forgotten now. Probably the cove who was slinging this fruit around has been dead for years. What's it matter to me how many oranges he had? What I say is . . ."

"Willie! Sit down!"

"Oh, all right! A bloke's got to sit here and just be a passive receptacle, eh?"

"Excuse me, sir!" said young Alfred, more or less saving a situation which looked like becoming tense. "May I ask a question?"

"Certainly, my boy! That's what I'm here for."

"Are those baggy eyelids of yours due to late hours or drink?"

"WHAT!"

"All right. All right. Don't do your block and set a bad example to the class. Let's get back to these oranges and things this chap was giving away. What was his name?"

"I don't see that it matters, Alfred."

"Oh, yes it does!" chipped in Oscar, the dux of the class. "If he's the same chap who bought ten pounds of two-inch nails, laid them end to end, and then wanted to know how many nails there were if it took him three minutes to ride past them on a bicycle going at twenty miles an hour, he ought to be certified. It's not safe to let those fellers loose. And another thing, I ask you, as man to man, what earthly use is all that guff to me? Am I ever likely to buy ten pounds of nails and a bicycle and ride . . ."

"That's enough! A man has three dozen oranges . . ."

"Struth, there he goes again! Couldn't you make it watermelons? If you knew what it was to have to sit here listening to you drooling about a maniac who doesn't know how many oranges he's got you'd have a bit more consideration."

"Hear! Hear!" muttered the class.

"Well, we'll try something different. I don't want to weary you, boys. There are eight horses in a race. The winner's price is five to four on. How much would you have to put on to win fifteen shillings?"

"I wouldn't be such a piker!" said little Thomas, indignantly. "If a man's going to bet like that he might as well stick to the Tote. Anyhow, you haven't given us the form or past performances. Nobody would bet in the dark like that. Might as well pick 'em with a pin. Have a bit of sense!"

"Oh, confound the lot of you! Class dismiss!"

"Why didn't you think of that before? Wasting our time burbling about oranges, and bicycles, and things when a man could have been fishing. The trouble with you is that you're behind the times. You won't co-operate."

"Go away!" moaned the teacher. "Oh, go away!"

"Come on, boys," said young Alfred. "Leave him alone. He looks about all in." And they slowly left the room, patting the sobbing teacher gently on the head as they passed.

Hooray, for the new education! What a pity it came too late for most of us.

7 How To Be A Lighthouse-Keeper Or Almost Anything

*Dont be a square pig in a round hole! If you
can't find your I.Q., you can always
become an M.P. or a journalist
or a banker or a removalist.
Let the Lower Coaching College show you
how. And how!*

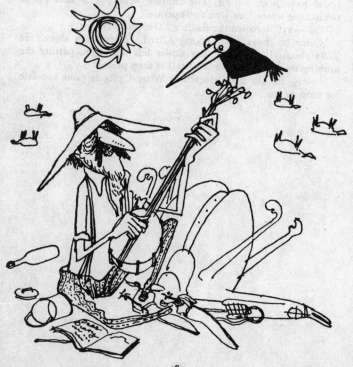

Journalists Are Born, Not Paid

Lately I have had a number of inquiries on the subject of "How to Become a Journalist."

Journalists are born. Why, nobody knows. The ambitious few become journalists by study. It is to these people who, tired of life, wish to become journalists, these few remarks are addressed.

For a start, if you'll just take an eyeful of that last sentence you can see that it's cockeyed. You will find all sorts of examples like that as we get along with the course.

To be a working journalist one needs tact, aplomb, a wide general knowledge, an inventive mind, a faculty for quick action, a nose for news, an ear for scandal, and a mouth for drinking purposes. Also a pencil and some paper. The three last items are absolutely essential.

Supposing you are walking along the street and a car full of passengers gets out of control, turns over three times and finishes up in a shop window. The first thing to do is to walk over to the first passenger who becomes conscious and say, "I represent the *Daily Terror*. Would you kindly tell me your name, age, height, weight and favourite author? Are you on a holiday or merely out for pleasure?" Other things will suggest themselves to you as you go along.

Then get into a tram, make straight for your newspaper office and fill in an expense account for your taxi fare.

In writing the story of the accident be brief, yet leave out nothing.

For example:

"Turning over four times *(there's seldom any argument among the passengers about the number of times)* a speeding car deposited its passengers in mangled heaps in So-and-so Street on *(leave out the date, for you're bound to be wrong. Anyhow, the printer will fix that)*. While the gruesome remains were being dragged, screaming madly, from the wreckage, which was not insured, our representative gave valuable advice from the other side of the street."

The rest is easy. Just follow on with the names, number of stitches, write "address unknown" next to the lot of them and then point out the danger of veranda posts and demand that all shops be equipped with cantilever awnings.

That's what is called ordinary, straight reporting. On the other hand we have descriptive writing. This is what is used to fill up the space where the advertising should have been.

"As the first pale pearly tints of dawn shimmered on the breeze-ruffled harbour and the wheeling gulls gracefully skimmed the jade-green, foam-flecked waters, s.s. Whatsthis, 12,000 tons, steamed majestically into port with a cargo of wire mattresses from the languorous shores of the romantic Bahamas. A feeling of yearning for the soft lap-lap of the wavelets on some sunny strand . . ."

You just go on like that till you think you've got enough.

Then, of course, there is the old standby, the Oldest Inhabitant. When things look blue and there hasn't been a murder for days and the insidious effects of the secret drug traffic have been done to a frazzle, then the true journalist turns to the Oldest Inhabitant as a weary child to its mother.

An Oldest Inhabitant will say ANYTHING. He remembers when he used to drive the mail coach and get held up three times a day between meals by bushrangers—a fine body of men, hounded by the police—and how the horses tied up to a rail where the General Post Office now stands kicked the slats out of the Governor's Vice-Regal buggy when they saw the first steam tram in Main Street, or Mulga Track, as it was known in those days.

The only difficulty about interviewing Oldest Inhabitants is getting away from them.

Speaking from some years of experience, I place these newspaper life-savers in the following order:

ACTRESSES: "I never expected such an overwhelming welcome from my dear, dear public. How wonderful it is to know that one is cherished in the hearts of all, from the lowest to the highest. Not that there are any lowest or highest in this wonderful land of yours. Tell everybody I am so happy—happy to be with you all again."

POLITICIANS: "What I'm telling you, boy, is for your ears alone. Or, if you publish it, don't mention my name. But if you do mention my name, remember the initials are F.P., not X.B. I've got a good picture of myself here you can use in your paper. Don't praise me up too much. It makes my colleagues in the House jealous."

"Supposing we call you 'The Genial Genius of Australia'?"

"That's it! That just about describes me. Have a cigar?"

Journalism is much easier than falling off logs.

Send for my illustrated pamphlet, *How to Become a Journalist and Owe Thousands of Pounds.*

Dark Doings In A Lighthouse

It has been brought to my notice that a young lady artist has a yearning to own a lighthouse in order to use it as a studio. So, for the benefit of this poor, deluded girl, I relate the following morbid story, suitable for adults only. Nothing "over the odds", of course, but keep it from the children.

I had been out all night, and the following morning I espied in a newspaper an advertisement for a lighthouse-keeper. Craven wretch that I am, I bethought me that 'twould be far, far better to be safely ensconced on an inaccessible lighthouse than to go home and say "Hullo dear!" to Mrs. Lower. Little did I suspect the tragic consequences of my foolhardiness. How was I to know that I was to lie, cold and stiff, battered beyond recognition on the cruel rocks of the lighthouse?

Woe is me! Woe! *(Put that horse down!)* I had taken Arburthnot, my grandfather, to act as assistant keeper. His main job was to act as a foghorn during fogs. All he had to do was to stand on top of the lighthouse and say, "Beep! Beep!" in a deep voice at regular intervals. Unfortunately, it became a habit with him, and he developed a nasty custom of beeping at his meals.

However, there we were isolated on the lighthouse surrounded entirely by walruses. For the first few weeks all was well. I used to gaze out from the lighthouse watching the waves pound on the rocks—I'd like to have a penny for every pound those rocks got—and watching the seagulls gullivanting about, but soon the job began to pall.

We had one of those intermittent lights, and, believe me, for sheer monotony you can't beat it. Blowing the thing out and lighting it again, blowing it out and lighting it, blowing it out and lighting it. There were times when I lost count and blew it out twice running without lighting it, and four ships were ground to pieces on the rocks before I could find the matches again. A rotten thing to read by, too.

In the daytime we had very little to do, and as Arburthnot had taken to singing "Many Brave Hearts Are Asleep in the Deep" and mournfully accompanying himself on his mouth organ (a rather difficult feat, now I come to think of it), I filled in my time unwinding the spiral stairway and winding it up again.

This is where the terror sets in. It gets very stark from now on, so if you're at all nervous you'd better get off here.

Madness crept in. The beeping of my grandfather became subtly hysterical. Time after time I noticed him glaring at me beneath his breath. The stairway no longer interested me, I knew the telephone book off by heart, and used to recite it out aloud until I got tired of it. I found myself leaping at shadows. Catching 'em, too, by cripes! Arbuthnot by this time spent every day sharpening the grindstone on his clasp knife. I tell you, things were looking pretty sinister.

Then came the terrible night. The wind was shrieking, the sea was roaring, my grandfather was singing, and the lighthouse was rocking from side to side. A dense fog swept up the channel and we couldn't see a yard in front of us, even if we'd had a yard. Soon, all too soon, the sea was lit up with distress rockets. Sirens blew and shattered wreckage piled halfway up the lighthouse.

"To your post!" I cried to my grandfather.

He dashed to the beeping department. I hurled myself to the match-locker.

"Beep! BEEP!" On went the light. Out again. On again. Out again. *(This is the sort of job I like, I get paid for this.)* On again. Out again. On again. Then suddenly the beeping ceased. Arburthnot staggered up to me.

"You fiend!" he hoarsed. "What have you done to me? I cannot beep! You hound!"

"Hush, Arbuthnot," I said, blowing the light out and lighting it again. "For all you know there may be ladies present on those helpless ships—HUP!" The worst had happened. I had got the hiccups!

"You HUP! blow the Hup! light out, I'll HUP! light it!" I screamed above the fury of the storm.

Seized with the urgency of the occasion, Arburthnot rose above all petty animosity and started blowing.

"Do you think you could manage a beep or two between blows?" I gasped.

"Well, I like that!" said my grandfather angrily. Demoniacal rage gripped me. I hurled myself at him, and we swayed to and fro. Especially fro. The light was out and not a sound came from the neglected lighthouse except the frenzied panting of two demented men. I got him down at last and choked him with his own beard. Then I set fire to the lighthouse as a warning to shipping.

Retribution overtook me with tragic swiftness. I had unwound the spiral stairway the previous morning, and had forgotten to coil it up again. I stepped out in the darkness and plunged straight to my doom.

Five years afterwards, when the supply boat called with our income tax assessments, they found me battered, as I warned you in the first place, beyond recognition.

Somewhere, under the wreckage of the lighthouse, lies Arburthnot. So, ladies and gentlemen, I ask you to be upstanding and drink a toast to British lighthouse-keepers. Thank you!

A Teller Tells

If you've got any money (don't laugh!) you'd better put it in our bank. Wep, who has a rather elaborate home in Rose Bay, pulled down his dog-kennel and he had a lot of marble pillars and mahogany woodwork left on his hands. I bought it for a song. At least I got half way through the song and Wep said he was quite satisfied and that he regarded himself as overpaid.

The only thing to do with marble pillars and mahogany woodwork is to make a bank out of it. I looked up Chambers' Encyclopaedia and found that the purpose of banking was to "invite moneyed men to lend to the merchants for the continuing and quickening of trade." This looked good to me, so I opened a bank. Wep was the teller.

We'd only been open an hour, when some poor, demented bloke walked in and said, "I want to see the manager."

Hastily getting dressed, I called him into my office. "I am the manager," I said, "what do you want managed?"

"I want to open an account," he replied.

"Open it outside," I said, "and then bring it in here and let me have a look at it. I don't want a mess in my office."

Well, he deposited twenty-five pounds with the bank. Wep was in a pretty good position as receiving teller, but he couldn't do much, because I had him covered with the bank revolver. He suggested, after the customer had left, that we shut up the bank and go. He also suggested that he ought to have a revolver in order to shoot any customers who wanted to draw money out of the bank. I reprimanded him and sent him back to his desk.

Then a fellow came in and wanted an overdraught. Wep came to me and said, "What's an overdraught?"

"How the devil do I know?" I replied. "Do your own crossword puzzles. There's a dictionary under the counter."

"This bloke wants one," said Wep.

"Well, open the fanlight and give it to him," I ordered.

The customer went away quite satisfied. I think he must have been used to it.

That was all the business we did for that day, but when you

come to think of it, twenty-five pounds whacked up between two of us is not bad for a day's work.

Next day, we decided to advertise, and we hung a large notice outside the building: "BANK AT LOWER'S BANK. THREE PER CENT. INTEREST! MARKED DOWN FROM FOUR AND A HALF! TRADE IN YOUR OLD PASSBOOK FOR THE LATEST MODEL!"

Did we do any business! We had to engage a boy to bite the two-bob pieces. He swallowed twelve, and as his salary was only 15/- a week we had to keep him on for nearly a fortnight to get our money's worth.

We had a certain amount of bother with cheques. For a start we wouldn't accept any cheques at all. Wep said to me, "Would you take a cheque of mine?" And I said, "No." And I said, "Would you take a cheque of mine?" And he said, "Do you think I'm mad?" So we thought that, going by past experience, it would be best to leave cheques out of the business.

Then, after we got going well, we thought that it wouldn't make any difference, anyhow, seeing that we were closing the bank any minute, so we decided to accept cheques from other banks.

By this time we had three tellers. I did all the listening. We also had a uniformed commissionaire with medals on. His medals alone cost us nine and six at the Mont de Piété. You can't run a successful bank on nothing. Look what it costs you for medals, for a start.

We are still in business, but if you want to deposit anything with us you'd better hurry.

Outgoing cheques at the moment are being marked N.S.F., which means Not So Fast, and we are sacking the paying teller and engaging two more receiving tellers. We are engaging them on piecework rates, and if you want to bank any money with us you'll have to make an appointment. Our passages are already booked for South America, so bank in our bank NOW, and get it over.

Rip out the coupon and mail today.

Removaling As An Inexact Science

When I had finished my studies and got my degree of Bachelor of Removalism at the Pantechnical High School I took Athelbert into partnership and started my own practice. Athelbert is my grandfather, of course, and it was a proud day when we hung up our plate, "LOWER & LOWER. REMOVALS AND STORAGE. BESPOKE FURNITURE SHIFTERS."

We charged £3/10/- for our first job. Worth it, too. I worked it out afterwards that it was £3 for putting up with my grandfather and 10/- for moving the furniture.

Starting on the light stuff first—crockery, and so forth—it was very sad to witness the breaking up of a home. As a matter of fact, when we were only half-way through the job the owner of the furniture was sobbing his heart out at the back gate.

And then, all of a sudden, we were taking down the pictures.

"What do you think of that?" I asked Athelbert.

" 'Stag at Bay'?" he said. "I can't see any bay."

"Do you like this one, 'Monarch of the Glen'? Or 'A Faithful Friend'? Does that convey any message to you? See the noble dog keeping vigil over the little child on the river bank; doesn't it stir you?"

" 'Sfar as I can see," replied Athelbert, peering at it, "the dorg is an 'arf-bred Shetland pony which, 'aving bitten the kid to death, is now waitin' to get his breath back."

"Sling it in the van," I said, wearily. Athelbert has no soul for Art. He doesn't even like Wep's drawings. That'll show you how low he's risen.

We had to blast the wall of the diningroom to get the sideboard out. When the smoke had cleared away we couldn't find the sideboard. This saved a great deal of trouble. But it was the piano which was the bedbug. All right, bugbear. Have it your own way.

After I'd been juggling with it for ten minutes I let it drop, and, wiping the sweat from my brow, inquired of the householder as to the whereabouts of my grandfather.

"He is under the piano," he replied in a weak voice.

Just like Athelbert. He always was fond of music. He was a bugler at the battle of Waterloo, and so infuriated the troops by indiscriminate bugling that they rose in their wrath and, failing to catch Athelbert, fell upon the enemy and smote them wondrously.

After I had extricated Athelbert I went into consultation with him. Ever been in consultation? Beautiful place. Drives, date palms, mosques, mosquitoes, pyramids. . . .

However, he suggested that he should get the piano out by sections, taking the white keys first, then the black ones, strings, pedals, etceteras, and, as he pointed out, by the time we'd got the main parts out whatever was left over could be put into a bag and slung over the balcony.

"Have you got an axe?" I asked the householder.

"I wish I had," he replied in what I thought was a rather ominous manner.

We procured a saw and converted the piano into two harmoniums. At this stage Athelbert had a marvellous idea. Seeing that we had blown the wall out of the dining-room, why not back the van into the house and just shovel everything into it?

Our brakes are not too good, and one of the mudguards got wedged in the kitchen sink, necessitating the removal of the sink, but, as I explained to the man we were moving, there was bound to be a sink where he was going so it made no difference. Getting out of the van, I inadvertently smashed the wardrobe mirror.

"That's seven years' bad luck!" I sighed.

"Smash another eight and then you'll know what to expect!" said Athelbert. "Save yer livin' a life of futile optimism. 'Smatter of fact," he added, "there's only one mirror left. All the rest seem to have got broke!"

"Smash it," I said. "It looks too untidy among the others."

We had a bit of a fight about who was going to take up the carpets. You never know in the removal game what you'll find under carpets.

We found two pawn tickets, a cash order book which was a complete surprise to the husband of the house, and a letter which my grandfather was reading out aloud when the householder snatched it from him. People have no manners these days.

There was some difficulty in getting the linoleum off the dining-room floor because the lorry was on it, but we managed to cut around the lorry and got quite a lot of it. Mostly in small pieces, but very handy for tacking on shelves and in cupboards.

Unfortunately there were a frightful lot of doors left over when we had finished. Have you ever counted the doors in your house? It's surprising, when you get them all in a heap, how many there are. And they look much bigger lying down than when standing up.

Talk about fun getting the van out of the house! Laugh! I thought I'd die. Wish you'd been there. Part of the balcony fell on Athelbert, and just as we were bumping over the kerb on to the roadway, all the furniture fell off the van.

The man who owned the furniture, he was laughing, too—laughing and crying at the same time. A strange sight. When I asked him for the £3/10/-, he trembled all over and broke down. He seemed to be upset. Didn't like leaving his old home, I suppose. He had a look at his furniture and then asked me if he could sleep in the van for the night. I covered him over with a piece of linoleum and left him to sob himself to sleep.

Do you know, for weeks after we had moved that man we kept finding odd pieces of chair and things in corners of the van.

We are still in business, and if any of you want to make a bolt for it remember "Lower and Lower. Civility, courtesy, cleanliness, promptitude and despatch."

Don't rush your orders in too early, as my grandfather is suffering at the moment from acute balcony of the neck.

Come On In — It's Just Divine

They tell me there's been a shortage of water in various parts of Australia. They should get me on the job. I was once a water diviner.

It was I who discovered the Burrinjuck Dam. I was walking along one day idly swinging my divining rod when the thing started barking like mad and pulling me along. I'd only gone half a mile, and sure enough there was the dam.

Of course, that's operating on a large scale. The beginner can get quite a lot of practice at home.

Supposing you've only been living in the house a few months and you don't know where the bathroom is, not having been there before. That's where the divining rod comes in handy. You've got to be an expert, though, otherwise you'll finish up in the kitchen sink.

And another thing. You've got to be very careful when using the rod in the house.

With so many water-pipes about, the thing is likely to go mad and dash all over the house knocking the furniture down.

I took it into an hotel bar once. The thing dragged me straight out the door again and stood me over a horse trough. Then I went back to the bar. I hadn't been in the hotel bar five minutes when there was a terrific commotion outside and a horse and cart came charging through the door and finished up on top of the cash register. Then the driver came in and said, "Who owns that thing in the trough that bit my horse?" And the publican said: "You take your blank blank horse off my cash register!" I saw that there might be some unpleasantness, so I left, dragged the stick out of the trough by main force and hurried off somewhere else.

Some say that it is the electricity in one's body that helps to make a good water diviner. Well, at the time of speaking, you could light lamps off me. They call me Illuminated Lennie down our street.

The main thing in water divining apart from electricity is confidence and faith in one's own ability. But you can overdo things in the divining business just as you can in anything else. After one of my clients had been boring for about a month without results he started to complain. I studied the problem and found that his farm in N.S.W. was right over Lake Geneva in Switzerland. After I had explained this to the farmer he apologized and went on boring. I believe he's still boring.

That is the only case of long distance divining I've heard of in this country.

Water is not the only thing you can divine. I was walking across a paddock on a dairy farm one day when the stick gave a sudden jerk and left my hand. It chased those cows for three days and they had to be fed by throwing bunches of grass at them as they went past.

Our milkman used to get quite offended when the stick rushed up the street each morning and clung to his cart. Reckoned it was ruining his business. He said that people were beginning to talk and that his cows had to drink water, so how could he help it if there was water in the milk? It was only natural, he said. I promised to keep the stick chained up until he'd finished his rounds.

There's a great future for water diviners in Australia. The work is pleasant, remunerative, and of benefit to the country. Perhaps you are casting around for a not too overcrowded profession for your son? Send for my booklet, *Water Divining—How It's Done*, by Professor Aqua Pura, celebrated Arabian water-finder.

Practice divining rods supplied free and repairs made at a nominal fee. Free practice bottle of water with each rod. What could be fairer than that? Hop in early! Don't let your son grow up to look back wistfully over the wasted years and mutter to himself: "If only my parents had made me a water-diviner — how different my life might have been!"

The time to act is now! You know the address. Just send in your application.

Yippee, I'm A Drover!

Gimme my boots and saddle! One of the greatest cattle-droving undertakings in Australian history is about to take the road. Some of the cattle will travel two thousand miles, and will be many months on the road.

Once again I feel the urge to have a good horse under me—which is a damned sight better than having it on top of you, as any cowboy knows.

Mark you! This is no game for mugs. If you have ever tried to round up a couple of fowls in the back yard around about Christmas time, you'll know what I mean. There's over thirty-two thousand head of cattle in this mob. From my experience of cattle-droving this should call for about sixty-four thousand drovers, apart from cooks, vets, SP men, ukulele players, two-up ring keepers, fight-settlers, bosses, jackeroos, horse-breakers, abos, swaggies who are going that way and the inevitable journalist or book-writer who will wish himself on to the company.

That looks like a job for me, by the way. Or, perhaps, I might be more useful as a stockwhip cracker. I use a fairly long whip. After I flick it—it's all in the wrist work—you don't hear the crack until about twenty minutes later. Of course, a man would need a longer whip than that even, for such a big mob. A man would have to get up at dawn so that the lash would crack up near the leaders about midday.

Then there's always the possibility of a stampede. There'd have to be somebody up in front to push 'em back if this happened. In the U.S.A. where I once went to demonstrate my method of stopping cattle without the use of the lariat, there were only three thousand head in the mob. It was an easy matter to smack down the first rush of bulls in the front ranks and that usually jarred the whole mob right through to the last straggling heifer in the rear. But, boy! Does it make your knuckles sore!

I think I'm getting too old for that now. They'd probably put me somewhere at the back. The only trouble about this is that a man would never have any breakfast. By the time a man got up to the nearest scran-wagon it would be just nice time to help wash up the dixies after dinner.

Of course one could live on dingoes and the like, but I've been reading about the spread of dingo fever lately, and I understand that it's worse than malaria.

That is another thing. The matter of supplies—fresh fish and lettuce and strawberries and all that.

Certainly there'd be no shortage of meat, but there's a catch in that, too. No conscientious drover would deliver a mob of cattle with most of their rumps and sirloins missing, and vealers with most of their chops removed. Apart from the untidy look of the thing, it's unprofessional. Not done.

What's more, I sincerely trust that any cow-bells attached to the animals will be removed at the start. I can stand a lot, but 32,000 cow-bells—No! I have heard the equivalent of 32,000 cow-bells on some Sunday mornings when the telephone rang, but in that case you can lift the receiver off and stagger back to your bed and resume your ice-pack in peace.

Getting up in the morning is another difficulty. Or maybe the difficulty would be in not getting up in the morning. You can't wind up a cow so that its cow-bell goes off at 6.30 a.m., or whatever it is. With a cow that suffers from getting up at nights and all that, one would never get any rest at all.

Speaking as an old-time stockman I will say that I will have no regrets if the old droving days come to an end.

"How?" you ask in your naïve way.

Well, my dear old boy, wouldn't it be much easier to can these animals on the spot and just post them or carry them to their destination in cars? A can of bully beef is much more tractable than a live bull. I suppose the suggestion comes too late now, but I think it should be kept in mind for some future occasion.

Anyhow, I'll bet that the boys who push the brooms and little barrows for our City Council are glad that this mob of cattle aren't being driven to the canneries via George Street.

Weather Or Not ?

One of the world's commonest topics is the state of the weather. Now, isn't it? Why is it then that we have so few trained meteorologists?

You never see a fond mother patting her little son on the dome and saying: "When he grows up he's going to be a meteorologist." Why? It's nice, clean, easy work. I don't know why I gave it up, except perhaps because there was not much money in it.

Take a simple thing like a wind gauge! What use is it, you might ask. What does it mean in my life?

Well, supposing there is a gale blowing where you are. You take a glance at the wind gauge and find that the wind is blowing at seventy miles an hour. That works out at— No, make it sixty miles an hour. That works out at a mile a minute. By simply walking backwards for two hours one would find oneself in a complete calm with the gale one hundred and twenty miles away. This shows you the practical nature of meteorology.

Then there is the rain gauge. No home should be without one. All that is needed is a tin can measured off in various places. It is best to have a fairly large tin because a small tin would get full too quickly and have to be emptied out, thus interfering with the calculations. Also, the tin should be raised a few feet from the ground, otherwise the dog might drink the entire week's rainfall.

Another instrument which should be studied is the barometer. This instrument is not for people of weak intelligence, nor for those of weak will-power. My own barometer has remained at "Set Fair" for the past twelve years through rain, hail, lightning, tornadoes, and blizzards. That's where the will-power comes in.

You've got to believe the thing or revert to the Dark Ages when they didn't have barometers to tell them if it was raining.

Thermometers are a different proposition. You need never travel abroad while you have a thermometer. Hang it near the kitchen stove and you're in the tropics. Lock it in the ice-chest and you're in Siberia so far as the thermometer is concerned.

One must adopt the right attitude towards these things, especially seismographs. These are very misleading. One judges by the needle markings on the chart that there is an earthquake in the vicinity of Siam. This is exciting news until you find out they're drilling the foundations of a new block of flats in the next street.

I will not speak of the barograph because I am not sure what it is.

We shall dismiss the sundial, too. I had a look at one this afternoon and it was an hour and a half fast by my watch and the park loungers seemed to be the only people who found any use for it. They were leaning on it.

Now what else is there? Egg-timers. We used to call them hourglasses in my day. They are full of sand at one end and nothing at the other end. The sand runs from the bottom of the instrument to the top when it is turned upside down, and from the top part of the bottom section when reversed, if you follow what I mean. This proves that an egg is cooked in three minutes. By having two egg-timers it is possible to cook an egg in one and a half minutes.

Strictly speaking, this is not meteorology, but it is so close to it that it doesn't matter. Like astrology! If you're born under the sign of Cancer the Scorpion your lucky number is twelve, and you should transact all important business on the ninth, or sooner, and beware of red-headed men over forty. Only Jupiter is in the ascendant.

I will now deal with telescopy. This is the best part of meteorology, astronomy, and astrology, and is one of the pure sciences.

Telescopy needs indomitable determination and fortitude. No man who has not lurked in a well-equipped observatory watching the transit of Venus can ever realize the thrill of waking up just when the thing is all over.

Astronomy is a neglected science. You read a report: "At approximately three-forty-eight a.m. the planet Saturn will be visible in the Western Hemisphere; this being the first occasion for three million years and eight months." What can you say to that? What I say is: "Go on! It just goes to show. I see Ajax has been scratched again." Nobody takes any notice of astronomical matters these days. Mention stars to people and they immediately start talking about Greta Garbo and Clark Gable.

Anyhow, I'm going to sell my telescope. I've just had a tooth filled. I mustn't eat for four hours, and my lucky month is September—— Oh, what's the use? Tomorrow will be fine with a slight breeze in the early afternoon from the N.N.E. The time now is three p.m. The moisture content around here is nil. Isn't it awful?

How To Settle Your Boy In A Career

Now that the school examinations are over and young Arburthnot has got his certificate, what am I going to do with him? I suppose many fathers and mothers are on the same raft.

I can't have him lounging around polishing telegraph poles with the back of his coat and cadging shillings from me every five minutes.

I suggested that he might get a job as an Indian in the Indian Army. But he merely sniffed at this. He has filled in an application form for a job in the Civil Service, but he will probably be an old man before he gets any reply. The whole situation is very difficult. I don't want to get him into one of those dead-end occupations like being a Prime Minister and just sitting at a desk loafing the hours away.

He seems to show a leaning towards engineering, having already irrevocably ruined two clocks. On the other hand he might be successful in the radio field, as he has taken our wireless set to pieces. He doesn't know how to put it together again, but he explained to me that that was a separate job entirely and he couldn't be expected to know everything. It sounded reasonable enough to me, but our wireless set is still spread all over the house.

His mother, of course, wants him to be a doctor. I don't know why it is that women always want their sons to be doctors. Arburthnot, if I know anything about him, would be up on a charge of manslaughter after his first case.

He mumbled something to me about wanting to be a radiologist, and I agreed that it would be a very nice occupation for him until I found out that he thought a radiologist was a crooner on the radio. There's been enough tragedy in our family already.

I have a lawyer friend who would give Arburthnot a job while he studied law, but I don't think he'd last the distance. He'd want to start saving people from the gallows or a fate worse than death straight away.

"What would you like to have a smack at, my son?" I asked him. He said, "I wanna be a sailor!" Just like his Dad.

"Oh, don't be a sailor, Arburthnot!" wailed his mother. "Your father was a sailor and look what it's done to him. All he got out of it was a lot of bad habits and tattoo marks!"

"Waddyer mean!" I exclaimed angrily.

"What about that time you were in Samoa? And when you started that brawl in San Francisco? And what about——"

"Belay!" I said, returning inadvertently to my old nautical manner.

"Tell me about the brawl in San Francisco, Dad," said Arburthnot, with his eyes glistening.

"There you are!" I said to the wife. "Now you've done it. Why can't you shut up? Now he'll want to go straight to San Francisco and start a riot." It's astonishing what little sense some women have when it comes to dealing with boys.

"You wouldn't like to be a journalist and work on a newspaper, would you, my boy?" I asked, patting him on the head.

"Don't you dare suggest it!" cried his mother. "Your own son —and you want to make him a newspaper writer! Have you no shame? There's sufficient depravity in this family already. *Two* journalists in the house! I couldn't bear it."

"Well, that's that, Arburthnot," I said.

"I don't think I'll ever get married," he replied thoughtfully.

"What do you mean!" said his mother.

"Aw, nothin'," said Arburthnot.

He's a great boy. A big help to me at times. I just gave the wife a triumphant look and walked out of the room.

But still, although that sort of thing gives the boy a grounding in domestic science, it doesn't help him to establish a career.

It's hard to know what to do. Here's the boy with his foot on the threshold of life, so to speak, and he can either march proudly out into the world or else trip over the aforesaid threshold and land on his ear.

Parents have a very grave responsibility. It was all right when Arburthnot was younger. Any difficulties could be solved by belting him on the chin and telling him to shut up and get on with his homework. I can't do that now.

You know how you lie in bed and talk to each other.

"Well, anyhow, if it comes to that, what opportunities did I have as a boy? None. Yet sheer grit and determination won the day. If that boy is anything at all like his father——"

"He'll be in gaol within a fortnight."

"Ah, what's the use of talking to you! Can't talk sense to some people. I'm going to sleep. Goodnight."

"I suppose you want to see him selling boot-laces in bar-rooms?"

"Goodnight."

"A lot you care. Any other father would see that his son——"

"Ah, shut up! Go to sleep."

"Do you think I can go to sleep when my son——"

"Good-night!"

"When my son has no future to look forward to? *You* are the one who is supposed to have so many influential friends in town. Ha! Ha! It makes me laugh."

"Listen! If you don't stop talking at me I'm going to get up and go and sleep on the lounge."

"That's right. Sing out at the top of your voice. You don't want to go to sleep, so everybody else must stay awake. And another thing——"

So I have to go and sleep on the lounge, folded up like a penknife.

We still don't know what to do about Arburthnot. He'll probably finish up as a bottle-oh's rouseabout.

8 Is There An Elf On Your Shelf?

*The do-it-your-sylph movement has spread even to
fairyland. Our special correspondent behind
the magic curtain reports on little giants who work
in biscuit factories, witches who train
plumbers, black dwarfs who keep vultures in
the bathroom, and other matters of municipal interest.*

A Grim Fairy Tale

This story concerns a little girl called Emily who lived in great squalor with her parents in the back yard of a disused iron foundry.

Emily's main joy was a little flower which she had nursed since it was a pup. One day she was digging around it, and mulching it, and prodding it when a wee, small voice said, "Hoi!"

"Lay off!" said the voice again.

Emily looked up and there, peeping out of the flower, was a dear little fairy.

"Say!" said the fairy. "Would you like me to cast a spell over you?"

"Sure! Throw it all over me. I haven't had any fun since the boy friend sold his motor-cycle."

Whereupon Emily felt herself getting smaller and smaller. Presently the fairy took her by the hand and led her into an old water-pipe.

"Where's this go to?" she asked.

"Fairyland," replied the little oaf . . . or rather, elf.

"You want to watch out for ogres coming around this bend. They're been pretty thick about here lately. As a matter of fact, things are pretty unsettled in these parts. Somebody pinched the wicked witch's wristlet watch."

"The wicish writches wash?"

"Oh, forget it!" said the elf. "What's the use of putting you under a spell when you can't spell? Here's the Fairy Queen. Good morning, Your Majesty!"

"Hullo, elf. How's yourself? Whom have we here?"

"This is little Emily."

"Welcome to our fair city, Emily. Don't take any notice of this cut over my eye. We had a bit of a party here last night. Come into the castle."

"What castle?" asked Emily, looking around.

"This castle," said the Fairy, waving her wand, and immediately a castle sprang up out of the ground.

"That's clever," said Emily.

"Phooey!" said the Queen. "You ain't seen nothin' yet. It's the wand that does it. See, it has a corkscrew at one end and a bottle-opener at the other. It can also be used as a folding camp-stool or a bicycle."

With a loud roar an ogre leapt out of a hole in the ground and the Queen dropped her wand and ran like mad. Emily picked up the wand, hit the ogre fair between the eyes with it and uttered the magic word, "SCRAM!"

The ogre went deathly pale and slunk away. Still clutching the wand, Emily retraced her steps along the gas pipe until she found herself once more in her own back yard. "This is where I get rid of a few of my inhibitions," she muttered to herself.

Her stepfather, catching sight of her, said, "Where the devil have you been?"

"Bingo!" said Emily, waving the wand at him. He immediately turned into a nail-file.

"Well, that's not a bad start," muttered Emily to herself. "It looks as if I might be able to coax a bit of glamour into my life with this thing."

"Emily!" bawled her mother from the door of the kitchen. "Come and finish this washing-up."

"That's just pie to me," said Emily, swishing the wand. "Bingo!" Straight away all the dishes were washed and dried and stacked away.

"Well, I'll be blowed!" said Emily's mother.

"S'easy," said Emily.

"Well, I wish you'd 'bingo' that loafing stepfather of yours. The landlord will be here any minute and we haven't a penny in the house."

"My stepfather has already been 'bingoed', but if you want to see me practise a bit of plain and fancy bingoing on the landlord just step this way. He's at the door now." Emily went and opened the door.

"I've called for the rent," said the landlord, gnashing his teeth, "and when I say I've called for the rent I don't mean maybe."

"Bingo," said Emily softly, and a remarkable change came over the landlord.

"Well, if it's not little Emily!" he said, smiling all over his face. "Have a chocolate, little girl. I was saving them up for my sick grandmother, but I think she can be sick enough without them."

"For the love of Mike!" said Emily's mother. "Bingo him again to make sure of him."

"Bingo!" said Emily again. The landlord burst into tears and said how ashamed he was of himself.

"Well, that's that," said Emily, closing the door on him.

"I see vast possibilities in that there wand," said Emily's mother.

"This," said Emily, "is where we women come into our own."

Isn't it wonderful? I mean wanderful.

Abracadabra And A Biscuit-Biting Giant

Once upon a time there was a small giant who worked in a biscuit factory. His job was to put the fancy edges on the more expensive biscuits, which he did by carefully and symmetrically nibbling them around the edges. Naturally, after some months he became full of small particles of biscuit.

One day the foreman, who in his spare time was a six-day bicycle rider, came to George (the giant's name was George) and said, "We've got a rush order for two hundred tins of our Ootsy Tootsy Specials. Spring to it!"

Well, these Oootsy Tootsy Specials were biscuits with a hole in the middle filled up with jam or jelly. And biting a round hole in the middle of a biscuit without touching the edges is a pretty ticklish job. So George rebelled.

"I'm fed-up with biscuits!" said George—which was no more than the truth.

"Very well," said the foreman. "You're sacked, dismissed, relieved of your duties and fired." The foreman always liked to do things thoroughly.

George the Giant then took a deep breath and told the foreman what he'd been wanting to tell him for months and months, and then, donning his coat and hat, strode out of the biscuit factory and back to his boarding-house which was kept by an old witch called Geranium.

"You're home early today!" she cackled, as George entered the house.

She couldn't help cackling. I think her adenoids had a lot to do with it. They say that a teaspoonful of honey and sulphur three times a day will prevent this. I can't vouch for it, but that's what I was told. Of course, if you were to listen to all you were told—*Sorry.*

"Yes," replied George proudly. "I'm sacked!"

"Ho!" said the witch.

Now this witch was no mug. You can't possibly be a witch, run a boarding-house, and be a mug all at the same time. "And what do you intend to do?" she asked in that frigid, antimacassar tone which is heard from landladies on such occasions.

"Oh, something will turn up," said George, airily. Worst thing he could have said.

"Look me in the eye," said the witch, whereupon she cast a spell over him. You can't trust women.

"You will stay in your room," said Mrs. Geranium.

"O.K.," said George.

Mrs. Geranium then disappeared in a cloud of pink smoke. She was always doing that, but George was used to it.

The smoke had hardly died away when George heard a soft tapping on the door. "It is I," said a soft little voice. "The girl who sat next to you at breakfast this morning."

"Ha!" said George. "Come right inside."

And in came the Fairy Queen! " Hush!" she said, gently closing the door behind her.

Have you ever noticed how, in all books, people coming into a room always gently close the door behind them? I suppose the reason for this is that if they closed the door in front of themselves they'd still be outside.

Anyhow, the Fairy Queen is in the room with the giant. The witch is downstairs in the kitchen boiling abracadabras in a cauldron. Good. I think we were up to "Hush!"

"I have heard all," said the Fairy Queen to George. "She has bewitched you. Come, take my hand. I will lead you away."

"Lead me away," said George, popping his eyes in and out.

"I can see," said the Fairy Queen in her low, sweet voice, "that you have been bewitched by that old witch."

Suddenly the door burst open. "Ha!" said Mrs. Geranium. "Nice goings on! Nothing like this has ever happened in my 'ouse before. What have you got to say for yourself, my young lady? If you can call yourself a lady."

"You've bewitched this man," said the fairy, pointing to the giant.

"And what about it?" said the witch, folding her arms. It looked like developing into a first-class row.

"Now listen, you girls," commenced the giant. I told you before that he had no tact.

"You!" they both said together.

"It's a pity you didn't go out and look for some work, you biscuit-biting loafer," said the Fairy Queen. "You're nothing but a parachute!"

"I was just trying to tell you——"

"Pah!" said the witch. "Come on, dearie," she said, taking the Fairy Queen by the arm. "Come and have a cup of abracadabra down in the kitchen."

"Men!" sneered the Fairy Queen bitterly, as they made their way to the kitchen.

"They're all the same," said the witch.

And in his room the giant scratched his left ear and said, "Well, I'm hanged if I know. There doesn't seem to be much difference between witches and fairies after all."

Which was a very profound remark. Ask your husband if I'm right.

Plumbob, The Magic Plumber

I must tell you about a most remarkable man—a plumber. His father was also a plumber, and had him christened Plumbob, but most people just called him Bob.

Some of those present may raise the point that there is nothing remarkable about plumbers. I will admit that; but Bob was different. By the way, his surname was Waterhouse.

He was handicapped early in life by being born very young, and for a number of months he was unable to walk and had to be carried about by his mother. Waterhouse, with indomitable courage, eventually overcame this difficulty. He even, of his own accord, laid on a hot and cold water system in his perambulator. His father used to give him a soldering-iron to suck and made him a teething-ring out of a length of gas-pipe. I am telling you this so you will understand that this man was a born plumber.

BUT—his mother, Waratah Waterhouse, was a very superstitious woman, and now that I look back I can see that she was the cause of all Bob's trouble. She consulted the local witch—you guessed this was coming, I suppose—and the witch advised her that if she wanted her son to be a really marvellous plumber she must bury a chop-bone in the churchyard at the full moon, together with one of her husband's bootlaces. It seems absurd, viewing it in the light of modern science, but "there are more things in Heaven and Earth than ever you dreamed on, Horatio" *(Henry Lawson)*.

Mrs. Waterhouse faithfully followed the witch's advice, and the results were astounding. Bob became a plumber practically overnight.

Of course, judging by the way one of them fixed our bath-heater, this is nothing unusual, but Bob became a real, super, streamlined plumber. What's more—this is the important point of the whole narrative—he was a magic plumber. He could make things leak just by waving a spanner at them. His father had taught him the fundamental ethics of plumbing.

"My boy!" he said, "uphold the traditions of the Waterhouses. When sent for to repair a leaky tap, make as much mess as possible, look suspiciously at the gas stove, smack it with a hammer in a vital spot and say, 'You should have had this fixed up long ago. You must have a pretty heavy gas bill, Mrs. Jones?'

" 'Oh, you've no idea!' she'll say. There is no one on this earth, my boy, who doesn't complain about his or her gas bill. It's a sure winner."

Shortly after this Bob received an urgent call. Waterpipes had burst and the house was flooded, said the customer. The gas pipes had also sprung a leak.

So Bob went to the races that day and the next day he went along to the house to have a look at things. He didn't have his tools with him at the time, so he said he'd be back the next day.

So far, as you may have noticed, he was behaving like any ordinary plumber. But the next day—what a difference! Bob arrived with two assistants and enough tools to build a battleship, and in no time—say, about four hours, not counting time off for afternoon tea—he had everything fixed.

There was a bit of an outcry about this from the Plumbers' Union, which resented these speed-up tactics, but Bob ignored them—or it. *Take your pick. A man in my job should know his grammar, but do I? Echo answers, "He don't!"*

I don't suppose you know anything about wiping a joint? No. I thought not. Anyway, it has nothing to do with cooking. As an ex-plumber, I will explain. You know those swollen, knob-things on waterpipes half-way up the wall? Well, all you have to do with them is slam on some kind of hot metal—melted-down saucepans, or something like that—and then you get a piece of thick rag and rub it all over the joint, and there you are. Easy!

It was very sad about Bob. He was a comparatively young man when he met his death. *Just a moment while I check up. No. He can't meet his death yet. I've got a bit more to go. Hang on. Won't be long now.*

He was doing a bit of guttering for a customer whose down-pipes had become cluttered up. You always find when the down-pipe is blocked that the guttering is full of birds' nests and tennis balls and pieces of newspapers.

Bob was on the roof this day examining the guttering and poking holes through the rusty parts with a screw-driver, so that he could say that entirely new guttering would be needed, when he lost his footing and crashed twelve feet to his doom.

The funeral was fine. Bob's ashes were put in a wash-basin and placed in a niche in the wall of the gasworks. Beneath the niche is a small brass plate bearing the inscription:

> *Here lies Plumber Bob.*
> *He died doing his job.*
> *Compliments from the mob.*

If that's not sad, what is?

The Goldfish And The Three Vultures

There once was a black dwarf called Basil D. Marmaduke Jones, who used to keep three vultures in his bathroom. He kept the three vultures in his bathroom in an effort to reduce the number of goldfish which infested the wash-basin.

If any officious naturalist wants to rush in with a denial that vultures eat goldfish, I would like to say that these were a different kind of vulture.

As time went on the goldfish developed a combative nature and started grabbing the vultures by the throat and holding them down in the wash-basin until they drowned.

Basil D. Marmaduke Jones was torn between his devotion to his vultures and his interest in the goldfish. His uncle, Aubrey Montmerency Jones, viewed the whole business with disfavour. He said that if young Jones insisted on being fish-minded why didn't he follow the precedent set by the British House of Parliament, where they have a Keeper of the Seals and a Lord Privy Seal?

You can imagine how this annoyed young Jones. He wanted to know how he was going to keep seals in his wash-basin and generally kicked up such a row that his uncle said that he would never darken Basil's door again. His aunt also said, "Don't talk to the boy like that!" You know how things start.

Anyway, just as Aubrey Jones got to the door, Basil said, "Stop!"

His uncle paused in the doorway with one foot in the air. "Take this spell off me!" he roared. "Making a man look ridiculous in front of everybody in the street!"

"Oh, all right," said Basil, who was a good-natured chap at heart. Then suddenly he turned pale. (*I thought you said he was black? Well, he turned a pale black. Anyhow, if it comes to that, who's writing this blinkin' story?*)

"My goodness!" he exclaimed, "I do believe I've forgotten the magic words!"

"What!" screamed his uncle. "Have I got to be stuck here like this for life?"

"Seems like it," said Basil. "I suppose I'll have to use the back door now that you're blocking up the front one. Terrible nuisance. I'll be around to feed you after I've fed the goldfish."

This well-meant remark only enraged the uncle more than ever. "Nice state of affairs!" he roared. "Running second to a goldfish! And I want a shave before I have my lunch!"

By this time a large crowd had collected in the street, blocking the traffic. Two policemen pushed their way through the gathering and one said, " 'Ere! Wot's goin' on 'ere?" And the other said, "Wot's all this? Makin' a public nuisance of yourself."

"And disturbing the peace," said the second policeman, getting out his notebook and pencil.

"And resisting arrest," said the first policeman as he tried to shift the immovable Aubrey off the doorstep.

"I'm not resisting arrest, you mugs! I can't move!" yelled Aubrey.

"Language," said the first constable, wetting his pencil. "We'll think of some more on the way to the station. The thing is—how are we going to get him off this here doorstep? He seems to be stuck."

"We'll have to get a couple of crowbars and a lorry and take him away, doorstep and all."

By this time Uncle Aubrey was quite speechless, and could only make queer, gurgling noises, but eventually a breakdown gang levered up the doorstep and Uncle Aubrey was loaded on to the lorry.

Basil followed in a P.D. car. On the way he had a brilliant idea. "Excuse me," he said to the sergeant next to him, "I have a brilliant idea."

"We've got no use for brilliant ideas in the police force," said the sergeant, gruffly.

"But this is so simple that even the police force might see it. Why not unlace his boots and lift him out of them?"

The sergeant was impressed but didn't intend to show it. "The best thing you can do," he growled, "is to mind your own business or you'll be getting yourself into trouble. As a matter of fact, I think you're in trouble already."

"What for?" asked Basil.

"Being in possession of goldfish and vultures without a licence."

Basil's cup of sorrow was full, but when they unlaced Uncle

Aubrey's boots at the police station and lifted him out of them, he felt much better.

Aubrey was subsequently fined £15 with costs and the boots and the doorstep were forfeited to the Crown.

Basil and Aubrey get on very well together now. Aubrey seems to have learned his lesson and has become very subdued. He even helps to feed the goldfish.

But he always leaves the house by the window now. He has a horror of doorsteps.

Which Witch Worried The Blacksmith?

Under the village doughnut tree,
The village baker bakes.
With soggy bread and cakes like lead,
The man his living makes.

What we need for this is grit and determination. Like a fowl laying an egg.

Anyhow, there was a blacksmith by the name of Izzy Isaacberg who kept a modest blacksmith's shop in one of the outer suburbs. It was near a school and the scholars, released from this den, used to crowd around and look in at the open door. It seemed that they liked to sticky-beak into the open door and hear the bellows roar.

This blacksmith had the effrontery to look the whole world in the face because he claimed that he owed not any man. This must have made him a bigger attraction for tourists than the Dionne quintuplets.

I'll admit that so far this is not a fairy-story. But have I ever let you down?

One day, when the village blacksmith was sweating his brow off at the forge an elf staggered into the place with a sprained pastern.

"Marry!" cried the blacksmith. "Zounds! This is a pretty pass. How now, good elf. Have at thee, knave!" That comes from something I read at school. But forget it!

INTERVAL

I just thought of that one. I'll be back in a few minutes.

"What did you want?" said the blacksmith on his return.

"I've got a moose out here that needs shoeing."

"We are not amoosed," replied the blacksmith.

"You'll shoe this animal—or elks!"

But this story is to be read to children. I always forget.

Well, the blacksmith was a very strong and sturdy man. His face was like the tan, if I remember rightly, and the muscles on his brawny arms stood out like brass bands. They stood nearly as far out as the Philharmonic Orchestra.

He said, "Well, my good elf, I will shoe your moose if you can remove the curse put upon me by the old witch over the road."

"What was the nature of the curse?" inquired the elf, idly tossing the anvil in his hand.

"Put that anvil down!" cried the blacksmith.

"I said, 'What was the nature of the curse?' " repeated the dwarf, rolling the anvil into a ball.

"She said I would break out in measles, one spot at a time. What's more, she said that she would have me looking like a set of dominoes before she'd finished with me."

"Sounds bad," said the dwarf. "Rotten anvil you've got. White ants in it. Well, if you like, I'll cast a spell over her."

"It's a deal. You go and throw this spell over her, and I'll shoe your elk free of charge."

"Attaboy!" said the elf, and disappeared. He had a handy habit of disappearing, especially when it was his turn to shout.

Before I go any farther! If, as I suspect, this Isaacberg started off as a baker and finished up as a blacksmith, it's got nothing to do with me. This is a fairy-story. And if there's any more complaints, I'll make him a plasterer. We can regard that as settled.

The elf went across the road and saw an old crone in black bombazine. "I understand that you're the local witch?" he said.

" 'At's me!" replied the witch.

"Well, this is where you get off," said the elf. "Remove the curse from the blacksmith or I'll turn you into a banana."

"*YOU* will! Ha! Ha!"

"Yeah—I will. Ha! Ha!"

At last the witch said to the elf, "What is this blacksmith to you? Is he necessary to your happiness?"

"He's shoeing my elk," said the elf, stubbornly.

Just then a little girl called Rose walked into the shop and ordered a penn'orth of hundreds and thousands. This rather upset the witch. I don't know whether you've ever tried to count out a penn'orth of hundreds and thousands, but it's very difficult. I've done it as a child, and usually found that I was one or two short. That's what's made me so cynical.

"What's going on here!" bawled the blacksmith, stamping into the shop."

This is getting a bit complicated.

"You take this spell off me," bawled the blacksmith, pointing at the witch, "and you," he said, turning to the elf, "come and take your elk away. I'm sick of this. Don't glare at me or I'll tear you apart."

As he strode out the witch sighed and said, "What a man! I must ask him over for a cup of tea."

"That's the finish of the blacksmith," muttered the dwarf, and he went across the road and saddled up his elk and said, "Mush!" And the elk mushed.

Little Jim And The Wizard

The full story of Little Jim, the collier's only son, whose cottage was a thatched one, has never been told. Very well! Uncle Lennie will tell it to you. Ready?

In due time Little Jim also became a collier like his father before him.

On his first day down the mine, he noticed a furtive-looking man staring at him in a strange manner.

"Lldw cwl yolticklylw?" asked Jim of a companion. I forgot to mention that this was a Welsh colliery.

"Shh!" answered his friend. "He might hear you. He's a wizard."

"And what does he do in the mine when he's not wizarding?"

"He sells race tips. We have races down here every day with the pit ponies. Seeing that you'll be in charge of the ponies hauling skips, you'd better watch him."

"Hmm," said Jim, thoughtfully. The evil seed had been sown.

One day, as Jim had expected, the wizard spoke. "Nice pony you've got there," he said.

"She can break even time for seven furlongs and with two tons of coal behind her," replied Jim proudly.

"Poof!" sneered the wizard. "If I had two tons of coal behind me I'd break all records. That nag has got to get a move on or be run over."

"Please yourself," said Jim and as he turned haughtily away he struck his head on a piece of coal jutting from the roof.

He turned on the wizard, his eyes blazing. It's a very foolish thing to let your eyes blaze in a coal-mine, but James was a quick-tempered youth.

"Did you do that?" he cried.

"Yes," said the wizard, calmly.

Every muscle in Jim's body tensed. His jaw jutted out and the veins throbbed in his temples. "I've got a good mind to go and tell the foreman!" he said at last.

"Listen, my boy," said the wizard, tapping Jim on the shoulder with his pick, "the foreman is in my power. And," he added, as he pulled the pick out of Jim's shoulder, "from now on, so are you!"

Poor Jim. One must remember that he was an orphan who had been brought up by parents whose outsides were old and mean. The prospects of riches glittered before him. Forgetting all his earlier training he chose riches. (*Time off, please. I have a visitor. It's all right. She came to the wrong place.*)

As time wore on, what with Jim training the ponies and the wizard acting as the colliery bookmaker, they both became very rich.

Jim, being on the inside, so to speak, and knowing that owing to strikes, stoppages, stop-work meetings and other amenities of the coalfields—knowing as I say that the mine was still chockful of coal, he bought the mine.

Now the wizard, like most wizards, was a niggardly man, and he demanded a half-share in the mine. Jim refused. He had visions of ultimately owning half the township, becoming parliamentary member for the district, and being knighted for buying Government bonds at seven per cent. when the next war broke out.

The wizard was incensed. "After all I've done for you," he said, shaking his diamond cuff-links and prodding the ground with his gold-mounted walking-stick. "Very well! I'll ruin you! Get that? Ruin you!"

Saying which, he climbed into his limousine and was driven away. Jim, feeling in need of exercise, drove home in his six-seater instead of the eight-seater.

In the meantime the wizard addressed a meeting of the Railway Employees' Union and told them that what they wanted was a three-hour week, spread over a fortnight. Next day all trains stopped. The miners had already struck on account of an injustice that had been done to a dairyhand in New Guinea.

Sir James (or Jim) said he would go back to the mine and work the thing himself rather than let the country go short of coal. Enraged, the wizard sought an interview with Sir James.

Nine hundred thousand strikers stood outside Sir James's mansion while the conference was held. Inside, the wizard was saying to Sir James, "So that's your last word? I get twenty thousand down now and five thousand a year? You're a hard man, Sir James."

Shortly after that the wizard appeared on the balcony of Sir James's mansion. "Fellow workers!" he said, holding up his hand.

(Loud cheers.) "Comrades!" he yelled. "I am glad to say that a settlement has been reached and you may all go home to your wives and families."

And that is the story of Little Jim. And, of course, the wizard.

What's In A Gnome ?

There has been some slight ado about fairy tales, and, as usual, I have been called upon to explain things. It has been said that Grimm's fairy tales are too grim. Giants tearing little boys' heads off and munching them with great relish, and cruel stepmothers hurling little children out into the snow. I agree that this sort of thing must stop, but, on the other hand, this wishy-washy stuff about Tootles, the Little Native Bear, and Tessie, the Tortoise, leaves the modern child cold. *What, then, do you suggest, Mr. Lower?*

Well, if you'll just sit here on the edge of the bed, I'll give you some idea of what a good fairy tale should be. You'll find the gin in the wardrobe, if you don't mind drinking out of the soap basin.

Once upon a time there was a retired tram guard who lived in a wood. On the outskirts of the wood lived a family of unemployed giants, all on the dole. One day, while the retired tram guard was out in the woods gathering nuts and May, he turned to May and said: "Have you heard from the Princess Maggie, lately?"

"I had a telegram from her only yesterday," replied May. "It appears that she has been turned into an S.P. bookmaker by a wicked witch."

"A wicked which?" asked the puzzled retired tram guard.

"That's what I said," replied May. Whereupon the retired tram guard was exceedingly bewildered.

However, he decided to go and see the princess himself, so the following day he packed a bottle of lunch and, taking all his money with him, he tramped off to the mountain, which, I forgot to mention, was in the middle of the wood. On his way he met a fairy who was sobbing bitterly.

"Wasser marrer wiz you?" asked the retired tram guard, who had just finished the last drop of his lunch.

"A confounded gnome has just pinched the cigarette card I wanted to make up the full set," sobbed the fairy.

"A gnome?" said the retired tram guard, "would you gnome again if you saw him?"

But the fairy was beside herself with rage and sorrow. Whenever she felt in need of company, she always got beside herself, which is very handy.

"Was it Ronald Colman?" asked the tram guard.

"Yes," sobbed the fairy.

"Here," said the tram guard, giving her some cigarette cards. "Here is a Ronald Colman, a Norma Shearer, and two Marlene Dietriches."

"Oh, bully!" said the fairy delightedly, "You may have any wish you like."

"I wish I was in the palace of the princess," said the retired tram guard, whose name, now I come to think of it, was Jack.

Taking her wand firmly in both hands, the fairy struck Jack a heavy blow on the left temple, and when he came round, there he was in the palace of the princess.

"Your Highness," he said as the Princess approached him.

"It's too late," said the Princess, "you can't get on. They're racing now. And I haven't got the scratchings for the next race, either."

"Wouldn't it drive you mad?" said the King, who had just arrived on the scene. "Whoever can remove the spell on her can have half my kingdom and half my youngest daughter."

"What have you got to do?" asked the tram guard.

"Bump off the witch and make all her fowls die. They lay eggs which hatch out dragoons."

"You mean dragons," said the tram guard.

"How dare you contradict me!" shouted the King in a great rage. "Ho! Varlets! Hurl this hellion into the moat!"

Well, after Jack had dragged himself out of the moat, he set off to find the witch. He found her living in a two-storey boarding house, and she was just packing up to leave, having won first prize in a lottery. "I'm gettin' out of this hole," said the witch. "I'm going to see life, I am. Me for the bright lights. WHOOPEE!"

"What about taking the spell off the Princess before you go?" said Jack.

"Spell, me eye!" said the witch, "she's having the time of her life. I suppose that old pot up at the palace promised you half his kingdom, and his youngest daughter?"

"Half his youngest daughter!" said Jack, who had a passion for correcting people.

"Have you seen the youngest daughter?" asked the witch, whose name was Ethel.

"No!" said Jack.

"Well, you haven't missed much. You've seen most of the kingdom, haven't you? What do you think of it?"

"It seems to be mostly bush!" said the tram guard.

"Listen, son!" said the witch, "forget it. You've got a good face. I like you. You come away with me and we'll hit it up. Got any money?"

"Yes!" said Jack.

"Oke!" said the witch. "Let's go!"

"What about those poor giants on the dole?"

"Boy!" said the witch, "the dole for giants in this State is three thousand a year. Come on!"

So they went away together and lived happily ever afterward, the only catch in it being that Ethel bewitched Jack and turned him into a teetotaller.

I don't know what happened to May. I did hear that she went off with the insurance collector after burning the house down. Bunky doo, children! And what, may I ask, is wrong with that?

Tick That Off!

You don't mind if I let my head go? If you don't get off the leash occasionally you're likely to go raving mad. Which is bad for the neighbours. *We start about here. Hold everything.*

Once upon a time there was a Swish washmaker. *One moment.* There was a Swiss watchmaker, called Carl. He invented a watch which, when worn in the top vest pocket, wound itself up by the palpitation of the heart. *Okay, so far.*

But Carl was ambiguous. *Ambitious—have it your own way.* He was a small, sandy-haired man about 45, with a slight limp and a black apron. He had a male father. He never had a mother. I suppose that warped him a bit. How would you like it? Wouldn't it warp you?

Carl was brooding in his little shop about people not smashing their watches and thus depriving him of a living, when in walked a little girl. Her name was Gravel. *Wipe that off.* Her name was Gristle. Her name was Gretel.

"Well, little Gretel," said the watchmaker, "what can we do for you today?"

"For a start," said little Gretel, "you can take that oily, smug look off your face." This the watchmaker did. They are like that. There are no militant watchmakers. They just drool around in cluttered-up cubicles with a telescope stuck in one eye and tell you to call back next week.

Little Gretel said, "I have here a watch. It will not go. It is sunk with all hands. It has no tick."

"You're telling me?" said Carl. "Neither have I. Hmm! Needs cleaning. What have you been doing to your main-spring? The cam-shaft and piston show signs of wear. You've burned out a big end. Also the carburettor is choked. But we can fix all that."

"When can I get it back?" said Gretel.

"Let me see—ah—this is October."

"Listen!" hissed Gretel. You can hiss a "listen". You can't do it with "Come here, mug." If you must hiss anybody it is a good thing to say, "Listen, you swine!" Good hissing there.

The trouble about giving you readers good advice is that I am not sure whether I am writing about a watch-mender or a car-minder. These extraneous matters tend to side-track one.

Reverting to Carl, the watchmaker. You may have noticed that I have not mentioned anything about getting things on tick. The nicest people don't do that. They leave it to radio celebrities. Poor Carl! He passed out in a manner befitting his profession. He was mending a grandfather clock and the pendulum knocked his brains out.

MORAL: *When inside clocks keep your head down. Then the swing will adjust itself.*

So Fur, So Good

Once upon a time there was a barber who was also a wizard. He didn't take up wizarding seriously until one day it dawned on him that he had hypnotic powers.

A customer would come into the shop for a shave, and the barber would talk and talk and talk until the customer went into a trance. When the customer came to, he would find that not only was he shaved, but he had also had a hair-trim, shampoo, face massage, violet ray, and manicure, and had bought two bottles of hair tonic and a quarter-share in a lottery ticket. Still slightly dazed, he would pay this barber about thirty shillings, and the barber would flick him twice with a clothes-brush and tell him two absolute certainties for the races which invariably ran fifth, and then say, "Necks Bees!"

The average barber is satisfied to let things go at that, but, as I said before, this one was a wizard. He was consulting his ouija-board one night, and it was revealed to him that there were fairies and elves about. He saw one on the mantelpiece. It had a long beard.

He dashed into his shop and had three or four gulps of bay rum, but when he came back to the room the elf was still there. Also a few fairies. They all had beards. Fortified by the bay rum, the barber said:

> *Elf, elf,*
> *Upon the shelf,*
> *Why don't you shave your blasted self?*

"That's what we've come to see you about," said the head elf.

"Righto, girls," he said, waving to the assembled fairies. "Let 'er go!"

The fairies then burst into song.

> *We have a slap-up notion,*
> *It is a magic potion,*
> *It grows hair,*
> *Bristles sprout*
> *Everywhere!*

To which the head elf replied: "All together in the barber's chair."

I'll spare you the rest. The barber sold his soul to the head elf in exchange for the magic potion. "Remember," said the head elf, before vanishing, "your sole is not your hone."

"You mean I can't strop my razor on my boot?" asked the barber.

"That shouldn't worry you, you heel," said the elf, and disappeared.

The next day the barber used the magic lotion. It worked splendidly but—there is always a but in these things—the barber had no soul. This made him mean and avaricious. He was not content to allow the customers to get out of the shop before their beards started to grow again, so he dabbed the lotion on in handfuls. *(Handsful. Thank you.)*

Beards shot out of faces before the customers could get out of the shop. They became jammed in the doorway. The shop was full of whiskers.

Madly the barber fought to stave off the encroaching beards. In vain. Cursing savagely, he tried to fight his way out of the shop, only to be dragged back, baulked, frustrated, and whimpering.

Madly he hurled the bottle of magic lotion through the window. It struck a horrified woman who had been standing in the street looking into the shop. She immediately had a fur coat, a thing she had been wanting for years.

A fire broke out. The barber wanted to charge everybody in the shop for a singe. Mad with rage, one of the customers strangled the barber just as the fire brigade arrived.

Too late. A blackened shell confronted them. "Well," said the captain of the fire brigade, "perhaps it's just as well, considering the water restrictions. It's no use squirting that."

MORAL: *Keep away from fairies. Remember what happened to Samson.*

Meet Jonathan Snow, The Bounder

This is about Jonathan Snow. You remember him?

Jonathan Snow was apprenticed to the barley-stick curling trade at an early age. He might have flourished at this, but unfortunately he developed the pernicious habit of twisting the sticks of barley-sugar to the left, instead of to the right, and was dismissed with ignominy.

But you must remember Jonathan Snow and his epitaph written by an illiterate friend of his which does not make it any the less poignant:

> *Poor Jonathan Snow*
> *Away did go*
> *Over the ragen main.*
> *With other mails*
> *For to catch wails*
> *And ne'er was seen agane.*

Anyway, when Jonathan was dismissed from the barley-stick curling factory with ignominy all he had were the clothes he stood up in and the ignominy which he wore in a chamois-leather bag next his skin.

He was an orphan, of course. All his people were orphans. It was fatal to be a parent in the Snow family, and Jonathan vowed, while still a youth, that he would never become a parent. Later he altered the vow slightly. He vowed he would never own up to being a parent. This saved him a lot of bother in after years.

Snow experienced a number of vicissitudes before his disappearance. He was standing miserably on the waterfront one day when a tall man with a beard approached him.

"Would you like to catch whales?" said the stranger.

"Why? Have you lost some?" asked Snow.

The stranger then slugged Snow with a section of gaspipe and the next thing he knew was that he was at sea in the fo'c'sle of a whaling ship.

The captain was known as Black McGinty, and he had a habit of bashing members of the crew in the face with whatever happened to be handy. Naturally, this made it pretty monotonous for the crew.

Snow, however, was a hardy lad, and soon he was diving overboard strangling whales with his bare hands and tossing them on to the deck.

In an excess of zeal one day he overdid things. He started throwing them aboard two at a time. The ship couldn't take it, and down she went.

That much is known. What happened to Snow has been a mystery up till now.

I am in a position to divulge that Snow is still alive and living in retirement in Australia.

He was washed up on an island. It was the first decent wash-up he'd had for months, and did much to improve his appearance.

Snow found that food was abundant on the island, so he set about building a hut.

Not knowing anything about the native flora, he attempted to chop down a native rubber-tree. The axe rebounded and cut his leg off at the waist, seriously inconveniencing him.

Thereupon he decided to make himself a wooden leg, and gnawed the tree down with his teeth. I told you before he was a hard man.

Once again his choice of timber was unfortunate, because every time he put his artificial leg down he used to bounce into the air. But he soon got used to this.

So long as he landed on his face he was all right. Landing on his feet meant, of course, that he just had to keep on bouncing. His progress was perforce somewhat erratic.

It didn't do his face much good, either, but Jonathan was tough. He could take it. He counted it a lucky day when he could land on something soft.

It was on one of his lucky days that he met a dusky maiden called Oolala.

She saw him bounding about and asked, with quiet dignity, "What's the big idea?"

Jonathan was pink with embarrassment.

"I beg your pardon, blast you!" he said in his rough, seamanlike way.

"You're a bounder!" exclaimed the maiden.

"Too right I am!" said Jonathan, pounding himself on the chest. "I'm the best bounder on this island! Watch me!" He then bounded.

"Marvellous!" cried the maiden. "But tell me, sailor—must you always land on your face?"

"It saves me shaving," he replied, gruffly.

"What a glorious big brute you are!" she cried, her eyes shining. "I feel that I could like you."

"Well," said Jonathan, thoughtfully, "if you do I could pouch a nice plate of steak and eggs." Jonathan had his dull moments.

"I am afraid you don't understand me," said the maiden, coyly.

"Why?" said Jonathan, "haven't you got any steak and eggs?"

"Say!" said the maiden, "do I look like a cafeteria?"

"There's no woman," said Jonathan in his cumbrous way, "that I wouldn't swop for a pie-stall."

A gleam came into his eyes. "Imagine the tomato sauce on the pie. And the steam coming out of it when you jab it in the middle with a fork. And the way the gravy runs down your chin. Oh, boy!"

"You are coarse, low, vulgar, beastly, and beneath contempt," said Oolala.

"Say that again and I'll knock you cold," said Jonathan.

She said it again and he bowled her with a snappy right cross. They were practically as good as married.

Snow is getting old now. He peddles bootlaces and back studs down at the Crown and Anchor. His wife runs a sly-grog shop in the suburbs. All the children are out of work.

Isn't life hell for the poor!

9 Whaling, Chess And Other Indoor Sports

There's sport in Lower's blood, as well as a few lonely corpuscles. No wonder, because his grandfather (q.v.) used to ride a roulette wheel, and his brother was a snakes-and-ladders champ. Lennie's forte was ludo. He won the under forte open.

The Dinkum Oil About Whaling

A lot of people don't know a thing about whales. This, to one who was practically born among whales, is a very serious matter. You might remark that you are never likely to be in need of a whale. But, you never know!

Having settled that part of the matter, let us proceed. The first mention of whales was when a man called Jonah swallowed one. Jonah, as you know, was a lieutenant in the Jewish navy and should have known better.

The catching of whales for commercial purposes is a large and thriving industry. I myself only catch them for sport. The trouble lies in getting them home. The last whale I brought home I had to leave out in the street as it was quite impossible to get it through the front gate. After about three weeks people started to complain. There was such a ridiculous rumpus about it that I have never gone whaling since. However, I don't mind giving anyone interested a few hints.

One needs a few small boats and a mother ship. This last is to put your mother on. The principal instrument used in whaling is the baboon, a barbed instrument something like a spear which is hurled into the side of the whale. One then just hauls the whale in. This is much simpler than fishing for them with ordinary rod and line.

After the catch has been hauled in to the side of the boat, it should be finished off with a belt between the eyes with a hammer and then inflated. Oh, of course, I forgot that you haven't done any whaling. Air is pumped into the carcase in order to make it buoyant.

A curious incident occurred on my last commercial whaling expedition. The man in charge of the air pump deserted his post for some reason or other and the whale burst and blew down the mainmast and the cook's galley. My word, I was annoyed. I was captain at the time, and the crew threatened to resign on the spot because of the language the cook used and the fact that there was no dinner that night.

"What's this I hear about there being no dinner for the men?" I said sternly.

"How can I cook when there's no cook-house?" the cook demanded when I said I'd keel-haul him.

"Get down to the stokehold and do your cooking there."

A quarter of an hour later, the chief engineer came up to me on the bridge. "Captain," he said, "there's trouble below. It's that cook. He insists on cooking the roast mutton in one furnace and baking the potatoes in another. He also says that another furnace is too hot for baking scones and refuses to allow the firemen to go near it, sir, until it gets down to the right temperature for scones. He's holding them off with the meat-chopper, sir.

"What's more, sir, we've lost so much pressure in the boilers through the cook that the engines are likely to stop at any moment."

"All right," I said. "Stop the ship until he's finished."

Just then there was a knock on the door. "Wuff!" I said. It must be explained to the land-lubber that this is a sea captain's way of saying "Come in."

It was the first mate. "I think you should come on deck, sir," he said. "The crew object to sifting the ashes from the stokehold in order to find the dinner. Able Seaman Smell—rather appropriate name for a whaler, what!—has already eaten three lumps of coke, thinking they were potatoes. He complains of severe internal pains, sir."

"Where's the ship's cook?"

"The—er—crew, sir, have lashed him to the end of a rope and are at present dipping him up and down in the bally ocean, sir."

"Outrageous! In about three-quarters of an hour—no, make it an hour—go and order them to cease such brutal treatment immediately. I can't have that kind of thing on my ship."

"No, sir. Very well, sir."

"Just a moment. Is there any tinned stuff aboard—sardines and things like that?"

"I would hesitate, sir, to give a member of the crew of a whaling ship a sardine."

"H'mm. Perhaps you're right, Mister Mate. I suppose I'd better address the crew. Have them muster on deck.

"Men," I said, "I order you all to go back to your work. We will make for the nearest port where we can have steak and eggs, blanc-mange, beer, fruit, rum——"

"Hooray!" they yelled.

Do you know, the way those men worked in the stokehold we hit the wharf with such force that the ship ploughed its way half-way up the town and stopped with its bows just outside the door of the saloon bar of the Senorita Cantata Hotel.

After that I gave up whaling. It's not a pleasant life. I wonder what fool thought of it first.

A Demon Polo Player

Now that the polo season is in full swing I would like to remind you that polo is a game for the idle rich. That's why I gave it up. I may be rich but I'm not idle.

I was first attracted to the game by the spectacle of beautiful ladies draped on the green sward covered all over with rugs and thermos flasks, with bits of leg sticking out here and there, all getting their photos taken for the social section of the papers. It made me ambitious.

I commenced by practising on the billiard table with a Barcelona nut and an ice-pick. I got so efficient that I could hole out in one in the top pocket from the baulk line.

My next step was rather more difficult. I procured a scooter and used to race up and down the hallway with an umbrella handle and a cricket ball, the object being to belt the ball through the front door with the umbrella handle without falling off the scooter. I became so proficient that one morning I caught the landlord fair between the eyes as he was coming up the front steps.

This made me more enthusiastic than ever, and I decided to buy a horse, one of those hammer things with the long handle on it, riding breeches, and a yellow woollen sweater. I also bought a couple of goal-posts, but I found out that this was unnecessary as they have them laid on at the polo grounds.

The idea of the game is this: You all line up facing each other and the umpire throws the ball on to the ground. Then your horse bolts, and while you're clinging on, terror-stricken, the ball comes near you and you lean over, swing your polo stick, and fetch your horse a most awful crack on the shins. You throw that horse away and get another one. That's what makes the game so expensive.

Then there are the chukkas. You're always breaking them or the handle comes off or the lining falls out or something.

I shall never forget the last big game I played in. I was coming down the field like the wind, that is, blowing like mad, with the ball in front of me. "Look out, Ashton!" I cried.

"Great Scott!" he gasped, "it's Demon Lower!" His face went white. Even his horse turned a bit pale. Summoning up all my strength, and believe me it takes a bit of summoning, I swung at the ball, straight for the goal. I didn't get it, which was perhaps just as well, because it was the wrong goal.

The head of my racquet flew off and struck Ashton's horse on the forehead. It gave a low moan, licked Ashton's hand, and then folded up and went prone all over.

"Now look what you've done!" he said.

"You shouldn't have been in the way," I replied. "You know my methods."

Then the umpire came up and said what about getting on with the game, so I picked up the horse and tossed it over the fence, and he got a fresh one.

The concluding part of the game was quite thrilling. Ashton's new horse was a bit too small for him. His feet dragged on the ground, and in moments of excitement he would stand up and the horse would just dash out from underneath him. It slowed the game up a bit until we got used to it.

We were running level at 3-all, when my horse decided to call it a day and rested on its left ear in among the spectators. Nothing daunted, I shouted in clarion tones, "I can play this blooming game without a horse!" and flung myself into the fray. What a game! When I'd finished winning the game for our side the field was strewn with recumbent horses, those of the players who were still capable of running were doing it, and the spectators were falling over each other to get out of the way. That was my last game.

I am sorry in a way that I gave it up because of the social side of the game. I mixed with all the best people at the time, and at polo teas and balls you should have seen the souvenirs I got! I got eight spoons and two cocktail glasses from one place alone. As a matter of fact, I accumulated so much crockery, cutlery, and general hardware that I decided to get married.

I should have stuck to polo, now I come to think of it.

Off To The Olympic Games

I never seem to get any time to myself. Always dashing hither and fro, saving situations. Now it looks as if I'll have to go to the Olympic Games again. One of our lads has a sprained ankle, another has busted his hand; another one has strained an abominable muscle in his abominan—half of them, it seems, are being wheeled about in chairs. Well, I suppose it's got to be done for the prestige of the country, and all that sort of thing.

My wife has nearly finished knitting me a hop, step, and jumper, and I have been practising the standing high jump at home. The standing high jump is the best thing I do. I just stand on top of the wardrobe and jump off. I am going to attack the world's record off the front veranda next Saturday.

I am a bit out of form for swimming, I must admit. The weather has been too cold for training, and it's so awkward swimming in your overcoat. Still, I think I can win the four hundred metres. I used to swim for the Gas Company.

It's the shot pushing event that I'm worried about. Javelin hurling—yes. Hurling the dishes—yes. Hammer throwing—definitely an expert. But shot pushing—no.

My old father said sadly to my Uncle Frederick in 1902, "I'm afraid the lad will never make a shot-pusher." My Uncle Frederick, who was a wealthy locksmith and had made a fortune by inventing a time lock for salmon tins (*I wish you'd come to the point! Dithering about like this. What do you think the public pays its money for?*)—Anyhow, my Uncle Frederick spent thousands of thousands of pounds trying to make me a good shot-pusher, but in vain. I haven't the knack.

Did I tell you I was the best euchre player in the Southern Hemisphere? I fancy I did. Well, the Southern Hemisphere, or the "Old Southern", as the boys call it, has changed hands now, and they've got a new girl in the saloon bar. Daughter of the house, I believe. Never shouts. (*Now, listen!* . . .) All right!

Pole vaulting! Girls, if you could only see me vaulting a pole, just ONCE! You'd be bringing along poles to me and saying, "Oh, do vault this one and autograph it afterwards." I'd just vault it vaultlessly and you'd be tickled pink. I don't mean that in a rude way, you know. I never wait till a girl goes pink before I tickle her. I always find . . . (*Get on with it!*).

Lot of interruptions I've got to put up with. The hurdles? I dare say you hurdle lot about my prowess over hurdles. As a matter of fact, the local athletic club, noting the effortless ease with which I sailed over hurdles, decided that it was useless to put the things about the place, and it was a sheer waste of hurdles. After that I did all my hurdling without hurdles.

One thing I can say confidently. The egg and spoon race is definitely in our grasp. I don't have to expatiate (*Eh?*). I don't have to tell the average well-informed citizen about my ability in this manly sport. Mention the name Lower and immediately one thinks of an egg. Or, in the case of vegetarians, a spoon.

Oh! Before I forget. I've got a new hat! Light grey with a black band. It's swell. I look like a bookmaker. (*I wish you wouldn't . . .*) Righto! Just wanted to let you all know that I've turned the corner as far as hats are concerned.

Getting down to hard facts, I want a masseuse. Blonde for preference. The situation is an honorary one, and applications will be received all next week. I also need a trainer, chaperon, manager, nurse and a driver of a steam roller (this last for the track events;

the track must be in perfect condition for me to put up my best times). I don't know how the devil I'm going to get my trophies home. And another thing. What about when I've just won the high-diving championship and have to dash on to the pole-vaulting arena in my swimming costume on my way to the wrestling tournament? My crikey, I'm going to be busy!

And now I'm going to put it on. "Put what on?" you ask. My new hat. I wish you could see me.

Avalanche ? Well, Alp Yourself

Winter is here again and I suppose we'll still have winter sports. A winter sport which may not appeal to all is to stay in bed or sit in front of the fire with a glass of hot toddy and a good book. That, of course, is a sign of old age and sloth.

Ski-ing is an outstanding winter sport. It consists of toiling strenuously up hills and then sliding down them again. Having done this, you pant your way up the hill and slide down again.

Seems a bit screwy to me, but then what sport isn't? Take ice skating, for instance! You just slide around and around either on your skates or on your ear, performing figure eights intentionally or accidentally. When you finally get sick of it you go home and rub liniment on the affected parts.

Ice hockey is one of the fastest games in the world, but I don't play. I don't like the method of scoring. They count up the number of broken ankles and dislocated knee-caps, and the side with the most injuries loses. That's how it looks to me, anyhow.

Football is more of a business than a sport. And another thing: what is a sportsman? People say, "Oh, he's a great one for sport. Never misses a match." That means that he sits all rugged up in the grandstand, munching peanuts and yelling out, "Come on, you little beauties! Stop him, Tiger! Oh! Nice work!"

One of the players might kick the ball over the picket fence and the sport, rushing to retrieve it, throws it back on the playing-field. Then he comes back to his seat and says to the chap next to him, "Nice to feel the old football again. Throws my mind back to the old days when I saved my side half a minute before the final whistle blew. I was on the left wing——"

"Aw, pipe down!"

"Who said that?"

"I did!" says an eighteen-stone onlooker in the next row.

"That's all right. I just wanted to know." Then he whispers to a friend, "I should have bowled that fellow over, really, but the stand is too crowded."

Boxing is not really a winter sport. As a matter of fact it's not a sport at all unless you win. If your opponent knocks you out, it's just a brutal display. If you knock him out it's a sport.

I am getting a bit old for Alpine climbing, but in the chalets and lodges of Switzerland my name is still mentioned with awe.

"Ah!" they say, "that man Lower was a devil! I have been a guide for many years in these parts but never have I seen his equal. I've seen him clinging to a rock with one hand, when suddenly an avalanche swept down on him."

"Good gracious! What did he do?"

"Held it back with his one free hand and shouted to the rest of us to get back and warn the villagers at the foot of the mountain. When he let the avalanche go it swept down and blotted out the entire village. A party went out to search for him and found him on the top of the mountain eating his lunch. All he said was, 'I thought I might as well finish the climb.'"

"He must be a remarkable man."

"He is. Iron-Man Lower, we used to call him."

Swimming has never been regarded as a winter sport, although there is a sort of a club called the Icebergs. They go to the baths all through the winter months and sit in the sun and play cards. One member accidentally fell into the water one day, so they made him Grand President of the club. The overcoat he was wearing at the time he fell in is one of the club's most cherished possessions.

The idea of all sport is to encourage tenacity, skill, restraint, and singleness of purpose. Bachelors can develop all these complaints in a very simple way. No elaborate equipment is needed. Just a needle and some cotton and a cold day.

The idea is to thread the cotton on to the needle while your fingers are half frozen. Sticking the needle into the table and then sneaking on it with the thread is barred. That is not sporting, and only a cad would do it. Also, the use of bag-needles is against the rules.

Quoits is a good game for the cold months. You just sit in front of the fire and throw the quoits on to the peg. The only trouble is that this is rather a strenuous game. When you've thrown all the quoits on to the peg you've got to get up out of your chair and collect them again. A game for young men, I should say.

I, myself, can get all the exercise I want out of a rousing game of draughts, or snakes and ladders, or ludo.

Play The Game, You Cadesses!

Women's district club cricket has commenced again. There are quite a few good women cricketers, I believe, but I think the game should be altered slightly to make it more feminine.

Polka-dotted bats with matching stumps is a suggestion. I have long thought that grass-green cricket balls would improve the game marvellously from the batsman's point of view. One could lie down and have a good rest while they were finding the thing. Cricket is a game most suitable for ladies, but I don't approve of football. I saw one ladies' football game, and I came away so shaken that it was days before I felt all right again. The idea seemed to be to grab somebody by the hair — it didn't seem to matter whom — hurl her to the ground, and then fall over her. Whoever gets up last has her guernsey torn to ribbons.

All women's football teams have a ball on the field just for the look of the thing. I wouldn't play in a woman's football team for all the coffee in Alaska.

It has been said that all women are savages at heart. It's quite true, too. Melt into your arms one minute, and belt you in the face the next. I know. That's why I think that women umpires should be employed at women's cricket matches. A love-sick umpire might be inclined to be a bit partial, whereas a woman umpire would be quite relentless.

"Oo!" says the batswoman to the wicketkeeper. "Did you hear what she said? Said I was out! The cat! And all because I won three and ninepence off her at bridge the other night."

"Never mind, dear. Smack her in the face as you're going back to the pavilion. She did the same thing to Amy Smith last week."

And another thing. Male scorers would be vitally necessary. I play billiards with ladies occasionally, and the way their score leaps from six to forty after they've scored four has often puzzled me.

"But you're not that much, surely!" I say.

"Well, there it is on the scoreboard."

What can a man do? That's why I think that the whole Board of Control should attend women's cricket matches to check up on the scores. Not that the scorers would be dishonest, you know, but they might want to do a girl friend a good turn out of pure goodness of heart.

Which reminds me — you know this one but bear with an old man's whim just this once — the bloke who walked into a butcher's shop; only a little, sad, bowler-hatted bloke, and said: "How's the steak today, butcher?"

"Tender as a woman's heart, sir," replied the butcher.

"Humph!" grunted the little man. "Gimme a pound of sausages."

My grandfather says that that always was a good joke.

One of my secretaries has just come in. I have dozens of them, all voluntary workers. They come and read the stuff I've written, mix it all up, look over my shoulder, go "Snff!" and walk out. It might be good for my soul, but it's very bad for my morale.

This one wants to know what the devil butchers' shops have got to do with the opening of the cricket season. I'll admit he has me there, but what's it got to do with him?

The world is full of busybodies. Thousands of them; and I know every one of them personally. Anyhow, they have fine cuts and glances to leg in butchers' shops, don't they? Know what he said then? "It beats me how you keep your job."

GO AWAY! He's gone away.

Pardon me while I lock the door.

There are two ways of playing cricket, in case you don't know. I don't suppose the knowledge will be of much use to you girls, but it might come in handy some time.

One is the grim, dour fight for runs against a failing light, with two to go and the match to win. Play up, and play the game, you cads. You know how it has been said that the battle of Waterloo was won in the billiard rooms of Eton. Or something like that. That is the grim, do-or-die method of playing cricket like they do in Test matches.

The other method is when a friend approaches you and says, "What about playing on our side next Saturday? We're playing the Associated Billiard Markers' Pastime Club. We'll have five nine-gallon kegs on the ground, and we can get more across the road."

"All right. You can count me in."

Where this kind of cricket is different to ordinary cricket is that the idea is to get out as quickly as possible before the rest of the players have finished off all the refreshments. Strangely enough, I play my best cricket on these occasions. I make a mad, wild swing in a desperate attempt to get bowled, and the ball swerves, the bat hits it, and away goes the ball into the next county.

From my vast store of cricket wisdom I shall pluck one or, perhaps, two items which may be useful to lady cricketers.

Never be bowled by a simple yob — I mean lob. Glance him to the off.

Always play a straight bat. Bent bats are practically useless.

To bowlers I would say, always carry a sharp penknife so you can cut a piece out of the ball in order to give it plenty of spin.

Fast bowlers who need a long run can save energy by doing the first couple of hundred yards on a bicycle, dismounting and then delivering the ball.

It is always best to aim for the wicket, but this is a matter of taste. Some think it better to aim for the batsman.

Mrs. Lower should make a splendid member for a women's cricket team. She never fails to bowl me out.

Well, put your pads on and keep your hair on. Cricket, remember, is a gentleman's game.

The Lowdown On Leapfrog!

There still seems to be some trouble about our Olympic Games team. That symbol of the Olympic Games, the five rings, always makes me feel inferior, because I never could play quoits, but still I have my ideas. Speaking as an old athlete (Welterweight Noughts and Crosses, 1928-30; Runner-up Hunt the Slipper, Patonga Beach Social Club, 1936), I should like to mention a few things.

In the first place, about the Musical Chairs team. We have a remarkable amount of talent going to waste. I have been watching the trams about knock-off time. Also suburban trains and buses. If we haven't got a world-beater or two in this country, I'm no judge.

As against that, however, we are, I'll admit, weak in leap-frog. Where are the leap-froggers of the good old days? I do not wish to boast, but frogs used to come for miles to learn from me. Could I leap? I was the most leperous bloke in Australia. Time took its toll, and I had to give the game up and take to practising the standing high jump. I could do the standing all right, but the high jump part had me tricked.

Disheartened, I turned to javelin hurling. Nothing is more soothing to the soul than hurling javelins. Give me a javelin and a thing to hurl it with, and I want no more from life.

It's so handy to be able to hurl a javelin, too. It can be used on the dog or to make toast or for picking up loose pieces of paper in parks, getting stones out of horses' hoofs — you've got no idea.

To get back to our Olympic team! We don't seem to have any really good discus hurlers. Improper training is, I think, the cause of it. A man who wants to hurl a discus in world competition should start off hurling aspirin tablets and work up through soup plates and gramophone records until he gets to the actual discus. He should then work himself into a violent rage. *(No! Not a violet ray! Don't interrupt)* and he will be able to crack a burly hurl.

As for running, I think we are fairly well represented. We won't win, but this is not our fault. For many years I have been picking at the Amateur Athletic Association about their starting guns.

In these days of furious rearmament it is ridiculous to use antiquated firearms. A machine-gun, or, better still, a small trench mortar, would give a better and bigger start to all concerned, including the spectators. I would even go further and have the whole track mined.

I have quite a number of ideas to submit to the Athletic Association. For hurdle races, for instance, I would have rubber hurdles. This would mean that any competitor who hit a hurdle (like the horse I backed on Saturday) would bounce back and have to have another go at it. Like Snakes and Ladders. Or one could have imaginary hurdles. This would be quite interesting. After all, what is the Hemp, Stop and Jup? Just a series of imaginary hurdles. And pole-vaulting. How much more interesting doing it without a pole!

How I delight in swimming! The smooth, swift plunge at the start when you land on your stomach, the half-hour you take to come up, the first mouthful of water, the glorious sensation when somebody comes and drags you out. You can't tell me anything about swimming. At least, you could, but I wouldn't listen.

Two-handed euchre is not bad, but, unfortunately, we have no one representing our country this year at the Games. It seems a pity, because I am the best euchre player in Australia. Except a chap I met in Narrabri. He used to cheat and crease the backs of the cards with his thumb-nail so he'd know them next time. I was creasing them in a different place, and it was most confusing.

I was never any good at draughts, because I get mad and sulk when people huff me. We'll pass that over. We will also pass over polo. All of which brings me to the most serious blot on our escut . . . escutsch *(Oh, spell it yourself)*. What I'm getting at is that Yo-Yo has been entirely overlooked. And behind it all is a story of jealousy and treachery unexampled in the history of our grand and noble Commonwealth. *(Whoa, there!)* I am the champion plain and fancy Yo-Yoer of Fitzroy and Woolloomooloo and surrounding districts, and apart from whether or not I yo to the Olympic Games, I hereby challenge all-comers to the best two out of three Yo-ho-ho's and a bottle of rum. The only condition I insist on is that challengers supply the whole of the rum.

Anyhow, I've had my say. Take it or leave it — as long as you leave the rum!

Fifteen Men On A Dead Man's Chess

Strange things occur. I suppose they always will. For instance, an Australian chess team is sailing for Argentina next month on a tramp steamer. When they get there, they're going to play chess. But don't ask me why!

What's more, they're going via Cape Horn in the middle of winter, which bears out a theory I have always held: *Chess is a form of madness.* You may have noticed how a chess-player will shift one pawn and then go into a trance for three or four hours. They get that way. And then they'll break into their theme song:

> *Fifteen men on a dead man's chess,*
> *Yo, ho, and a couple of pawns.*

I wouldn't care to be captain of that tramp steamer. Or even a member of the crew. If the captain has any sense he'll break all records for the crossing to Argentina.

Then there'll come the time when they'll actually be in Argentina. They'll find things very different over there. People are inclined to be a bit temperamental in those parts. Scenes will undoubtedly occur.

"Ha! You castle my bishop! Name of a dog! Name of two dogs! One thousand curses on you, gringo!"

"Put that gun down!"

"Castle-bishoper! I hate you to the back of your teeth!"

BANG!

And that will be one visting chess player who won't be coming home.

Speaking personally, I think the whole scheme is one of the biggest ramps I've ever heard of. Just fancy if I started to pack a bag or two and the wife said, "Where do you think you're going?"

"I'm going to Argentina, my dear, to play chess."

"You're going to *what?*"

"I'm going on a tramp steamer to Argentina to play chess."

"Blime!"

"Really, my dear! Most unladylike."

"Well, blow me down! Are you sure you're all right in the belfry? This certainly is a new one. I fell for that one about going to the country to see about buying a greyhound, but this one's nutty. You just unpack those bags and get on to the lawn-mower. And make it snappy."

There is something pathetic and heroic about this chess expeditionary force. Some of these poor men may finish up like my poor brother, Lemuel. He went to Algiers to defend his title as world champion snakes and ladders player; beat a colonel of the

Spahis, was immediately imprisoned and later forced to join the Foreign Legion, where he served with great distinction and was awarded the Cafe Noir with bar, but later died in action covered with Arabs.

I myself am more of a ludo fan, and won the Borneo Gold Bowl in '89. I was much younger then, of course, but the rigours of the climate sapped my health. That and the baboons crawling all over me. Very unnerving.

Still, these games abroad make for a good deal of goodwill and understanding between nations. I wouldn't be surprised if we signed a non-aggression pact with Argentina after the chess season. As the old adage says, "There is many a true word spoken in chess."

It is a noble game. You can't cheat at chess because everything is spread out for all the world to see. That's why I prefer poker. There have been some catty remarks about the extraordinarily good luck I have when it's my deal; but what I say is, if you can't do a bit of fancy dealing for yourself, why deal at all? Nobody has ever invited me to go to Brazil to play poker, but I have been told to go to other places.

Chess, like all games, has a language of its own. Gambits, and all that. You've only got to knock over a chess board when in play and you learn the whole lot.

"Gambit all, sir! You clumsy, lumbering oaf!"

Another good thing about chess is that you can play it by telegram. It's very matey that way.

You have messenger-boys ringing the door-bell and presenting telegrams at 3 o'clock in the morning.

"Pawned your castle. Stop. Hope all are well at home. Stop. Rook in top right-hand corner. Hope hear from you next month."

Then you beam-wireless back: "Wife packed up chessmen. Stop. Said looked untidy. Stop. Better start over again. Stop. Best wishes may best man win. Stop."

You couldn't do that with poker. When it came to a show-down who'd believe a telegram like: "Sorry, old boy, have royal routine flush. Stop. That makes you three bob my way." No good at all.

Backing horses by phone is different. When settling day comes the bookmaker says: "Bad luck, son. You're up for seven pounds ten."

"Who? Me!"

"Yes, you rang me up on Saturday. Remember?"

"Well, what do you know about that? I wonder who that could have been? Said he was me, did he?"

Of course, it's not as easy as all that. But you can usually get away with it once. When you run out of bookmakers you just give up betting. It's one way of getting out of the gambling habit.

But about this flitting off to Argentina to play chess. Watch your husband closely and carefully. If you see him poring over a book with the title, *Chess, And How to Play It*, knock him down and take the book away.

Or, on the other hand, if you're sick of the sight of him, give him a chess board and a book of rules and then hope for the best.

Carrying An Elephant Across Australia

All over Australia, and particularly in Victoria, people are pushing each other up mountains in wheelbarrows. There's a farmer in Yackandandah who intends to pull a sulky 190 miles with a fourteen-stone passenger in it. They are doing these things for a bet.

That kind of thing is child's play to me. Now, if the fellow who is pushing the chap up Mount Buffalo in a wheelbarrow took the wheel off the barrow and then pushed it there'd be some merit in the thing. Myself, I'm prepared to carry the *Encyclopaedia Britannica* up Mount Everest and then read it out loud with two hard-boiled eggs in my mouth.

I was challenged to stay out all night three times in one week, but the wager was only a measly £10,000, and I had a good look at the wife and decided it wasn't worth it.

All these stunts show a high degree of intelligence in those who participate in them. Also I have noticed that a certain class distinction is creeping into the industry. Extract from a Sydney paper:

> *CHRISTCHURCH, Tuesday.—Two men here have undertaken a 50 miles in 8 days wheelbarrow stunt for a wager of only £5.*

The sneer in that last bit! Only five pounds! No sooner do the upper strata of the intelligentsia start something exclusive but the blinking rabble start imitating it.

One record I made remains unbeaten. It was when I carried an elephant from Perth to Brisbane. One of my elephants — I kept a herd of them to keep the grass down on my back lawn — took sick and it was apparent to my skilled eye that he needed medical attention. I merely mention this in order to convince you that the feat was not carried out in a spirit of frivolity, but rather was it a matter of urgent necessity.

I set off from Perth at dawn with a man walking in front with a red flag. We ran so short of provisions on the way that the man ate the flag. As a matter of fact, by the time we got to our destination there wasn't much left of the elephant on account of me gnawing at him from time to time.

It was a bitter struggle, tramping across the pitiless desert in the blinding sun. The only shade I had was the elephant. At night I would cover it up with my coat and sleep in my singlet beneath the stars. Later, it got so cold at nights that I used to pull the elephant over me. It was much warmer that way.

As the days wore on he became feverish, and one night he started whimpering. I got up and gave him his paregoric, but it didn't seem to do him any good and, would you believe me, I had to walk up and down all night with him. You wouldn't believe me? All right, then. Anyhow, I got him off at last, but he lost a ton and a half in less than a fortnight.

Needless to say, I was worried to death. I would sit beside him holding his paw and listening to his breathing. Every now and then I'd take his pulse out and wash it in an antiseptic, after which I would have to fold up the antiseptic, replace the wheels on it, and grind its valves.

After about three weeks, the man with the red flag went mad, and the antiseptic bolted in terror. I shot the man and, carefully placing the elephant on the ground, I marked the place with a stick so I could find him again, and set off after the panic-stricken antiseptic.

I caught it at last and led it back to where the elephant lay bleating pitifully. I applied a torquinet in order to stop him bleating to death, and, gathering him up in my arms, I staggered on, followed by the thoroughly chastened antiseptic.

It was at about this time that I started eating small pieces of the elephant. I started on his ears as they were pretty ragged anyhow, and he didn't seem to mind, but when I commenced on one of his front legs he looked at me with such a pitiful expression that the tears welled up in my eyes and ran down my face, and that was the first drink I'd had for four days.

On the fourth week I was so emancipated *(Don't show your ignorance!)*, so emaciated that I was compelled to remove my spurs, fasten them on to the elephant's tusks, pick up his hind legs, and wheel him.

It was in this fashion that we staggered into Melbourne. *(I thought you were going to Brisbane?)* That, my girl, is the fault of the printer. Printers are always making mistakes like that. Uncle Lennie NEVER makes mistakes.

When I took what was left of the elephant to the vet, he said, "What was this?"

"My elephant," I replied weakly. I was almost spent. As a matter of fact, I had hardly any loose change.

He rolled my elephant up and handed him back to me. "I can do nothing for you," he said.

Sadly I put him in his trunk and left him at the Railway Parcels Office. Sometimes, in the long winter evenings, I take the ticket out and look at it. Ain't life hell?

By Rook And By Crook

I am not playing in the world chess championship this year. I had enough trouble last time. We were playing at Geneva some years ago and the continual brawling among the players upset the League of Nations to such an extent that they applied sanctions to me and my grandfather.

And once you get a sanction on you it's very hard to get off. I tried kerosene and cloudy ammonia, and even sand paper, but you can still see signs of it on me now. You see, it was this way:

My grandfather had just beaten the Yugoslavian welterweight, Katznitzo, and was standing behind my chair while I played Upsa Dazie, the Turkish Tiger. I led off using the Alsatian gambit, and pawned Dazie's queen in the first half-hour.

Perhaps I'd better explain the game before we go any farther. Chess is played on a black and white board. All the white squares are next the black squares, and all the black squares are next to the white squares. This is to keep them separate.

Then you are given a handful of rooks (not the kind you know) and pawns, and kings, and queens, and bishops, and castles which you spread out on the board indiscriminately. You then go to sleep. The first to wake up moves something on the board, and then it is the other player's turn.

Well (*Stop shuffling your feet!*) as I say, I pawned Dazie's queen with a clever feint with the rook, and a right-cross with the king behind the touch-lines. Dazie was furious, and said that if I did it again he was going home, and taking his board with him because it was his board, and he was only letting me play on it as a favour. I said what about the fishing rod I lent him two years ago, and he said I'd never had a fishing rod.

My grandfather in the meantime had pinched Dazie's rook, and hid it behind the clock. Then someone tipped the table over and we had to start all over again. We were lucky to get out of the place alive.

Nothing like that ever happened when I was running the Casino at Nice. The only thing that jarred during the whole of the time the Casino was under my management was that my grandfather would insist on riding on the roulette wheels. Ultimately I had to have a special roulette wheel made for him, and the clients used to gamble on which hole my grandfather would roll into when the wheel slowed down. One day he had ten francs on the black, and dislocated his hips trying to roll into the right hole. He has never been the same since.

I put him on burying the suicides, but he used to upset the customers too much, tramping around the rooms with his shovel over his shoulder, and singing out, "Next, please!" He was never of much assistance to me in my sporting career.

It was just the same when I ran the billiard saloon. He used to give the customers axe handles for cues and spot up an egg on the table occasionally. He said it made the game more interesting.

Then there was another time when I was secretary of the Foozle Golf Club. He was greenkeeper and he went around one day and plugged up all the holes on the course with the exception of the nineteenth. The result was that the members had to carry picks and shovels in their golf bags. It led to a lot of bitter recriminations because, at the end of the day, there were 785 holes on the course.

We decided, after a meeting of the club committee, that we would change the game so that the object would be to hit the ball without getting into a hole. It was not a great success, because one of the members, making a swing on the edge of one of the holes, fell in and was not missed for some days.

Food was thrown down to him as often as possible, but somebody hit him on the head with a tin of salmon, and when we at last got him up he was suffering from concussion and covered all over with butter and eggs — things which well-meaning friends had thrown down to him.

When I was running my S.P. establishment he was even worse. He was handed a two shillings and a note: "Shilling e.w. Rogilla." He jotted it down in the book, "One shilling every week from Mr. Rogilla, pd. fortnight in advance." You know you can't run a business that way.

Another time I was running a shut-the-door and butterscotch tournament. (*Battledore and shuttlecock, thank you.*) On the eve of the finals he left the door of the cage open and all my shuttlecocks got out. It spoilt everything.

People who had booked ringside seats months in advance

demanded their money back. There was a riot at the turnstiles. The chief of police came to me and said, "I'm afraid I can't hold them back much longer."

My grandfather said he could quieten the crowd by singing them a pathetic song about mother and silvery hair and being far from home and all that. Well, I let him have a shot at it, and by the time they had finished with him they were too exhausted to do anything else and I was able to escape.

I took the old gentleman flowers and fruit while he was in hospital, but he didn't seem at all grateful. There's not much gratitude or kindliness in this world. You ask them for bread and they give you fourteen pounds.

Anyhow, you can see that it is chess as well I'm not playing in the chess tournament. (*All right! ALL RIGHT! I heard you the first time.*)

10 Science, Medicine And Other Lurks

An appendectomy performed on a tandem bicycle. A catapult for putting the cat out at night. Is the scientist human? Ask the abdominal Snow man.

The Phrenzied Phrenologist

I have become interested in phrenology.

Ever since the last time I got a belt on the head — which, I might add, took a whole tram to do — I have been interested in bumps on the head and phrenology generally.

Where, I said to myself, would Napoleon have finished up if his nurse hadn't dropped him on the floor of the bathroom at the age of four months?

This history maker, this lucky little boy, fell slap on his nut.

Napoleon was dropped from a height by accident, and struck the floor of the bathroom with his cranium. Josephine rushed in — no, I'm a bit in front of myself.

The result of this bathroom incident was the development of a horrible lump which a phrenologist said was the bump of organisation. Hence the retreat from Moscow.

Becoming, as I said before, interested, so to speak as it were, though far be it from me and speaking as a disinterested observer and a member of the public (don't stop me) and a mother of eight and indignant taxpayer, constant reader, public welfare and anonymous (Finished! Shut up!) I have taken up the study of phrenology.

The reason — or one of the reasons — is that I can spell it right every time. It's a gift. You walk up to any policeman and say, "Go on. Spell phrenology."

He'll say, "You get on home or I'll put you in!"

This shows that he's ignorant and can't spell. Awful, the high level of ignorance our police force has achieved.

But I was going to tell you.

When I first became a phrenologist (I never miss, do you notice?) I had to use a mallet on most of the clients as they didn't have the appropriate lumps.

Later, I just invented lumps. Saved trouble all round.

Once I examined a man who had a head on him like a custard apple. "Last time you had a haircut — if ever — did they use a stump-jump plough on you?" I asked.

I got thoroughly rebuffed that time. "My name is Joe Stalin," replied the client with great dignity. "And those are not bumps — they're callouses."

Of course I tried to keep my profession a secret from Sir Gravel Lower, the head of the family. I called myself Professor Lennie

Lower and for a long time he thought I taught the banjo and rhumba.

But the dread moment came. He was pacing the huge library. As a rule, he did it on a bicycle, but it was away being repaired.

"So!" he said, glaring, "You're a phrenologist — huh! Disgraced the family! And all the time I thought you were teaching the banjo to the masses, you cad!"

"Father!" I cried.

"Go and die," he muttered. "If I had a shilling I'd cut you off with it. Look at you! Covered with dandruff and smelling of hair-oil! My son! As I said once before, I'd like to cut you off with a shilling. How much have you got, you bounder?"

"Eightpence, sir," I replied.

"Oke!" said Sir Gravel. "Pass it over and if ever I can rake up another fourpence, you're cut off with a shilling — understand?"

"Yes, sir," I replied.

"Very well. Go to one of the colonies. Australia is pretty remote. There become a journalist."

"But, father! Not that!"

Sir Gravel merely summoned the butler. "Atkins," he said (the butler's name was Atkins. I think this is why Sir Gravel called him Atkins), "hurl this renegade into the snow."

"If I may make so bold, sir?" inquired Atkins.

"Very well, Atkins," I replied.

Then he hurled me.

And here I am.

Wouldn't it drive you mad?

Don't Cry Over Spilled Onions

I said to Marconi only the other day, we inventors don't get any kudos for our inventions. And I love kudos. With a dash of tomato sauce they are delicious.

Who invented the catapult for putting the cat out at night? I did. Has anybody ever come up and patted me on the back for it? No.

Then there was the machine I patented for beating up the hen in order to get positively fresh egg drinks. There was another machine which cried for you while you peeled the onions. Then there was Perkin's Ponderous and Perfectly Puerile Potato Peeler. The potatoes were simply inserted one at a time and the peel went one way, the eyes went another way, pieces of your finger-nails went another way and all you had to do was to find the potato.

I got the idea for one of my best inventions while hunting gristly bears in the Rockies far away. The gristly bear is so called because it is very sinewy. It has a habit of sinew before you see him. *(Oh, Mr. Lower!)* Its nostrils are placed so far apart that it is bandy-legged and has to back up to anything it wants to smell. *(Get on with your work.)*

Yes. I invented a robot for taking the blame for cigarette burns in the carpets. And do you know what I did? I INVENTED A GUN TO SHELL PEAS WITH! Good graziers!

Here among my test tubes and retorts — a test tube is a thing used by international cricketers and a retort is a back answer, I won't be so technical in future — I carry out experiments which stagger the imagination. And if you've ever had an imagination with the staggers, you can sympathize with me.

And what about the rubber rubbish tin — the dustman's bane? They can kick it until they're black in the face and it still resembles a rubbish tin. I'd have made a fortune out of that if it wasn't for the objections raised by the Sports Committee of the Rubbish Carters' Union.

Did I ever tell you about the luminous sun-dial which could be lit up at night? Wasn't it me who invented *(Just a minute. That "me" should be "I". Who's writing this stuff, anyhow? All right! All right!)* . . . who invented that priceless boon to the proletariat, the alarm clock that won't go off? Need you ask? And the indestructible conversation lolly. And the rubber jujube. And water wings for teetotallers.

Bah! What have I got out of it? Nothing but obloquy. *(What!)* I said obioquy, and if there's a woman here who wants to deny it, let her stand forth.

In collaboration with Mr. Edison some years ago, I produced a keyhole that would follow the key about and pounce on it. We sold thousands of them.

I was responsible for the installation of the hundreds and thousands counter in one of our wealthy clubs. Elastic blankets for boarding houses was another of my triumphs. My laboratory assistant has recently perfected an electric rat catcher. It rings a bell and wakes the wife who rushes into the kitchen. While wife is in kitchen wondering why no rat in trap, husband who has rung bell from front gate has gone to bed and is so asleep that he has been there for hours to great astonishment of wife of the first part, heretofore mentioned.

I was the first man to prove that perpetual commotion was not only possible, but almost unavoidable.

Why I haven't been knighted has got me beat. That's the worst of these governments. Class-biased, that's what they are. Although

I was class-biased myself at school. Always stuck at the bottom of the class. In the circumstances, one can't complain.

For the past eleven years I have been working on an apparatus to shut the wife up when I come home late. I think I have over-estimated my inventive powers. There are some things which are beyond human ingenuity.

Excuse me. I think my mortar and pestle is boiling over.

Surgery Surges On

Spirit of progress in the medical profession seems to be getting a little out of hand.

I have just been reading about the eminent surgeon who whipped out a patient's appendix in 1 min. 35 sec., thus beating the previous record by seven and four-fifths seconds.

This sort of thing has got to be stopped. Otherwise we may hear of further strange feats, brought about by the spirit of emulation.

"Did you hear about Smith?" one young surgeon will ask another.

"What's he done now?"

"Removed a man's kidney with only a nail-file and tack-hammer while suspended from an electric-light cord by one foot."

"Old stuff!"

"He's claiming a record, anyway. The B.M.A. is investigating."

"I still think it's old stuff. What about Sir John Macdougal?"

"What has *he* done?"

"Haven't you heard? Don't you read the Sports Supplement of *The British Medical Journal*?"

"I must have missed that issue."

"Well, it was an appendectomy."

"Child's play!"

"But listen! He did it on a tandem bicycle. The anaesthetist rode in front and Sir John at the back. Only two laps around the operating table from a standing start in five and three-fifth seconds and the last eighteen inches on a flat tyre."

"That's pretty good! Yes, I'll admit that's pretty good!"

"And what's more, the patient put up a record, too. Four seconds after the commencement of the operation he was dead."

"Well, that's fine! That's what I call co-operation."

I cannot see how surgery can make such great strides while suspended by the legs, but the modern trend should be a great source of entertainment to medical students, as well as instruction.

"Gentlemen," says the surgeon to the goggle-eyed students, "I am about to perform a delicate brain operation with merely a tin-opener and two bag needles."

"Hey!" says the patient feebly.

"You see, gentlemen, the patient is cheering already. Lie down, mug!"

"Shall I give him another dash of ether?" asks the anaesthetist.

"Yeah! Splash it over him. Not too much on the floor. The matron doesn't like it. Now then, gentlemen, I insert the can-opener here, just above the left eyebrow — so. Round we go! Off she comes!

"Now inside here we have the brain. Pass the brain around, Jones!

"Dammit, I've forgotten my penknife. Ah, thank you!

"Now, we slice a piece off here — and here — and here. Slap she goes back into the skull. The bag needles, sister! I shouldn't have to tell you."

"Sorry, sir!"

"This twine sterilized?"

"Of course, sir! It's been soaking in sheep-dip for ten minutes."

"Good. Now we just go Zip! Zip! Zip! Dammit! This twine's rotten, sister! Ah, well! Anybody got a safety-pin? Thanks, sister. I hope you don't inconvenience yourself? Well, there you are, gentlemen.

"Okay. Chuck a sheet over him and wheel him away. Any questions, gentlemen?"

"Er, yes, sir," mumbles one of the students. "How is the patient to get on with only half a brain?"

"He'll be happier than ever he was before."

"Will he be able to think?"

"Good Lord, no That's why he'll be happy. By the way, what was my time for that one?"

"Two and three-fifths, sir, but I think my stopwatch is a little slow. I usually put it on a quarter of an hour before I go to bed."

"Tut! Tut! And you forgot about it last night, I suppose?"

"I'm terribly sorry——"

"Never mind. Just go to the door and yell out for another patient. Sterilize the can-opener, sister."

"I'm afraid, doctor, you left it inside his skull."

"Ah, well; it was blunt, anyway. Get me another one. This next case I intend to do one hand, kneeling, gentlemen."

"You beaut!"

I do hope Wirths' circus comes around shortly. I've got to have my tonsils out and I'm a busy man.

Recipe For Radio Operations

On a ship which carried no doctor, a man's life was saved recently by instructions received by wireless from a doctor. This is nothing new; neither is it clever. It even may be positively dangerous. In similar circumstances I operated on my grandfather.

During the depression, which some of you may remember, my grandfather was sporting on the village green (with a hey nonny nonny) when he fell down and broke his wishbone.

He was picked up and towed home by the local ambulance, to the great delight of the village constable, who regarded my grandfather as the bugbearer of his life, and had frequently toed him (my grandfather) home himself (the constable).

The poor old gentleman lay on a bed of pain for weeks. Which, if you don't mind me intruding these intimate details, seriously interfered with his occupation, which was that of a corner-turner. He had a permanent job while the depression was on. Now, my grandfather regarded himself as a self-made man. I don't know whether this was a boast or a complaint; anyhow, it suited everybody because no one else would take the responsibility. Like all self-made men, he had his little idiosyncrasies, which he kept in a small bowl in the dining-room, and the peasants regarded him as "queer."

When he tucked the ends of his serviette into his top vest pockets he imagined that he was a Mason, and insisted on eating with a gavel. He could never get used to modern ways. As a matter of fact, when he heard the phone ring he used to wonder whether it was a fire or an auction sale, or just someone at the front door. Of course, I don't want this to go any farther.

Anyhow, he wouldn't allow any doctors near him, which hurt me more than it would have hurt him, as I was his sole heir. He had the largest collection of feather dusters in the country and at one time offered the collection to the Museum. The Museum people refused, saying that they had no use for the collection, as they never dusted anything. After they had been rejected by the War Museum, my grandfather was very annoyed and became an ardent pacifist, and used to spend hours down at the waterfront poking his tongue out at battleships.

Where the devil are we? (*You were about to operate on your grandfather.*) Yes. Well, I made arrangements to have instructions broadcast by a well-known doctor, and having thoroughly sterilized the axe and other instruments, I laid my grandfather out on the table and turned on the radio.

"The appendix," said the radio, "is below the waistline." Which was a bit tricky as my grandfather has no waistline.

"Make an incision low down on the left side."

I did this.

"Place the hands on the head and swing backwards and forwards from the hips." I did this, also. "Be sure," it went on, "to get your boots at Gumbles'." And then, very harshly it said,

"Beat up the white of an egg! Remove the appendix. Cover with finely grated cheese. The hands should be thoroughly rubbed with lemon juice. Then out popped the little bunny rabbit three times a day between meals and garnished with lettuce. The patient should be kept in a warm place and well corked."

"What the hell are you doin'!" said my grandfather.

"Add a tablespoonful of olive oil a drop at a time!" yelled the wireless.

"Chatham is making a great run on the rails, and don't forget that Garg's biscuits are the best."

It was then that I began to think that there was something wrong with the wireless cabinet. Hastily throwing a sheet over my grandfather, I went to it and examined it. My gridleaker had short-circuited with the revolving gaffle plate, thus disconnecting the directional gibbler, causing the gyratory snugging flap to fuse! I switched the thing off and went back to my grandfather, who was pacing up and down the room in a great rage.

There he was, covered with grated cheese and breadcrumbs, wringing the lemon juice out of his beard. "What the devil am I going to do with this?" he shouted, holding out his appendix.

"Let me stitch you up before something else falls out," I said.

"Be damned to you," bellowed my grandfather. "Gimme a safety-pin."

Well, I won't weary you with all the details, but the old gentleman recovered and now goes every day on his tricycle to meet the train. *I say! How awfully jolly!* Yes. And, what's more, he wears his appendix as a watch fob. *You don't tell me!* Yes.

Excuse me. I smell something burning.

Slick Go The Cheers

What an interesting world we live in! Things going on all around. What we journalists describe as a bombshell has been launched. Just a minute. You can't launch a bombshell.

Well, a movement is afoot. The Australian conference of Master Hairdressers has spoken:

"We want to raise the status of hairdressers, who are now looked down upon as common barbers, to that of professional men, such as doctors and lawyers."

That's madness. Fancy a decent respectable barber wanting to be on the same level as a lawyer.

Still, the time may come. One will go into the barber's waiting room and be greeted by an attendant."

"Yes, sir?"

"I wanna shave."

"Have you an appointment?"

"No. I just wanna shave."

"I see. Name and address, please."

"Bill McCauly, 'The Pines,' Bondi — but what the——"

"Occupation?"

"Barman. But listen——"

"The barber will see you shortly."

After about an hour the barber is ready for you.

"Ah! Mr. McCauly, I presume? Sit down and tell me your trouble."

"I just wanna shave!"

"Hmm! A shave, eh! Lie down here and take your shirt off. Hmm — yes — distinct hirsute growth on the face. Who is your next-of-kin?"

"But listen——!"

"I'll have this drafted out properly for you.

"Whereas I, William McCauly, hereinafter referred to as the party of the first part, do voluntarily and, of my own wish, and without malice aforethought, desire to be shaved——

"Read it over yourself and sign here, and here. That copy is for yourself. Now when did you first feel this coming on?"

"I tell you I want a shave."

"Yes, yes. Calm yourself. I'll give you a sedative. Have you any witnesses? Anyone who can testify that you grew this hair yourself? You can speak quite plainly to me now that I have taken up your case. For instance, I take it that this is your own face? Not illegally acquired, borrowed, or hired for an illicit purpose? Good. Now then, just sit down in this chair. Relax. . . . Nurse!"

"Yes, sir."

"Robe and lather the patient, please, while I sterilize the instruments. Short at the back and sides, old boy, I suppose?"

"I don't wanna haircut! I wanna shave!"

"My dear chap. Lots of patients come to me totally ignorant of the fact that they need a haircut. Only expert diagnosis can tell. You have come to me just in time. Tut! Tut! A moustache, eh? Strange that I never noticed it before. That will have to be removed. I think I shall have to call in my colleague, Hairdresser Frawley. He's a moustache specialist. His fees are a little higher than the ordinary practitioner, but he's a good man. The razor, nurse. . . ."

Mind you, I have seen this coming for a long time. I have never yet met a barber who didn't know everything, and such being the case it is only right that he be given his proper social and professional status in the community.

I defy anybody to stun a barber with a question he can't answer, be it foreign affairs, skin diseases, horses or hangovers. Just the same, it seems a pity that barbering should be degraded to the level of the medical and legal professions.

Barbers who know their ancient history will tell you that barbers were the first doctors.

Leeches, they were.

Laid Low With Punjivitis

My word, I showed up some of the delegates to the Medical Congress last week. The place was littered with dermatologists, otologists, toxicologists, ophthalmologists (try that on your zither), and I think there was a doctor there, too. During my lecture I had them all spellbound. They were due for a spell, anyhow.

Gastritis was my first subject. Gastritis is brought about by putting the head in the gas oven. It is becoming increasingly prevalent lately. The kitchenettes in some flats are so small that the housewife sometimes thinks that she would have more room to do the washing-up inside the gas stove. This is very foolish. It is far better to do the work out in the street.

Where a gastritis patient has been in the oven for an extended period, he should be laid firmly on his back. A match is then applied ,and any hot water needed for hot foments, etcetera, may be quickly and economically obtained by standing the kettle on the patient's face. An emetic is then applied to the back of the neck. A linseed poultice should then be taken after every meal.

Gastritis was not the only subject I dealt with. I proceeded on to the dermatological section and discussed such things as warts and yaws; hence the term, "Warts yaws?"

Yaws is brought about by malignant yawning, and is usually caught at concerts in aid of the church bazaar. It is a very yawful complaint.

Warts may be cured by the application of red-hot foments. These must be kept applied until the wart reaches 100 degrees centigrade. It is then a boil. And if anyone doesn't know what to do with a boil he doesn't deserve to have one.

Conjunctivitis is another insidious disease. It is due to too much use of conjunctions and is very common among journalists. One such patient was at death's door and his dying prepositions were taken as he could only breathe noun then.

I treated him with frequent strong doses of catgut and had him almost cured when we ran out of cats. One of the nurses made the unfortunate mistake (although well meant) of ringing in some dog gut.

The result was dreadful. The patient leapt out of bed and started biting himself. He then tried to climb up the bed-post, but was unable to follow himself. At last, frothing at the mouth, he lapsed into a comber from which he never recovered.

Which shows that even in medicine one has to be careful.

About this time I was interrupted by a delegate who had been heckling me off and on for hours. He wanted to know what I would do in the case of hereditary typhoid of the left ventricle of the glosso-pharyngeal nerve.

"The glosso-pharyngeal nerve," I explained, "must be removed and spread out to dry in the shade. The ventricle may then be upended and searched for typhoid germs. In some cases it is necessary to smoke them out. As each one emerges it must be thoroughly donged with a small surgical hammer and laid to one side.

"The nerve and ventricle are then replaced and fixed in position with some good antiseptic glue. The patient may then be allowed to go home, if he has a home. If he hasn't got a home, don't treat him. There's no money in it."

"Thank you, sir," he said, and sat down, thoroughly abashed.

"What do you think is the cause of colic?" asked a lady chronicologist.

"Too much handling of colic dogs. Same as ringworms, tapeworms, and so on. Children should not be allowed to play with worms. A ringworm is a worm that has turned. Anything else you'd like to know?"

"Yes, doctor. The Congress has requested me to inquire if you would honour us by laying the foundation gallstone in the new wing of the B.M.A. boiling-down works. We feel that after all you have done for medical science something should be done in recognition of your sterling services."

"What about a bob in?" I suggested.

The whole Congress turned pale, and for a moment I thought that I would have to treat the lot of them for pernicious anaemia. I explained this to them, and they went even paler, and there was an unseemly scramble for the exits. Only one lady doctor remained.

"Doctor," she said, "I think you're marvellous." Coyly she laid her cheek on the coracoid process of my scapula, and I could feel her auricles and ventricles flapping madly against my left lung.

Arm in arm we left the building. What goitre thing is there than love?

Ah, well, nux vomica sclerosis qui mal y pense. (That'll cure your catarrh!)

New Noses For Old

I have never bothered much about my nose, but this morning, while shaving, I observed it closely. It would be useless re-shaping it. It should be removed entirely.

My ears also stick out a bit. Of course, a man needs ears so he can breathe in comfort with his hat on, but there should be some way of folding them back.

I was thinking that a dab of seccotine behind each ear might make them look neater if they were pressed flat until the gum dried.

Now, if I had been born with someone else's face, I could have gone around being me just the same and nobody would have suspected it. (Hold tight here.)

According to physiognomists (Okay, relax), your features reveal your character.

For instance, a prominent hooked nose reveals virility, ruthlessness, and anaemia, or something.

Thick lips denote a lascivious nature. A high forehead means that you're a genius and likely to be dumped in the rat-house any minute.

It has frequently been observed that a woman who has had her face lifted develops a completely new personality.

I'm not surprised. A woman with her hair down is a different woman to the same woman with it dolled-up, if you get what I mean. I mean you can notice a change when she sheds her apron and puts on her fur coat.

In a dinner-suit and boiled shirt I become so gentlemanly that I am almost unapproachable. In full evening rig-out, tails and white tie and gardenia and all that, I am practically insufferable.

It's psychological, that's what it is. Look what a new hat does to a woman. She wants to go places and do things.

It just goes to show something or other.

Speaking for myself, I would like to get in on the ground floor for a new stomach. My present one just can't take it.

I'd like a stainless steel one with asbestos lining. The shape is not so bad—I hope you don't mind me talking about my stomach like this—but it is lacking in performance.

If some blokes I know had their stomachs lifted they would have a remarkably good chest measurement. The trouble would be that you'd have to lift everything else with it. I will not go into details about this phase of the matter, but a man might find that his feet wouldn't touch the ground.

Perhaps I shouldn't have started this. At any moment I might think of some possible feat of plastic surgery which will get me the sack on the spot. They're pretty prudish in this office. That is, during working hours.

As a matter of fact, for a bloke with a mind like mine this subject is a honey. I must write it fair dinkum some time and show it to the boys in the bar.

Face-lifting is fairly new and is regarded as a modern miracle, but elbow-lifting has been going on for hundreds of years and nobody has ever thought of it as extraordinary.

Now I come to think of it, I have been the subject of various slight facial alterations in the past. I once came home with a black eye and a split lip, but did anybody compliment me? No. The only comment in the old home was, "It's a pity he didn't blacken your other eye."

You can't please everybody. Indeed, there are times when you can't please anybody.

I have resigned myself to going through what remains of my life with this same face. What little alterations I make from time to time are not really radical, and are mostly due to crook razor blades.

I would remind you of Shakespeare's remark:
A nose by any other shape will smell just as good.
This, I think, is from *Romeo and Juliet*.

Something To Beef About

The clinical congress of the American College of Surgeons has announced that cows' blood is quite all right for blood transfusions for human beings.

This I doubt, though among my friends I number a few who have never had a cow transfusion but are cows just the same.

The effect of such treatment on a sensitive subject such as myself is hard to foresee. I fear that the sight of a patch of grass would make me feel the urge to lie down on it and chew, or amble around on it and moo.

Other more serious complications occur to my mind. One day a man might find himself in court charged with assaulting a police officer.

"This is a very serious offence," says the magistrate. "While Constable Jones was on traffic duty at the intersection of King and Pitt Streets, you were seen to put your head down, rush across the street, and wilfully and violently butt the constable in the stomach.

"Have you anything to say in mitigation of this offence?"

"Yes, your Worship. I had just had a bull's-blood transfusion up at the abattoirs."

"Well!"

"The constable behaved in a very provocative manner. During a lull in the traffic, he pulled out a red bandanna handkerchief . . ."

"Hah! I see. Case dismissed."

After several transfusions goodness knows what might happen.

A man might find himself engaged to a pot of meat extract or in moments of depression he may wander into the local butcher shop.

"Yessir?" says the butcher, sliding sawdustily up to the counter.

"I've come to give myself up," you reply sadly.

"How much do you reckon I'd be worth on the hoof? Moo!"

"Just step into the freezing chamber, please. Hmm. About a hundred and forty-seven pounds. Very light. Drought where you come from?"

"Yes. The grass is very dry. No nutriment in it."

"I see. Yes. H-mm. Might be able to use you for soup bones. I'll give you one and eightpence."

"What about me suit?"

"All right. Two and eightpence."

"What! A lousy deener for a good suit like this! I wouldn't think of it. I'll go to some other butcher." Then you flounce out of the shop.

"He'll be back," says the butcher confidently to his assistant.

Then you wander sadly away to the cow pastures and lie down and chew some more until a young heifer comes along and looks at you in that solemn way cows have.

You lumber cumbrously to your feet and, bowing, say, "Pardon me, but haven't we met somewhere before? Your face is very familiar."

"And *you* are too familiar. Buzz off before I call the rouse-about!"

And there you are, a ruddy outcast.

I have no ambition to finish life as a batch of rissoles. The prospect is displeasing and undignified. If, on the other hand, these cow transfusions, taken in moderation, give one that satisfied placidity which most cows seem to have, I'm all for them.

Now if some of my bosses could only have about thirty gallons of peaceful bovine blood pumped into them, life would be much easier for me. But that is too much to hope for.

Every one of them lives on raw tigers and in the pub next door they put on a special rattle-snake counter-lunch in the saloon bar. At least that's what I suspect.

The picture is rather gloomy, but fancy getting first prize at the Royal Agricultural Show! Lalapalloosa Lower of Interlochen the Second. Grand champion. Oh, boy! Welcome in all the best circles. Blue ribbons to hang over the fireplace. The only bull-minded bloke in a whole paddock full of cows. (Of course you would bring that up.)

Anyhow, I'm willing to have a go at this cow-transfusion. I can't be any more milked and mulct than I am now.

Charge Your Hypodermics!

The Australian Dental Association has just held a convention. Quite a shivoo! Lunches and lectures and dances and dinners for five days.

How jolly! Dentists, mark you, who ought to be banned from decent society and branded on the forehead.

I've often wondered how people become dentists. Probably some sadistic urge due to ill-treatment in early youth. If they had been put in a Borstal institute when showing the first signs of mental dentality or dental mentality or, anyhow, becoming jaw-minded, they might have been cured. As it is they are permitted to roam at large and have conventions.

The luncheon should be interesting. The waiter comes along, looks at the guest and says: "Tut! Tut! You should have come to me months ago. Open wide. This is only asparagus soup. It won't hurt a bit." He pours the soup into the dentist, stands back and says: "There now. That wasn't so bad, was it? Just spit into this bucket."

Conversation will sparkle about the table. "A most interesting molar, Mr. Wasley. Nearly broke my wrist on it. And then—you'll laugh at this—it turned out to be the wrong molar!"

"Ha! Ha! Mr. Frizell, you slay me! What did you do?"

"Just hauled out a couple of bicuspids in the way of apology, if you know what I mean . . ."

"Damn sporting of you."

"Aw, I dunno. Ethics of the profession and all that."

"Gentlemen!" announces the chairman. "I'd like you all to charge your hypodermic squirts and have an injection in the upper gum. The King!"

"The King!"

"And now, gentlemen, it is my great pleasure to introduce our guest of honour, Mr. Hiram K. Oates, of Oklahoma, one of the leading dentitians in his home state."

"Hear! Hear!"

"Speak up!"

"Quiet! Will the noisy gentleman at the end of the table kindly keep his canines covered?"

"Wal, boys," says Mr. Oates, "it sure gives me a great thrill to be here among you boys. Much as I have appreciated your great country, it fills a cavity in me to be among you boys. Your luncheon has sure been very toothsome." (Laughter and feet-stamping.)

"I guess you've all heard of the great advances in American dental research." (Yes! Yes! Hear! Hear!)

"I assure you gents here assembled that the old technique still holds good.

"Drill 'em; fill 'em, wait a while, then drag 'em out. Then in goes the falsies!" (Prolonged cheers.)

"I note that a gentleman third from my left is holding his face. Could it be . . ."

"No! No!" shrieks the gentleman third from the left.

But it is no use. They are on him. He's down! He's up again! Five to one. It's not fair. He's trying to break out of it. Down again! Dentist Wasley leads with his forceps! Connects! He's got it!

Then they all stand around holding up the tooth and sing: "For He's a Jolly Good Fellow."

As for me! I do not wish to be in it. If you can think of anything worse than a dentists' dinner, please don't tell me.

Diabolical Dan McGrew

There once was a dentist called Daniel McGrew, and he grew and he grew and he grew and he grew. Anyway, he was no relation whatever to Dangerous Dan McGrew. To me he was simply Deadly Dan McGrew, the Diabolical Dentist.

As a small boy I liked reciting that one about Dangerous Dan McGrew. Especially the part where you say, "For one of you is a hound of hell! And that man is Dan McGrew!" Being able to say "hound of hell" out loud was as good as a week's holiday to me.

But we were speaking of dentists, I think. I shall have to tread softly here. I am at present having some teeth filled. A boring business.

This dentist I started to tell you about was no ordinary dentist. He was not one of those dentists who bored holes in your teeth, plugged them up with clay, told you it was a temporary filling and to come back next week and he'd do it all over again.

It was strange how I came to meet this dentist. The editor was a bit annoyed with me one day. Well, he's annoyed with me every day, but this was a very bad case, and chancing to meet this McGrew, the dentist, I asked him if he could concoct me a love-philtre which I could slip into the Boss's morning tea and make him a pal for life instead of a raging hyena. Cocaine, or something like that.

I should never have spoken to that dentist. He looked at me with eyes like a dead cobra and said, "You have two defective bicuspids."

Up till then I had always thought that a bicuspid was a two-handled spitoon or cuspidor, as we say in the States.

"You should have them attended to," he went on. "I might be able to save the right molar for you, but the one on the left will have to come out, I'm afraid."

"*You're* afraid!" I said. "It's me that's afraid."

"Do you know that bad teeth can so affect your health that they can wreck your whole life? If you don't have those teeth attended to you'll probably finish up as a leprous, raving lunatic in some foul gutter."

I went home and told my wife about this and she said the dentist was quite right. She said that if I had looked after my teeth with the same thoroughness with which I studied racehorses we could have had a car by now. I don't know what my teeth have got to do with racehorses and motor cars, but that's women for you.

Anyhow, I made an appointment with McGrew. Having had some previous experience of doctors' and dentists' waiting-rooms, I brought along my own magazines, a packet of sandwiches, and a thermos flask.

I didn't know that this man was a magician. But I had been waiting only half an hour when his lady assistant opened a door and said, "Mr. Lower?"

Sweat broke out on my face. But—"Just step inside, please," she said. And I was in.

"Ha!" said the dentist. "Sit down in that chair and make your-self comfortable, old man. Head back. That's it. Open wide. Hmn!

"Any bleeding from the gums?"

I said that I hadn't been bleeding from the gums and he looked so disappointed that I wished I could start bleeding from the gums straight away. He then got some kind of chisel and started knock-ing chips off one of my good teeth. My best tooth, as a matter of fact.

"Yes," he said, "I think we might be able to save that one for you. The phenodrochical solution, nurse."

It was then that I should have telephoned for the police. But, as I said before, this dentist was a magician.

I just cowered in the chair. Me!—Lasher Lower! The Terror of the Tropics!! Following which this McGrew did everything to me except give me a haircut and shave.

As I tried to stagger out of the place, the nurse handed me a card. "What's that for?" I feebly moaned.

"Next Thursday at eleven-thirty," she replied brightly.

And this is where the magic comes in. I went, although I swore by all my ancestors that next Thursday would find me in Madagas-car, where I believe they hunt dentists with bows and arrows.

I suppose you want to know what happened to McGrew at the end. Rather dramatic it was. Pathetic also. A patient with the hiccups coughed a pair of forceps into the right eye of McGrew and they came out just below the left ear.

Only a young man, too. On the surface, it seems a pity, but it's O.K. with me.

Water On The Brain

There is far too much fuss about water in this country. Latest scheme seems to be to switch the Snowy River down to Mel-bourne. This will cost millions, and I fail to see any sense in it whatever.

If we're short of water, what's wrong with cocoa? It's more palatable and much less dangerous. You never hear of people drowning in cocoa like they do in water.

I will forestall your objection which I perceive quivering on the lips. It is not the custom in this country to bathe in cocoa. Why be hide-bound?

The time may come when mother will say: "Willie!"

"Yes, Mum."

"Have you Cadburyed yourself yet?"

"No, Mum. Father's Bushelling himself in the bathroom, and I can't get in."

You have all heard of these prominent actresses who every now and then bathe in champagne. That's a swell idea. If any actress is thinking of taking a bath I would like to be invited along.

A champagne bath, I mean. With a whole bath full of champagne you could invite a few friends along. It would be a bit of a squeeze, I suppose, and you might find yourself washing somebody else's knees, but you could drink your way out of it, unless some lousy teetotaller pulled the plug out first.

A bishop, whose name I can't spell, said that praying for rain was a waste of time if we have no dams. Pretty tough words for a bishop. You can't kneel down and pray, "Give us some rain, dam it all." I couldn't, anyhow. All right for bishops. Me! I wouldn't be so familiar.

It should not cost a great deal to bring water from Alice Springs What a lady! Admittedly the distance is great, but pumping stations dotted here and there would fix that.

I would like to be a night watchman at a pumping station. Maybe the gurgling and splashing would get on my nerves and I would turn the thing off.

Then I would get long-distance calls, I suppose.

"That you, Lower?"

"Yes, sir."

"Turn that blasted water on! I want to wash."

"You had a wash yesterday."

"Well, as a matter of fact, it's not for me; it's a friend of mine."

"Do I know her?"

"No. It's a cousin of mine just down from the country."

"Oh, yeah? I can let you have a pint. Stand by."

The more I think about that job the better I like it.

But I never get jobs like that. Perhaps I vote for the wrong people.

It's a strange thing that a man doesn't value a thing until he hasn't got it.

Of course, that doesn't go for smallpox and things like that, but believe me, the time will come when members of the Melbourne Club will sit and sip their water with relish and gusto. (You must try that one of these days. Just call for a Relish and Gusto.)

"Steward!" the oldest member will say, "this is not Snowy River!"

"You asked for Murray with a dash of Yarra, sir."

"Well, take it away and bring me a Hawkesbury."

"The Hawkesbury is off, sir. Fish stuck in the main. Would you care for a Pittwater Lagoon?"

"All right. Not too much mud. I don't know what this confounded club is coming to. Different when Smith was secretary. Inefficiency, that's what it is. Look at Jones.

"The other day I called for a Snowy River and found a trout-fly in it.

"They don't sieve the stuff properly, that's the trouble. I always strain mine through my handkerchief."

"By the way; heard about Simpson? Lucky beggar. Won a bath full of water in the lottery."

"You don't say. It's to be hoped he doesn't wash in it all at once."

"Oh, no. He's bottling it for his old age. Beastly business about Cholmondely, eh?"

"What's that?"

"Haven't you heard! Caught watering his **geranium**. He pleaded that it was some soup he'd been using for **shaving** water, but they shot him just the same." Sorry to be gruesome.

I must hurry home now, before the washing-up starts. You get bits of cabbage and stuff in your ears if you arrive too late for a wash.

For your next bath try a can of tomato soup. It gives you that schoolgirl complexion all over. You wouldn't know what a schoolgirl's complexion looks like all over, perhaps, but you can take my word for it.

Weighs And Means

Do you want a figure like a bean? People in all walks of life, and some who find it hard to walk at all, keep pestering me for information on how I preserve my sylph-like figure. I will explain it here, once and for all. After this I don't want to be bothered any more on the subject.

With me, I suppose, it's a gift. I can reduce my bust measurement by about two inches simply by taking all the things out of my vest pockets. Exercise and diet are the main things.

As regards diet, Marlene Dietrich recommends stoned raisins soaked overnight in lemon juice. I have not tried this, but think it should be good. Ladies who are bad shots should get someone else to stone the raisins for them. Moderate sized stones should be used, and the stoning should take place in the open, where the risk of breakages is less. Oranges and lemons were used in days gone by by the belles of St. Clement's, who found them very beneficial.

Coconuts are good. By the time you have finished one coconut the day is done, the light has fled, and you are too worn out to try to eat anything else. People with tender gums should soak the coconut in warm water before eating, as it softens the shell. Starchy foods, such as potatoes, stiff collars, and dress shirt-fronts, should be avoided.

Exercise should be taken in moderation. Here is a good one for reducing the hips: Stand erect with the hands on top of the head, and slowly raise the left leg to the level of the shoulders. Keep it there for five or ten minutes, then gently lower to the ground. Do this ten times with the left leg and ten times with the right leg. Then do it with both legs at once. You will actually feel a difference in your hips almost immediately.

There is an excellent vibratory massage machine on the market. The lady is not supplied with the machine. Superfluous flesh taken off by means of the vibrating belt falls into a container attached to the chassis.

A brisk walk each morning will work wonders; or failing that, a brisk drive around town in the limousine. This, however, does not take in bending and stooping exercises, which are essential for the maintenance of a good figure. I have found that the best way for a husband to persuade his wife to go in for bending and stooping is to make the fence which stops the view into the next door neighbour's yard about ten feet high, and then to block up all the cracks, leaving only a few peep holes about one foot from the ground. The husband next door should bear half the cost of alteration, as the scheme works both ways.

I diet very strenuously myself. First my breakfast, then diet; lunch followed by a fairly light diet in order to prepare for afternoon tea, which should be followed by a fair amount of dieting until dinner time. If the system can stand it, one should fast from then until supper.

After supper, to bed. A little exercise may be had by getting up a couple of hours after retiring and wandering around the house wondering if there was any of the rice pudding left over.

Don't be misled by weighing machines. Weighing machines are the most lying things on earth, and should be treated accordingly. When you see "16 st. 10 lb." on the dial, think of the number you first thought of and stick to it. And don't be disheartened if results do not come immediately. Slim women may look slick, but a fat woman stays. Ask any corset manufacturer.

Epilogue

The Melancholy of Lennie Lower

By ALEXANDER MACDONALD

Lennie Lower passed this way—but all too hurriedly, and in the nervous, scurrying fashion peculiar to men of his trade; a trade which, as James Thurber once remarked, impels its practitioners to the very edge of the chair of Literature, where they ply their craft with much uneasy twitching, as if half-afraid that some Big Bogeyman—an editor or a publisher, perhaps—is going to snuff them out of existence at the drop of a single laugh.

While he was around, of course, some rare old entertainment was had by all—by all, that is, except perhaps by Lennie Lower himself, who habitually wore the slightly haunted expression of the literary flagellant who is obliged to thrash some five hundred words a day out of himself to supply the highly critical demands of *every* type of reader, from the dustman to the dowager.

This aspect of the humorist's art has been persistently overlooked. The serious novelist, for example, is more or less safe within his own circle. He is not expected to cater for the taste of the urger or the bar-fly. Conversely, the pot-boiler authors are unperturbed by the scorn of the literati. By and large, and within their own limits, most men of letters are allowed a fair measure of self-satisfaction.

Not so the essayist in comedy—that is to say, the sort of comedy which Lower used to write, without apparent effort, week after week, year after year. Like another national Australian comedian, the late Roy Rene, Lower was required to be all things to all men. The same line with which he fetched a chuckle from a doctor of laws was also calculated to draw a guffaw from a barrowman.

In short, Lower was expected to—and *did*—furnish a sort of readers' common room, to be shared with equal pleasure by fans of Mr. F. J. Thwaites, readers of the *Sporting Globe,* and earnest students of Feodor Mikhailovitch Dostoievski.

The knowledge that this phenomenon must be brought about, and the constant effort of *bringing* it about, time after time after time, preyed upon Lower's never robust nervous system to a degree where strangers in pubs found it hard to believe that here, in person, was the redoubtable wag, the effervescent word-spinner—the gay, the laughter-loving Lennie Lower.

Like so many humorists, he didn't look the part. He was a smallish, dark, morose man, who would light up at intervals, like an erratic neon-sign, with a violent sparkle of high spirits, which often produced some rather fey behaviour.

The mere sight of a straw hat, for example, could always lure out the hobgoblin in him. "Aha! Breakfast!" he cried, on one occasion, observing his friend Norman ("Tibby") Cotter, wearing one of those fashionable creations of the early 1930s. Wrenching Mr. Cotter's boater from his head, Lower took a large, semi-circular bite from the brim, returned the headgear and departed, masticating with enjoyment, leaving Mr. Cotter dancing a *pas seul* of rage.

I also recall an incident in the bar of the Assembly Hotel, in Phillip Street, Sydney, involving the moustache currently sported by the artist "Wep", W. E. Pidgeon. Wep, in a passing fit of vanity, let it be known that he was growing a Guardsman's Moustache. Lower, somewhat contemptuously, dismissed it as a toothbrush job.

"It's a Guardsman's Moustache, I tell you!" said Wep heatedly.

Lower was seized by a gust of inspiration. "It's a *toothbrush* moustache!" he said. "And I'll prove it's a toothbrush moutache! I'll bloody well brush my teeth on it!"

Grasping Wep by the ears, he proceeded to do so, until such time as anxious friends prised them apart.

This sort of whim, admittedly, is not liable to inspire either confidence or admiration; but it does give some inkling of the slightly demented turn of mind which could evolve such a definition as: "Bread: Bread is a large number of small holes entirely surrounded by bread"—or have a Noble Earl address his valet with the words: "Go, bring me a glass of rum with an emerald in it, and a dish of prawns."

Lower's long periods of depression were, I suspect, a sort of germinating process somehow necessary to the creation of his wildest and funniest ideas. To quote Thurber again, on the subject of professional humorists, "The little wheels of their invention are set in motion by the damp hand of melancholy." This melancholy, in Lower's case, was so painfully evident during his creative shifts (the tools were as often as not a blunt pencil and the back of an envelope) that you might have supposed him to be working on a blank-verse tragedy rather than a carefree piece entitled "Can You Bite the Back of Your Neck?" or "A Whale's Best Friend is its Blubber."

Unlike the tragedian, however, Lower wore his royal purple mood only in private, never in the public place of print. "Blood is thicker than water," he wrote, at the beginning of *Here's Luck*—a theme on which certain latter-day authors have luxuriated for thousands of words on end. Not Lower. With pure and infinitely less tiresome logic, he rounded off his premise with the sublimely relevant conclusion, "But then, so is soup."

Another outcome of Lower's dark introspections was the vital ingredient of all satiric comedy—the intense awareness that human beings are, in themselves, so ludicrous that it is impossible to treat them seriously. In the case of many distinguished wits, this awareness has not always been absolute. Oscar Wilde, for example, was prepared to be devastating about anybody and everybody—with the exception of Oscar Wilde, for whom he sustained a warm, almost sentimental regard to the end.

In Lower's *De Profundis*, on the other hand, Lower—alias J. Gudgeon, hero and buffoon of *Here's Luck*—was whipped just as hilariously as the other figures of fun, including the floosies, the Darlo Road Demons, the Randwick Daggers, and that dead lair to end all dead lairs, Stanley.

Indeed, Lower's prevailing mood of total irreverence, with its occasional note of self-derision and a never too distant undertone of actual cruelty, seemed to sum up, for the first time, a recognizable manifesto of the Australian sense of humour, as distinct from the English, the American or the Continental sense of humour. Once or twice (in the past, admittedly) a glint of the callous streak within us had shown through the overlay of innocent fun. As a matter of fact, Australia's true embodiment of Puck is neither a jolly old Punch nor a folksy old Uncle Remus. He's a lethal old prankster called the Bastard from the Bush. (And, for grim pleasantry, it would be hard to beat the much-quoted comeback: " 'Will you have a cigarette, mate?' said the Leader of the Push. "I'll have the flamin' *packet!*" said the Bastard from the Bush.")

Unfortunately, this sharp, hard-bitten and highly individual attitude was obscured, only too often, by images of dying stockmen, tipsy drovers and sentimental swaggies—who all looked more or less like colonial caricatures of Wordsworth's Old Leech Gatherer.

Lower, however, had no eye for such blurred outlines as Cumberland folklore superimposed on these bright, bleak antipodean landscapes, nor any ear for either the gentle joshing of English drawing-room comedy or the sophisticated college humour then popular in the United States.

Consider him on almost any topic that is generally venerated elsewhere. On Parenthood, for example. "I would rather rear a platypus than a boy," wrote Lower; adding sombrely, "The greatest problem of all is to know in what trade or profession the boy will be best fitted to support his old father at a later date."

Or, on the Professions:

Judging by the number of divorce cases doctors become entangled in, it would seem that the only way some of them can keep their names untarnished is by the application of a little metal polish to their brass plates.

Or, on the Church:

He [Stanley] did show some interest in the subject of the revision of the prayer book. His suggestion was to insert crossword puzzles on alternate pages with blank leaves interspersed here and there for sketches and notes to be passed along to fellow-sufferers during the sermon.

Or finally, on Old Age:

She is an old lady, and the age of chivalry is not dead while a Gudgeon lives. Perhaps a different son-in-law might have described her as a senseless, whining, nagging, leather-faced old whitlow not fit to cohabit with a rhinoceros beetle. But I wouldn't.

Lower's line of jesting does not tinkle; it clashes, like flint on steel. For, with all his inspired word-play, and his matchless gift of rationalizing insanity until it took on the form of a pellucid truth, with all his brilliant verbal caperings, Lower was never a man for mere elfin laughter. Beneath the rippling absurdities was the fierce and erratic merriment of a pioneer in a harsh and lonely world of humour; of a man who was well aware—to quote Thurber once more—that the claw of the sea-puss was a moral to get him in the end.

And it did.